From Slavery to the Cooperative Commonwealth

This book reconstructs how a group of nineteenth-century labor reformers appropriated and radicalized the republican tradition. These "labor republicans" derived their definition of freedom from a long tradition of political theory dating back to the classical republics. In this tradition, to be free is to be independent of anyone else's will; to be dependent is to be a slave. Borrowing these ideas, labor republicans argued that wage laborers were unfree because of their abject dependence on their employers. Workers in a cooperative, on the other hand, were considered free because they equally and collectively controlled their work. Although these labor republicans are relatively unknown, this book details their unique, contemporary, and valuable perspective on both American history and the organization of the economy.

Alex Gourevitch is an assistant professor of political science at Brown University. He has previously served as an assistant professor at McMaster University, a postdoctoral research associate for Brown University's Political Theory Project, and a College Fellow at Harvard University. Gourevitch is the coeditor of *Politics Without Sovereignty: A Critique of Contemporary International Relations* (2007). His work has been published in *Political Theory, Modern Intellectual History, Constellations, Public Culture, Philosophical Topics,* and the *Journal of Human Rights*. He has also written for magazines such as *Jacobin, Dissent, Salon, The Chronicle Review, N+1, The American Prospect,* and *Washington Monthly,* and he is coauthor of the blog *The Current Moment.*

From Slavery to the Cooperative Commonwealth

Labor and Republican Liberty in the Nineteenth Century

ALEX GOUREVITCH
Brown University

CAMBRIDGE
UNIVERSITY PRESS

32 Avenue of the Americas, New York, NY 10013-2473, USA

Cambridge University Press is part of the University of Cambridge.

It furthers the University's mission by disseminating knowledge in the pursuit of education, learning, and research at the highest international levels of excellence.

www.cambridge.org
Information on this title: www.cambridge.org/9781107663657

© Alex Gourevitch 2015

This publication is in copyright. Subject to statutory exception and to the provisions of relevant collective licensing agreements, no reproduction of any part may take place without the written permission of Cambridge University Press.

First published 2015

Printed in the United States of America

A catalog record for this publication is available from the British Library.

Library of Congress Cataloging in Publication data
Gourevitch, Alexander.
From slavery to the cooperative commonwealth : Labor and republican liberty in the nineteenth century / Alex Gourevitch, Brown University.
    pages cm
Includes bibliographical references and index.
ISBN 978-1-107-03317-7 (hardback) – ISBN 978-1-107-66365-7 (paperback)
1. Labor movement – United States – History – 19th century. 2. Wages – United States – History – 19th century. 3. Cooperation – United States – History – 19th century. 4. Republicanism – United States – History – 19th century. I. Title.
HD8072.G764 2015
331.880973′09034–dc23   2014026552

ISBN 978-1-107-03317-7 Hardback
ISBN 978-1-107-66365-7 Paperback

Cambridge University Press has no responsibility for the persistence or accuracy of URLs for external or third-party Internet Web sites referred to in this publication and does not guarantee that any content on such Web sites is, or will remain, accurate or appropriate.

In dedication to my father, Peter Gourevitch, and in memory of my mother, Lisa Hirschman.

Contents

Acknowledgments	*page* ix
Introduction: Something of Slavery Still Remains	1
1. The Paradox of Slavery and Freedom	18
2. "Independent Laborers by Voluntary Contract": The Laissez-Faire Republican Turn	47
3. "The Sword of Want": Free Labor against Wage Labor	67
4. Labor Republicanism and the Cooperative Commonwealth	97
5. Solidarity and Selfishness: The Political Theory of the Dependent Classes	138
Conclusion: The Freedom Yet to Come	174
Bibliography	191
Index	207

Acknowledgments

Although my name is on the title page, this book is not mine alone. It started as a dissertation, nearly a decade ago, so it is only right for me to begin by thanking my dissertation advisors, Jean Cohen, Nadia Urbinati, and Ira Katznelson. In their different ways, they helped me realize I had an idea worth developing and then pushed me to develop it. Jean's razor-sharp questions kept me focused and spurred me to find my own voice. Nadia's feel for the sweep of history was an inspiration well past the dissertation phase, and her mentorship when I was first starting out is something I will continue to treasure. Ira's feel for how to move between history and theory is a model I continue to follow. I am also grateful for the comments of my two other dissertation readers, Corey Robin and Andreas Kalyvas, who were the first to help me understand how I might turn my project into a book. In fact, Corey continued to provide much needed counsel well into the late stages of the book's completion. I also must thank Daniel Kato and Ian Zuckerman. Their comradeship during our dissertation writing group was essential during the otherwise long and solitary months of writing during that early phase.

Aziz Rana has been not only a great friend and a close reader but an inspiration throughout this project, from its inception right up until just about the very last day. In certain ways, this book continues a conversation we began more than a decade ago. In the long process of turning my dissertation into a book, so many other people read chapters and papers that I hardly know where to begin acknowledging their contributions. I am sure I have, unconsciously, left some people out, but I would especially like to thank Chris Bickerton, Corey Brettschneider, Daniela Cammack, Philip Cunliffe, Sandipto Dasgupta, Prithviraj Dhatta, David Estlund, Isabelle Ferreras, Nicholas Frayn, Pablo Gilabert, David Grewal, Javier Hidalgo, Sean Ingham, James Ingram, Carlo Invernizzi, Sharon Krause, Matthew Landauer, Charles Larmore, Bruno Leipold, Chris Mackin, Tamara Metz, Laura Phillips, Peter Ramsay, Danya

Reda, Corey Robin, Genevieve Rousseliere, Emma Saunders-Hasting, Lucas Stanczyk, Scott Staring, John Tomasi, Jeppe von Platz, Kevin Vallier, Daniel Viehoff, Stuart White, Suke Wolton, and Carla Yumatle.

The Montreal Political Theory Manuscript Workshop was easily the most rewarding and intense experience – really a crucible – during this book's writing. The participants not only read the entire manuscript; they then spent a full day carefully helping me eliminate errors and clarify crucial ambiguities. They all deserve thanks, but I would like to especially mention the commentators and the organizers: Arash Abizadeh, Evan Fox-Decent, Pablo Gilabert, Jacob Levy, Victor Muñiz-Fraticelli, William Clare Roberts, and Robert Sparling. I would also like to thank the two reviewers for Cambridge University Press for their many helpful suggestions on improving the manuscript and deep thanks also to Lew Bateman and Shaun Vigil for believing in the book and for shepherding me through the production process.

Looking back, I can truly say that whatever truths this book contains would not be there without the help, perhaps I should say cooperative efforts, of others. Whatever errors still remain are mine alone. One other person deserves more than acknowledgment: my wife, Tal Astrachan. Gratitude does not even begin to describe how I feel about her support.

Introduction

Something of Slavery Still Remains

In the fall of 1887, the Knights of Labor, the largest organization of workers in nineteenth-century America, attempted to organize sugar cane workers in and around the town of Thibodaux, Louisiana. The mostly black plantation workers were paid next to nothing and labored long hours in brutal conditions. Worse yet, many worked for bosses that just a few decades earlier had been their slave masters. Although they now had to make contracts with their former slaves, these masters-cum-bosses were still accustomed to exercising unquestioned control over their labor force.

The labor association suddenly challenging the plantation-owners' authority was first organized in 1869 as "The Noble and Holy Order of the Knights of Labor" by a small group of Philadelphia garment workers. The Knights' Preamble and Declaration of Principles said they had come together "for the purpose of organizing and directing the power of the industrial masses."[1] The phrase "industrial masses" was meant to communicate a certain egalitarian idea. The Knights believed that all workers, skilled and unskilled, white and black, had the right to defend their interests collectively and, as such, they had a common interest in belonging to a single labor organization. In fact, the Knights were the first national labor association ever to organize black workers together with whites on a mass basis – an effort not meaningfully duplicated in the United States for nearly a century.[2] They aspired to draw disparate groups of workers together under the idea that everyone should have not just higher wages, shorter hours, or better conditions, but full economic

---

[1] Terence V. Powderly, ed., "Knights of Labor Platform – Preamble and Declaration of Principles," in *Labor: Its Rights and Wrongs* (Washington, DC: The Labor Publishing Company, 1886), 30.
[2] Leon Fink, *Workingmen's Democracy: The Knights of Labor and American Politics* (Urbana and Chicago: University of Illinois Press, 1985), 150–72; Claudia Miner, "The 1886 Convention of the Knights of Labor," *Phylon* 44, no. 2 (1983), 147–59; Robert E. Weir, *Beyond Labor's Veil* (Philadelphia: Pennsylvania State University Press, 1996), 46–51.

independence. A life spent working should not be a life spent working under someone else's will.

In pursuit of their emancipatory project, they had established assemblies of Knights everywhere from the male-dominated mines of rural Pennsylvania to the mostly female garment factories of New York to the railroads of Denver. The Knights' expansion into the American South began in 1886 at their general assembly meeting in Richmond, Virginia. In a conspicuous show of racial solidarity, a black Knight named Frank Ferrell took the stage to introduce the Knights' leader, Terence V. Powderly, before Powderly's opening address. In defense of his controversial decision to have a black Knight introduce him, Powderly wrote "in the field of labor and American citizenship we recognize no line of race, creed, politics or color."[3] After the assembly, a number of Knights met with local contacts in Southern states such as South Carolina, Virginia, and Louisiana to organize workers and set up local assemblies.

Their plan in southern Louisiana was to organize the sugar workers and to present plantation owners with a choice: raise wages or face a crop-threatening strike. After the summer growing season, sugar had to be cut relatively quickly or be lost to frost, so a threat to withhold labor carried real weight. The Knights' organizing drive in Louisiana quickly turned into one of the boldest, and most catastrophic, challenges to the plantocracy since the end of Reconstruction ten years earlier.[4]

Initial letters from local organizers in the sugar parishes showed little awareness of the looming danger. From late August to early November 1887, *The Journal of United Labor*, the official paper of the Knights of Labor, received mostly positive updates from organizers in Louisiana. A message dated August 29, 1887 reports "three new Local Assemblies, located at Thebodeaux, Chacahoula and Abbeville." After mentioning employer threats to replace potential strikers with convict laborers, the Louisiana Knight concludes with the assurance that "an amicable settlement, satisfactory to both sides, can be arranged."[5] A week later, a letter from Terrebonne, Louisiana mentions a success at organizing, despite "employers on plantations" having "taken all possible means to harm the Order." The reporting Knight also observes that employees receive their mere 50 cents per day in "pasteboard tickets" redeemable only at over-priced local plantation stores. Widely used throughout the United States at the time, these tickets or "scrip" had the sole purpose of keeping workers bound to a specific employer. Small wonder a Knight from Terrebonne said their effect was to "make you a slave" and reported that they had become an

---

[3] Terence V. Powderly, *Thirty Years of Labor 1859–1889* (Columbus, OH: Excelsior Publishing House, 1889), 659.
[4] Rebecca J. Scott, *Degrees of Freedom: Louisiana and Cuba After Slavery* (Cambridge, MA: Harvard University Press, 2009), 61–88.
[5] "Morgan City, LA., Aug. 29, 1887," *The Journal of United Labor* VIII, no. 11 (September 17, 1887), 2491. *The Journal of United Labor*, hereafter *JUL*.

issue in negotiations with planters.⁶ In a September 21 message, an organizer in another sugar town wrote that, despite having to keep their membership in the Knights a secret, the local workers are "doing splendidly." A similar report from a neighboring parish on October 3 stated "we are progressing rapidly down here."⁷

Knights had good reason for their initial optimism. By late 1887, one district assembly in the bayou region claimed 5,000 black members, more than forty local assemblies were spread across New Orleans and planter country, and the membership included some of the most influential black leaders from the heady days of Reconstruction.⁸ A spirit of self-assertion not seen for more than a decade blew through the cane fields. If planters would not raise wages and pay in currency rather than pasteboard tickets, then the Knights were ready to call a strike for November 1. The planters refused, threatening to use convict labor to replace ordinary workers. Uncowed, thousands of workers struck.⁹

Soon after, reports that found their way to the *Journal*'s main office up north in Philadelphia had turned noticeably darker. On November 17, the *Journal* printed a letter from Franklin, Louisiana saying, "we are having some excitement ... on account of a strike. The planters and the Governor, with the militia, are endeavoring to crush the Order out of existence." Despite these ominous signs, the author still hoped that "by January 1 we will be in good trim to lease (on the co-operative plan) a good plantation."¹⁰ In the face of military threats, the Knights continued to believe not only that they could raise wages but, more remarkably, that they could organize black workers to own and manage a plantation for themselves. This was no mere pipe dream. Just 400 miles away, near Birmingham, Alabama, Knights had founded two cooperative settlements. Named "Powderly" and "Trevellick" after leading Knights, these towns were to serve as organizing hubs and, by the time of the sugar strike, included a cooperative cigar works and iron foundry.¹¹ We shall return shortly to the wider significance of this "co-operative plan."

On November 26, the *Journal* printed a letter describing the Knights' defiance of the "many companies of State militia, with their Gattling [sic] guns," who were attempting to force the striking workers back to the fields. Little did

---

⁶ "Terrebonne, LA., Sept. 5, 1887," *JUL* VIII, no. 12 (September 26, 1887), 2496.
⁷ "Little Cailliou, LA., Oct 3, 1887," *JUL* VIII, no. 15 (October 15, 1887), 2508; "Hocma, LA., Sept. 21, 1887," *JUL* VIII, no. 13 (October 1, 1887), 2500.
⁸ Scott, *Degrees of Freedom*, 61–93.
⁹ According to Scott, the oft-repeated number of 10,000 striking workers is exaggerated but it is still very likely the numbers were in the thousands. Ibid., 81.
¹⁰ "Franklin, LA.," *JUL* VIII, no. 20 (November 17, 1887), 2528.
¹¹ Clare Dahlberg Horner, *Producers' Co-Operatives in the United States, 1865–1890* (Pittsburgh: University of Pittsburgh Press, 1978), 40–1; Steven Leikin, *The Practical Utopians: American Workers and the Cooperative Movement in the Gilded Age* (Detroit, MI: Wayne State University Press, 2004), 73.

the *Journal*'s editors know that by the time they had printed that letter the Louisiana state militia had broken the strike and corralled thousands of strikers into the town of Thibodaux, where a state district judge promptly placed them all under martial law. State militia then withdrew, intentionally leaving the town to a group of white citizen-vigilantes called the "Peace and Order Committee," who happened to have been organized by the same judge that declared martial law. Upon meeting resistance from the penned in strikers, the white vigilantes unleashed a three-day torrent of killing, from November 21 to November 23, on the unarmed cane-workers and their families. "No credible official count of the victims of the Thibodaux massacre was ever made," writes one historian, but "bodies continued to turn up in shallow graves outside of town for weeks to come."[12] Precise body counts were beside the point. The question of who ruled town and country, plantation and courthouse, had been answered. As a mother of two white vigilantes put it, "I think this will settle the question of who is to rule[,] the nigger or the white man? For the next 50 years ..."[13] A few months later, the Knights continued to organize in parts of Louisiana and elsewhere in the South, but the slaughter at Thibodaux put strict limits on the black worker's struggle for economic independence and equal rights in the South. Farming a plantation "on the co-operative plan" was not even a dream deferred; it was easy to forget it had ever been a possible world the cane cutters might live in. The Knights, meanwhile, were soon reduced to an historical footnote.

The officially sanctioned mob violence at Thibodaux was one of many over the course of Southern history. In each case, a challenge to race-based class rule was met with vigilante justice in the name of white supremacy. In this case, however, it is worth noting that the Knights articulated their challenge in a specific, not well-remembered, language of freedom. From the abolition of slavery to the end of Reconstruction, many freed slaves sought more than legal recognition as equal citizens. They felt their liberation included the right not to have a master at all. They refused to work for former masters, even when offered a formal labor contract and wages.[14] Instead, when possible, they seized or settled land set aside for them and worked it individually or in joint "labor companies."[15] Former slaves asserted their independence at all levels by organizing their own militias to protect their rights, by working their own property, by voting as they wished, and by holding local and national office. This

---

[12] Scott, *Degrees of Freedom*, 85.
[13] Quoted in ibid. 87.
[14] For accounts of the fraught attempt to impose the wage-labor form on freed slaves see Eric Foner, *Nothing but Freedom: Emancipation and Its Legacy* (Baton Rouge: Louisiana State University Press, 2007), 79–90; Amy Dru Stanley, *From Bondage to Contract: Wage Labor, Marriage, and the Market in the Age of Slave Emancipation* (Cambridge: Cambridge University Press, 1998), 1–137.
[15] Scott, *Degrees of Freedom*, 36; Foner, *Nothing but Freedom*, 79–90.

radical moment of Reconstruction was quickly suppressed and the collapse of Reconstruction in 1877 spelled the end of any but the narrowest interpretation of what emancipation would mean.[16]

When the Knights of Labor swept into Louisiana a decade later, they not only revived old hopes about self-organization and economic independence. They also integrated these regional aspirations of former slaves into a recast national ideology of republican freedom. The aforementioned hopeful parenthesis – "by January 1 we will be in good trim to lease (*on the co-operative plan*) a good plantation" – speaks to this ideological shift. No doubt black laborers and local leaders heard echoes of the short-lived Reconstruction-era "labor companies" and black militias in this new language of self-directed "co-operative plans." Their enemies certainly did. The *Thibodaux Sentinel*, a racist local paper hostile to the Knights' organizing efforts, warned "against black self-organization by trying to remind whites and blacks of what happened a generation earlier, in the days of black militias, and white vigilantism" and evoked "the old demons of violence and arson by 'black banditti.'"[17] But former slaves were now also modern workers, and the Knights trumpeted the same emancipatory language throughout the nation, heralding "co-operation" as a solution to the problems facing wage-laborers everywhere. If their message carried special historical resonances in the South, the Knights added a new universalizing and solidaristic note.

This program of liberation through cooperative self-organization, articulated in the transracial language of making all workers into their own employers, scared northern industrialists just as much as Southern planters. In fact, if we see the Thibodaux massacre as just a Southern race story, then we run the risk of unintentionally and retrospectively ceding too much to the plantocracy and its attempts to control labor relations by transforming economic conflicts into questions of racial superiority. After all, wherever the Knights went and wherever their message of cooperation and independence took hold, they were met with violence not all that different from that of Southern vigilantes. Throughout the 1870s, 1880s, and 1890s, the Knights faced private violence from employers and their hired guns, most notoriously the Pinkertons. The Pinkertons operated in legal grey zones, sometimes with outright legal sanction from the courts, and often in cooperation with National Guards or even Federal troops. In fact, on occasion it was the public violence of the state that was responsible for spectacular acts of legally sanctioned murder and coercion.[18] Labor reformers labeled

---

[16] Foner, *Nothing but Freedom*, 90–110. On the black militias in Louisiana, see Scott, *Degrees of Freedom*, 50–58.
[17] Scott, *Degrees of Freedom*, 80.
[18] Philip Taft and Philip Ross, "American Labor Violence: Its Causes, Character, and Outcome," in *The History of Violence in America: A Report to the National Commission on the Causes and Prevention of Violence*, ed. Hugh Davis Graham and Ted Robert Gurr, 1969; William Forbath,

this unholy alliance of the state with the "Pinkerton Armed Force," its spies and "provocative agents," as a kind of "Bonapartism in America," threatening to turn "the free and independent Republic of the United States of America" into the "worm-eaten Empire of Napoleon the Third."[19] Just as in Thibodaux, the lines between vigilante violence and legal coercion sometimes blurred into indistinction. What, then, was the idea of freedom that triggered such extreme responses?

The Knights of Labor represented the culmination of a radical, labor republican tradition. Their starting premise was that "there is an inevitable and irresistible conflict between the wage-system of labor and the republican system of government."[20] Wage-labor was considered a form of dependent labor, different from chattel slavery, but still based on relations of mastery and subjection. Dependent labor was inconsistent with the economic independence that every republican citizen deserved. That is why, in the name of republican liberty, these Knights sought "to abolish as rapidly as possible, the wage system, substituting co-operation therefore."[21] Here was the source of their "co-operative plan," which they found as applicable to the cane fields of Louisiana as to the shoe factories of Massachusetts.[22] The Knights wrote the cooperative program into their official constitution, the Declaration of Principles of the Knights of Labor, and, at their peak, organized thousands of cooperatives across the country.[23] The cooperative ideal threatened Southern planters, Northern industrialists and Western railroad owners alike because it struck at the dominant industrial relations between employer and employee. Affording all workers shared ownership and management of an enterprise, whether a sugar plantation, newspaper press, or garment factory, was – according to the Knights – the only way to secure to everyone their social and economic independence. The abolition of slavery two decades earlier was but the first step in a broader project of eliminating all relations of mastery and subjection in economic life. Although these ideas had been around well before the Civil War, it was only the abolition of chattel slavery and the rise of industrial capitalism that allowed the republican critique of wage-labor to come forward as a unifying, national cause. As

Law and the Shaping of the American Labor Movement (Cambridge, MA: Harvard University Press, 1991); Louis Adamic, *Dynamite: The Story of Class Violence in America* (New York: Chelsea House Publishers, 1971); Barton C. Hacker, "The United States Army as a National Police Force: the Federal Policing of Labor Disputes, 1877–1898," *Military Affairs* 33, no. 1 (April 1969), 1–11.

[19] John Swinton, "Bonapartism in America," *John Swinton's Paper* II, no. 100 (September 6, 1885). Hereafter *John Swinton's Paper* cited as *JSP*.
[20] George E. McNeill, *The Labor Movement: The Problem of to-Day* (New York: The M. W. Hazen Co., 1892), 459.
[21] S. M. Jelley, *The Voice of Labor* (Chicago: A. B. Gehman & Co., 1887), 203.
[22] On the cooperatives in Stoneham, MA, see Leikin, *The Practical Utopians*, 89–115.
[23] For the constitution, see Powderly, "Knights of Labor Platform – Declaration of Principles of the Knights of Labor," 30–3. Best estimates are that the Knights established approximately 500 producer cooperatives and thousands of consumer cooperatives. Leikin, *The Practical Utopians*, 2.

Ira Steward, a child of abolitionists and prominent post-war labor republican, wrote in 1873, "something of slavery still remains ... something of freedom is yet to come."[24]

Labor and Republican Liberty

Although not nearly the topic of scholarly interest they once were, labor historians have long known about the Knights of Labor and their predecessors. These "labor republicans" are usually, and fairly, seen as something of a hopeful or utopian moment in the growth of an otherwise more conservative American labor movement.[25] Their meteoric rise was only outpaced by their collapse. By the time of the Thibodaux massacre, the Knights were beginning their rapid decline. The more enduring, if much less radical, American Federation of Labor overtook them by the end of the century. But the Knights were not just a passing phase in American working-class formation. Their rise and fall is not only of importance to scholars of American political and labor history. The Knights were also a local, American chapter in the wider development of what has come to be known as republican political thought.[26]

The aim of this book is to interpret labor republicans as a substantial contribution to this republican tradition. Although labor historians have documented the way the language of republican liberty and civic virtue articulated class grievances in a peculiarly American vernacular, historians of political thought have failed to register the significance of this labor scholarship, let alone of the nineteenth-century voices themselves. Perhaps that is because historians of political thought assume there is nothing here but one of those peculiarities

---

[24] Ira Steward, "Poverty," in *Fourth Annual Report of the Bureau of Statistics of Labor*, ed. Massachusetts Bureau of Statistics of Labor, vol. 173 (Boston: Wright & Potter, State Printers, 1873), 412.

[25] The major investigations into the Knights are mostly from the late 1970s to the early 1990s. Norman Ware, *The Labor Movement in the United States, 1860–1895: A Study in Democracy* (New York: Vintage Books, 1929); Weir, *Beyond Labor's Veil*; Kim Voss, *The Making of American Exceptionalism: The Knights of Labor and Class Formation in the Nineteenth Century* (Ithaca, NY: Cornell University Press, 1993); Gerald N. Grob, *Workers and Utopia: A Study of Ideological Conflict in the American Labor Movement, 1865–1900* (Evanston: Northwestern University Press, 1961); Fink, *Workingmen's Democracy*; Susan Levine, *Labor's True Woman: Carpet Weavers, Industrialization, and Labor Reform in the Gilded Age* (Philadelphia: Temple University Press, 1984); Leikin, *The Practical Utopians*; David Montgomery, "Labor and the Republic in Industrial America: 1860–1920," *Le Mouvement Social* 111, no. Georges Haupt parmi nous (1980), 201–15; Herbert Gutman, *Work, Culture and Society in Industrializing America* (New York: Vintage, 1976); Richard Oestreicher, "Socialism and the Knights of Labor in Detroit, 1877–1886," *Labor History* 22, no. 1 (1981), 5–30.

[26] The literature is massive and will be discussed later. Leading statements are Quentin Skinner, *Liberty before Liberalism* (Cambridge: Cambridge University Press, 1998); Philip Pettit, *Republicanism: A Theory of Freedom and Government* (Oxford: Oxford University Press, 1999); Michael Sandel, *Democracy's Discontent: America in Search of a Public Philosophy* (Cambridge, MA: Harvard University Press, 1996).

of American history. If so, then they make a serious mistake. Those supposedly exceptional features of American history – race and slavery, immigration and the frontier, industrialization without a major socialist party – are better seen as elements of historical experience that sharpened labor reformers' focus on what republican liberty could mean in a modern economy. Precisely because Americans fought such a vigorous and intellectually productive battle over the relationship between slavery and freedom, they also uncovered long-standing paradoxes as well as conceptual resources in the republican tradition itself. These peculiarities of American history gave them a special sensitivity to the problem of slave labor, and through that, to the connection between republican liberty and labor relations generally. The claim that wage-labor was inconsistent with republican government reflected something more than a judgment about the Deep South or the United States. It also showed the usefulness of republican language when speaking to new, intercontinental experiences of domination in the modern economy as a whole. That is likely one reason why the Knights were able to organize assemblies not just in the United States but also in Canada, Belgium, England, France, and New Zealand. A political tradition that, in the hands of originating figures such as Cicero, once sanctioned deference, inequality, and slavery,[27] had now become a serious threat to existing forms of domination and inequality. How did this happen? What were the ideological transformations that allowed for such an inversion of what had once been an aristocratic tradition?

Republican Political Thought

The answers to those questions require us to revise our understanding of the republican tradition. However, I should note that, although this book is a contribution to scholarship on republican political thought, it did not begin that way. Originally, I conceived it as a critique of that scholarship from a broadly speaking Marxist standpoint. I noticed that the major works of republican political philosophy and legal theory had little distinctive to say about the social question in general, and about modern forms of labor domination in particular.[28] The landmark works on the history of republican thought had an

---

[27] On these topics in Cicero, see Peter Garnsey, *Ideas of Slavery From Aristotle to Augustine* (Cambridge: Cambridge University Press, 1996), 40–43; Andrew Lintott, *The Constitution of the Roman Republic* (Oxford: Clarendon Press, 1999), 220–32; Neal Wood, *Cicero's Social and Political Thought* (Berkeley: University of California Press, 1988); Eric Nelson, *The Greek Tradition in Republican Thought* (Cambridge: Cambridge University Press, 2004), 57–59. See the discussion in Chapter 1.

[28] These were, at the time, Pettit's *Republicanism*, Sandel's *Democracy's Discontent*, and Dagger's *Civic Virtues*, as well as a few essays on economic regulation and basic income. For example, Philip Pettit, "Freedom in the Market," *Politics, Philosophy & Economics* 5, no. 2 (June 1, 2006), 131–49; Philip Pettit, "A Republican Right to Basic Income?," *Basic Income Studies* 2, no. 2 (December 2007), 1–8; Nien-hê Hsieh, "Rawlsian Justice and Workplace Republicanism," *Social Theory and Practice* 31, no. 1 (2005), 115–42; Richard Dagger, "Neo-Republicanism

analogous defect. They limited themselves to the early modern period, roughly the fifteenth to the eighteenth centuries, which spans the recovery of classical republicanism by the Italian humanists and the transmission of their ideas to the British commonwealthsmen and American rebels.[29] Although these works showed in different ways that some classical idea of freedom was revived so as to criticize various forms of 'political slavery,' such as absolute monarchy and colonial government, scholars fell well short of discussing the history of reflection on actual slavery, let alone the importance of the nineteenth-century labor question. The prevailing historical scholarship gave the strong impression that nothing conceptually meaningful happened in the republican tradition after the American Revolution.

Originally, I thought these scholarly limitations reflected real limitations. It appeared that the republican tradition simply lacked the theoretical resources to comprehend, let alone provide a coherent response to, the modern forms of economic domination and the corresponding demands for freedom. In particular, it seemed that the republican tradition remained too strongly wedded to two institutions, private property and slavery, to generate a significant, modern response to industrial capitalism. The republican defense of the rights of property against the propertyless, even when stretched to include small property-owners seeking protection against speculators and rentiers, seemed incapable of addressing the needs of poor workers, let alone the wider questions of how to organize production and consumption on an egalitarian basis. As for slavery,

---

and the Civic Economy," *Politics, Philosophy & Economics* 5, no. 2 (June 1, 2006), 151–73; Richard Dagger, *Civic Virtues: Rights, Citizenship, and Republican Liberalism* (Oxford: Oxford University Press, 1997). On legal republicanism, see the symposium in the 1988 Yale Law Review, especially Sunstein's and Michelman's essays. Cass Sunstein, "Beyond the Republican Revival," *Yale Law Journal* 97, no. 8 (July 1988), 1539–90; Frank I. Michelman, "Law's Republic," *Yale Law Journal* 97, no. 8 (July 1988), 1493–537. Also Bruce Ackerman, *We the People: Foundations* (Cambridge, MA: The Belknap Press of Harvard University Press, 1991); Morton J. Horwitz, "Republicanism and Liberalism in American Constitutional Thought," *William & Mary Law Review* 29 (1987), 57–74. Only William Forbath and James Pope gave labor republicanism any sustained attention in their important essays. William Forbath, "Ambiguities of Free Labor: Labor and the Law in the Gilded Age" *Wis. L. Rev.* (1985), 767; James Gray Pope, "Labor's Constitution of Freedom," *Yale Law Journal* 106, no. 4 (January 1997), 941–1031.

[29] Quentin Skinner, "Machiavelli's Discorsi and the Pre-Humanist Origins of Republican Ideas," in *Machiavelli and Republicanism*, ed. Gisela Bock Maurizio Viroli Quentin Skinner, vol. 120 (Cambridge: Cambridge University Press, 1993), 121–41; J. G. A. Pocock, *The Machiavellian Moment: Florentine Political Thought and the Atlantic Republican Tradition* (Princeton, NJ: Princeton University Press, 2003); J. G. A. Pocock, "Review: Virtue and Commerce in the Eighteenth Century," *Journal of Interdisciplinary History* 3, no. 1 (Summer 1972), 119–34; Maurizio Viroli, *Republicanism* (New York: Hill and Wang, 2002); Nelson, *The Greek Tradition in Republican Thought*; Mark Jurdjevic, "Virtue, Commerce, and the Enduring Florentine Republican Moment: Reintegrating Italy Into the Atlantic Republican Debate" *Journal of the History of Ideas* 62, no. 4 (2001), 721–43; Caroline Robbins, *The Eighteenth Century Commonwealthman* (Indianapolis, IN: Liberty Fund, 2004); Gordon S. Wood, *The Creation of the American Republic, 1776–1787* (Chapel Hill: University of North Carolina Press, 1998); Pettit, *Republicanism*; Skinner, *Liberty Before Liberalism*, 17–50.

even if modern republicanism was not inescapably tied to the institution itself, its conceptual apparatus was too linked to the peculiarity of that experience to make sense of the market. Slavery, as an experience of personal subjection to a specific master, was rather different from the forms of domination a person might experience in the anonymous labor market. The shift to the modern labor market, the rise of an industrial proletariat, and the transformation of property composed elements of a historical reality that could not fit the republican vocabulary. That, I thought, was why republicanism had no *intellectual* history beyond the eighteenth century, even if it had a political and labor history. There was good reason why Marxism eclipsed the republican demand for liberty, both in theory and practice. Or so it seemed.

However, episodes such as the Thibodaux massacres, and figures such as Ira Steward, gave me pause. After deeper investigation, it became clear to me that those working in political philosophy and the history of political thought had simply overlooked the dynamism of the very tradition they sought to recover. By ending their narrative with the American Revolution, they let the curtain fall on the drama of modern republicanism just as a new set of actors took the stage and as another act was about to begin. The nineteenth century was a period of intense self-reflection for the republican tradition because of internal class challenges to some of its deepest assumptions. As artisans and wage-laborers seized the language of republican liberty and civic virtue, they brought to the fore a series of paradoxes and puzzles. They also exploited and developed conceptual possibilities that had, until then, remained dormant or marginal to the republican tradition's primary concerns. These labor republicans developed the conceptual material both for criticizing "wage-slavery" and for generating a demand for a cooperative commonwealth. Although not quite the same language as Marx, this was clearly no stale mode of thought incapable of responding to the times. Any reckoning with the republican tradition would first have to reconstruct the political ideas of these nineteenth-century labor republicans and give them their full place not just in American history, but in modern political thought.

Rehabilitation and Renewal

Reconstructing labor republicanism as a form of political theory is not just a matter of filling gaps in our historical knowledge. Instead, it goes to the heart of the republican revival's central aspiration: the rehabilitation of a lost language of freedom. Quentin Skinner, one of the leading figures in this scholarly movement, argues that, "we have inherited two rival and incommensurable theories of negative liberty."[30] The dominant, liberal theory defines freedom as "non-interference." The lost, republican theory defines freedom as

---

[30] Quentin Skinner, "A Third Concept of Liberty," *Proceedings of the British Academy* 117, no. 237 (2002), 262.

"non-domination."[31] Whereas liberals worry only about the narrow case in which others *actually* interfere with our choices, republicans, it is said, are concerned with the wider condition in which others *can* interfere *even if* they never actually do.[32] That is why for republicans, but not liberals, dependence on another's will is the defining condition of unfreedom. As Philip Pettit, another key neo-republican scholar, puts it, the great virtue of this tradition is that "enslavement and subjection are the great ills, and independence and status the supreme goods."[33] Yet, say neo-republicans, the conceptual distinction between these two theories of freedom is hardly even recognized.

According to these scholars, there was once an out-and-out struggle between these two theories of liberty, which took the form of an early modern political conflict between republican parliamentarians, represented by figures such as Algernon Sidney, and liberal monarchists, represented by figures such as Thomas Hobbes. On Skinner's account, "Hobbes's counter-revolutionary challenge eventually won the day."[34] Worse yet, says Pettit, the liberal view "succeeded in staging this *coup d'etat* without anyone noticing the usurpation that had taken place."[35] Thus, when Isaiah Berlin famously said there are only *two* coherent ways of speaking about liberty, one negative and one positive,[36]

---

[31] On the language of "non-domination" see Pettit, *Republicanism*, 51–79. I only received Pettit's latest restatement, *On the People's Terms: A Republican Theory and Model of Democracy* (Cambridge: Cambridge University Press, 2013), too late to incorporate in any meaningful way into this book. But it would not have forced any large changes to my argument, especially because Pettit's book, even though it refines the language of "non-domination," is not a rewriting of the history of republicanism or the problematic of slavery and freedom.

[32] The conceptual twists and turns involved in cashing out this distinction are complex and ongoing. See Quentin Skinner, "Freedom as the Absence of Arbitrary Power," *Republicanism and Political Theory* (2008), 83–101; Philip Pettit, "Republican Freedom: Three Axioms, Four Theorems," in *Republicanism and Political Theory*, ed. Cecil Laborde and John Maynor (Oxford: Blackwell Publishing, 2008), 102–30; Cecil Laborde and John Maynor, "The Republican Contribution to Political Theory," in *Republicanism and Political Theory*, ed. Cecil Laborde and John Maynor (Oxford: Blackwell Publishing, 2008), 1–28. For important critiques, see Charles Larmore, "Liberal and Republican Conceptions of Freedom," in *Republicanism: History, Theory and Practice*, ed. Daniel Weinstock (London: Routledge, 2004), 96–119; Alan Patten, "The Republican Critique of Liberalism," *British Journal of Political Science* 26, no. 1 (January 1996), 25–44; Robert E. Goodin, "Folie Républicaine," *Annual Review of Political Science* 6, no. 1 (June 2003), 55–76; Eric Nelson, "Liberty: One Concept Too Many?," *Political Theory* 33, no. 1 (February 2005), 58–78; Matthew H. Kramer, "Liberty and Domination," in *Republicanism and Political Theory*, ed. Cecile Laborde and John Maynor (Oxford: Blackwell, 2008), 31–57; Ian Carter, "How Are Power and Unfreedom Related?," in *Republicanism and Political Theory*, ed. Cecil Laborde and John Maynor (Oxford: Blackwell Publishing, 2008), 58–82; Sharon Krause, "Beyond Non-Domination: Agency, Inequality, and the Meaning of Freedom," *Philosophy and Social Criticism* (2012); Patchen Markell, "The Insufficiency of Non-Domination," *Political Theory* 36, no. 1 (February 1, 2008), 9–36.

[33] Pettit, *Republicanism*, 132.

[34] Skinner, "A Third Concept of Liberty," 247.

[35] Pettit, *Republicanism*, 50.

[36] Isaiah Berlin, "Two Concepts of Liberty," in *Four Essays on Liberty* (Oxford; New York: Oxford University Press, 1979), 118–72.

he reproduced at the conceptual level a political defeat. This defeat has been naturalized. According to Skinner, we have become "bewitched into believing that the ways of thinking about [concepts like freedom] bequeathed to us by the mainstream of our intellectual traditions must be *the* ways of thinking about them," which then constrains our political imagination.[37] The task of historical scholarship is to denaturalize this way of thinking about freedom by making us aware that the present constellation of values and conceptual possibilities is neither necessary nor self-evidently the best.

After all, say neo-republicans, the unnatural strictures on our way of thinking about freedom serves certain interests. The liberal concept of "freedom as non-interference remains tied to the sector of interest and opinion that first gave it prominence and currency." This original sector is the "class of profit-seeking entrepreneurs and professionals," self-servingly blind to certain kinds of unfreedom that appear in the private economic domain.[38] The predominant theory of freedom is indifferent to certain forms of unfreedom that deserve our attention, especially in areas such as the economy and the family. Although neo-republicans acknowledge that their concepts were also once tied to a privileged sector of society, "freedom as non-domination transcends its origins."[39] The general hostility to "enslavement and subjection," they say, drives republicanism to "articulate grievances which far outrun the complaints of its founding communities."[40]

Surprisingly, despite these broad claims about the critical power of the republican theory of liberty, these scholars have given us few clear historical examples of moments in which republicanism fully "transcends its origins." Although there is extensive historical scholarship on the early modern republican argument for self-government, these works are of limited use in showing how republicanism goes substantially beyond its classical origins. Were American colonists, who invoked their republican liberty against the arbitrary power of the British Crown in Parliament, really attacking "enslavement and subjection" itself or were they interested in self-government because it protected their own private domination of slaves and Native Americans? Did colonists seek their independence in order to be more secure in their ability to deprive others of their independence? Doubts such as these are why neo-republicans have been subject to the bruising counter-criticism that their own tradition is inescapably inegalitarian and aristocratic.[41] Critics argue

[37] Skinner, *Liberty before Liberalism*, 116.
[38] Pettit, *Republicanism*, 132.
[39] Ibid., 133. For a similar theory of the origins of the liberal view, see also Sandel, *Democracy's Discontent*, 168–84.
[40] Pettit, *Republicanism*, 132.
[41] John P. McCormick, "Machiavelli against Republicanism: On the Cambridge School's 'Guicciardinian Moments,'" *Political Theory* 31, no. 5 (October 2003), 615–43; Eric Ghosh, "From Republican to Liberal Liberty," *History of Political Thought* XXIX, no. 1 (2008), 132–67; Daniel Kapust, "Skinner, Pettit and Livy: The Conflict of the Orders and the Ambiguity

that republicanism is an ideology that is tied to the uncompromising defense of private property against redistribution,[42] whose theory of liberty is compatible with various forms of undemocratic political life,[43] and whose political culture is deeply implicated in conservative traditions of patriotic unity and caste-like customs of deference.[44] What makes these criticisms so forceful is that they draw on actual historical examples of the demand for republican liberty being coupled with self-conscious defenses of these inegalitarian political and social arrangements. Where exactly is the "transcendence of origins"?

Neo-republicans such as Skinner and Pettit readily acknowledge the deep roots of their thinking not just in the classical republics but in one of their most unjust institutions: slavery. As Skinner reminds us, modern republicans "owe their phraseology entirely to the analysis of freedom and slavery at the outset of the *Digest* of Roman law."[45] The Roman law says that, "the fundamental division within the law of persons is that all men are either free or are slaves."[46] In the master-slave relationship, the slave is under the arbitrary power of the master: "[T]he master's power is said to be arbitrary in the sense that it is always open to him to govern his slaves, with impunity, according to his mere *arbitrium*, his own will, and desires."[47] Given this description of slavery, it is no wonder dependence on another's will is the condition to be avoided. In fact, as neo-republicans frequently observe, the republican tradition gets its grip on the social world through the extension of these classical metaphors of mastery and subjection. If "the lack of freedom suffered by slaves is not basically due to their being constrained or interfered with in the exercise of any of their specific choices" but because "they remain subject to the will of their masters,"[48] then the category of "slave" has potentially enormous scope. It is applicable to any relationship bearing these basic features. The origin of republican thinking in Roman jurisprudence appears here not as a liability but as an asset, the fulcrum for its ability to pry open and criticize subjection in various domains of social life.

---

of Republican Liberty," *History of Political Thought* XXV, no. 3 (December 24, 2010), 377–401; Graham Maddox, "The Limits of Neo-Roman Liberty," *History of Political Thought* XXIII, no. 3 (2002), 418–31; Ellen Meiksins Wood, "Why It Matters," *London Review of Books* 30, no. 18 (2008), 3–6.

[42] Wood, "Why It Matters"; Nelson, *The Greek Tradition in Republican Thought*, 1–18.

[43] Kapust, "Skinner, Pettit and Livy"; McCormick, "Machiavelli against Republicanism"; Patchen Markell, "The Insufficiency of Non-Domination."

[44] Richard A. Epstein, "Modern Republicanism, or, The Flight from Substance," *Yale Law Journal* 97, no. 8 (July 1988), 1633–50; Ghosh, "From Republican to Liberal Liberty;" Maddox, "The Limits of Neo-Roman Liberty."

[45] Skinner, "A Third Concept of Liberty," 248.

[46] *The Institutes of Justinian*, trans. J. B. Moyle (BiblioBazaar, 2008), I.iii.

[47] Skinner, "Freedom as the Absence of Arbitrary Power," 86.

[48] Ibid., 89–90.

Nevertheless, if "in the republican tradition ... liberty is always cast in terms of the opposition between *liber* and *servus*, citizen and slave,"[49] it is notable how little neo-republicans say about the actual *servus*. There is almost a sleight of hand whereby the formal acknowledgement that the republican theory originates in and draws its inspiration from slavery excuses the need for any further reflection regarding how, in the classical republics, the freedom of citizens *presupposed* the unfreedom of slaves. These scholars sometimes make it appear that because their theory of freedom arises from a conceptual opposition with slavery their tradition is naturally disposed to say, "enslavement and subjection are the great evils." But the opposite is just as true. Historically and conceptually "enslavement and subjection are the great evils" not because the free citizen hates slavery but because he thinks he does not deserve the servitude that others *rightfully deserve*. Or, at least, the *liber* seeks his *libertas* even if that means others must remain *servi*. Whether liberty is consistent with equality, whether republican liberty can be universalized, is at best an open question. The question of whether republicanism can be egalitarian and critical in the way that its defenders hope and its critics deny hinges on settling this central ambiguity.

The best chance republicanism had of "transcending" its aristocratic origins and of developing an egalitarian critique of enslavement and subjection was when someone other than society's dominant elite used republican language to articulate their concerns. That is precisely what happened when nineteenth-century artisans and wage-laborers appropriated the inherited concepts of independence and virtue and applied them to the world of labor relations. The attempt to universalize the language of republican liberty, and the conceptual innovations that took place in the process, were their contribution to this political tradition.

Over the course of the next five chapters, we trace this complex process of conceptual change and development. This process involved a series of overlapping steps, each of which required real intellectual effort not to mention significant political conflict. This was no straightforward or unproblematic extension of republican concepts to a new domain. No, something conceptually and politically meaningful happened after the American Revolution. The following telling example gives us a brief preview of this process of ideological extension. In June, 1882, the *Journal of United Labor* published the following definition of "slavery":

> The weight of chains, number of stripes, hardness of labor, and other effects of a master's cruelty, may make one servitude more miserable than another; but he is a slave who serves the gentlest man in the world, as well as he who serves the worst; and he does serve him if he *must* obey his commands and depend upon his will.[50]

---

[49] Pettit, *Republicanism*, 31. See also Chaim Wirszubski, *Libertas as a Political Idea at Rome during the Late Republic and Early Principate* (Cambridge: Cambridge University Press, 1968), 1–2.

[50] "Slavery," *JUL* III, no. 2 (June 1882), 248.

All the hallmarks of republican thinking are there. The great evil is dependence on another's will; the benevolence of that will is irrelevant; servitudes vary in their form and misery but they are servitudes all the same. Remarkably, it turns out that these lines are taken verbatim from Algernon Sidney's staunchly republican *Discourses on Government*, which was written exactly 200 years earlier, between 1681 and 1683.[51] The *Discourses* were an attack on monarchy by way of a page-by-page critique of Robert Filmer's famous monarchist tract, *Patriarcha*. Sidney's work earned him an arbitrary trial and summary execution at the hands of Charles II's despotic magistrates.[52] The *Discourses* are shot through with the language of freedom and slavery,[53] announcing at the very beginning the core distinction that structures the work as a whole: "[L]iberty solely consists in an independency upon the will of another, and by the name of slave we understand a man, who can neither dispose of his person nor goods, but enjoys all at the will of his master."[54]

Yet Sidney, like many republicans before him, was primarily concerned with forms of government. The relevant slavery was to a public magistrate, prince, or king, uncontrolled by law and public opinion. However, two centuries later, the Knights were putting these same words to use to criticize a different subjection altogether: the domination of employers. Like Sidney, they thought that the republican definition of slavery made it possible to criticize a wide range of power relationships, not just chattel slavery, but they could rely on much less historical precedent for their practical use of this language than Sidney and his predecessors could.[55] In fact, Sidney himself seems to have thought public freedom was consistent with a large degree of private domination. He wrote, with respect to "my house, land, or estate; I may do what I please with them, if I bring no damage upon others." That is because a republican society "leaves me at liberty to take servants, and put them away at my pleasure. No man ... can

---

[51] Algernon Sidney, *Discourses Concerning Government* (Philadelphia: C. P. Wayne, 1805 [1698]), II:21, p. 181.

[52] Blair Worden, "The Commonwealth Kidney of Algernon Sidney," *The Journal of British Studies* 24, no. 1 (January 1985), 1–40; Alan Craig Houston, *Algernon Sidney and the Republican Heritage in England and America* (Princeton, NJ: Princeton University Press, 1991), 3–98.

[53] The most careful analysis of Sidney's use of these metaphors is Houston, *Algernon Sidney and the Republican Heritage in England and America*, 101–45.

[54] Sidney, *Discourses Concerning Government*, I:5, p. 17.

[55] Although, of course, these earlier figures altered their heritage in important ways. For instance, as James Hankins notes, the idea that a self-governing republic was the only legitimate form of government was an early modern invention. James Hankins, "Exclusivist Republicanism and the Non-Monarchical Republic," *Political Theory* 38, no. 4 (July 27, 2010), 452–82. However, note the important qualification that many modern defenders of republican liberty did not think active self-government was a necessary condition for enjoying non-domination. Werner Maihofer, "The Ethos of the Republic and the Reality of Politics," in *Machiavelli and Republicanism*, ed. Quentin Skinner and Maurizio Viroli Gisela Bock (Cambridge: Cambridge University Press, 1990), 283–92; Daniel Lee, "Popular Liberty, Princely Government, and the Roman Law in Hugo Grotius's De Jure Belli Ac Pacis," *Journal of the History of Ideas* 72, no. 3 (July 2011), 371–92.

tell me whether I am well or ill served by them. Nay, the state takes no other cognizance of what passes between me and them, than to oblige me to perform the contracts I make."[56] In fact, not only did Sidney further believe that propertyless servants did not deserve the vote, but he repeatedly argued that "if there be a contest between me and my servant concerning my service, I only am to decide it: He must serve me in my own way, or be gone if I think fit, tho he serve me never so well; and I do him no wrong in putting him away."[57] The private realm of voluntary contracts remained a place where some serve others "at their pleasure," where servants must accept their employer's "own way" and expect no reciprocal consideration, and where they can claim "no wrong" in the treatment to which they agreed. This is a picture of arbitrary rule by one man over another. For Sidney, private economic domination was perfectly consistent with, even an inextricable part of, his program of quasi-regicidal republican insurrection. No man was a king, but every leading citizen was a minor despot. Sidney could not have better articulated the view that labor republicans would later attack using Sidney's own language.

We can see, then, the transposition of the republican program to the domain of private labor relationships was no simple matter. Despite Sidney's popularity among some later radicals,[58] there were many twists and turns before the kinds of arguments he had made could be carried into mines and factories, not to mention the Louisiana sugar country. The labor republicans had to solve a number of interrelated problems if their tradition was to remain a universalizing language of emancipation. The structure of this book reproduces the progressive unfolding of these various challenges.

As Chapter 1 shows, modern republicans inherited a special dilemma, which I call the "paradox of slavery and freedom." Simply stated, this paradox was a conflict between two propositions. The first was that the independence of the republican citizen presupposed the dependence of slaves. The second was that belief in human equality required that political values be applicable to all, or "universalizable." Republican liberty seemed to conflict with human equality. This was no mere logical paradox; it was an out-and-out historical confrontation over the institution of slavery itself. It was not without reason that American slave-owners thought *they* were the true torchbearers of classical republicanism. However, one important resolution of the paradox, emerging in the confrontation with those slave-owners, was the idea of a republic of free laborers. This free labor ideal defined independence as a condition of self-controlling labor that all could enjoy. The ideal was meant to resolve the tension between freedom and equality in favor of a universalizable conception of economic independence.

---

[56] Sidney, *Discourses Concerning Government*, II:41, pp. 337–38.
[57] Ibid., 339.
[58] On Sidney in America, see Houston, *Algernon Sidney and the Republican Heritage in England and America*, 223–78.

However, as Chapter 2 shows, the free labor ideal was beset by a further ambiguity. Was wage-labor a form of free labor? The wage-laborer had been a liminal presence in early modern republicanism, but the rise of industrial capitalism pressed on this question with new intensity, even before the slavery issue was settled. The anonymous interdependence of the labor market and the growth of large-scale industrial labor processes seemed to eliminate all forms of purely personal dependence. But it also put new dependences in their place, not to mention threatened the small-scale proprietorship that had given the free labor ideal its social basis. One response to this dilemma, offered by nineteenth-century "laissez-faire republicans," was to say that the wage-laborer was economically independent in the morally relevant way. The wage-laborer controlled his labor the way any property-owner controlled his property, thus wage-labor was free labor and the paradox of slavery and freedom finally resolved.

Labor republicans rejected this position. As the final three chapters show, they incorporated conceptual elements from political economy and cooperative socialism to argue that the wage-laborer, though not a chattel slave, was still subject to various new kinds of economic dependence. Wage-labor was in fact wage-slavery. Only the cooperative commonwealth, a condition in which all workers exercised joint ownership and control over industrial enterprises, could offer everyone a condition of free labor. This vision not only responded to laissez-faire republican arguments, but overcame the nostalgic agrarianism of earlier generations unwilling to think through what republican liberty could mean in an industrial society.

These ideas about cooperation and independence spilled over into a new conception of civic virtue. Republicans had conventionally argued that virtue was a set of qualities whose purpose was to preserve existing free institutions and that had to be coercively inculcated by the state. Labor republicans, in contrast, reinterpreted these virtues as habits of cooperation and collective action that the dependents cultivated in themselves so as to transform society. Civic virtue became a principle of active solidarity. The cooperative commonwealth would make wage-slaves free, but only if wage-slaves brought this cooperative commonwealth into being themselves. This was the full force of Ira Steward's pronouncement that, "something of slavery still remains … something of freedom is yet to come."[59] Once we reconstruct the ideas of the labor republicans, we might come to see not just the force of their words in their own time, but that something of freedom is yet to come for us as well.

[59] Steward, "Poverty," 412.

I

The Paradox of Slavery and Freedom

> *No legislator of antiquity ever attempted to abrogate slavery;*
> *on the contrary, the people most enthusiastic for liberty –*
> *the Athenians, the Lacedemonians, the Romans, and the Carthaginians*
> *– were those who enacted the most severe laws against their serfs.*[1]
>
> Voltaire

Voltaire's assault on ancient liberty, which forms the epigraph to this chapter, contains a familiar liberal criticism of the classical republics. The "most enthusiastic" advocates of liberty in the classical republics were some of the most ardent slave-owners. A half-century and a French Revolution later, Benjamin Constant plowed the same ground: "[W]ithout the slave population of Athens, 20,000 Athenians could never have spent every day at the public square in discussions."[2] Polemical as these formulations were, they carried a strong grain of truth, enough to worry modern inheritors of republican ideas. Some, including slave-owners in the American South, bit the bullet and defended their peculiar institution on the grounds that they were the true defenders of republican liberty. As John C. Calhoun, a Senator from South Carolina who served for seven years as Vice President, put it, "I fearlessly assert that the existing relation between the two races in the South ... forms the most solid and durable foundation on which to rear free and stable political institutions."[3] Even after the abolition of slavery in the United States, the

---

[1] M. De Voltaire, "Slaves," in *A Philosophical Dictionary Vol. 2* (London: W. Dugdale, 1843 [1764]), 460.

[2] Benjamin Constant, "The Liberty of the Ancients as Compared with That of the Moderns," in *Constant: Political Writings*, ed. Biancamaria Fontana (Cambridge: Cambridge University Press, 1988 [1816]), 314.

[3] John C. Calhoun, "Speech on the Reception of Abolition Petitions," in *Slavery Defended: The Views of the Old South*, ed. Eric L. McKitrick (New York: Columbia University Press, 1963 [1837]), 14.

compatibility of slavery and republican liberty remained a guiding concern. George McNeill's *The Labor Movement: The Problem of To-day*, an authoritative collection of late nineteenth-century views on the labor question, opened with the observation that, "in Greece and Rome slavery was recognized as a fundamental institution of the state – the absolute condition of any progress in the arts and sciences." It is "not likely to be true" that "the free citizens of the Roman Empire supported themselves in agriculture by their own labor without the assistance of slaves."[4]

However they judged ancient society, many modern republicans knew they faced a particular kind of conflict between freedom and equality. It appeared to any interpreter of republican liberty that the independence of free citizens presupposed the dependence of slaves. Yet, if freedom could not be enjoyed by all, if some had to be slaves so that others could be free, then respect for human equality required abandoning republican liberty.

I call this dilemma the paradox of slavery and freedom. The paradox can be stated logically as a contradiction between two propositions. The first proposition is that republican liberty is a socially constituted condition of independence made possible by the servitude of others. The second proposition is that human beings are equal and thus all legitimate political values must be universalizable, or enjoyable by all. The particularism of a commitment to republican liberty – independence for a particular class, dependence for another class – logically conflicts with the universalism of the commitment to human equality. Hence a paradox. Although we can state this paradox logically, it is not a free-floating intellectual or moral dilemma. It was a practical problem that emerged historically as modern republicans reflected on the theory and practice of classical city-states. As the labor question came to the fore in the nineteenth century, the paradox of slavery and freedom became the site of a struggle over the fate of the republican tradition itself. As concrete political challenges to slavery and then wage-labor developed, it became all the more urgent to resolve this paradox – to decide whether and how republican liberty can be universalized, or whether human slavery is the necessary price of liberty. The ideal of free labor was, in part, the fruit of this ideological struggle.

This chapter shows how the paradox of slavery and freedom emerged as a historical problem and why "free labor" appeared as an answer to the paradox. The first section shows how both the theory and practice of the ancient republics communicated the idea that freedom presupposed slavery. In the classical republics, however, there was at most a dilemma, not a paradox, because there was no requirement that liberty be available to all. The second section then shows how the rise of a modern commitment to human equality generated the paradox itself, and how the ideal of free labor emerged as a response to this struggle.

---

[4] McNeill, *The Labor Movement: The Problem of to-Day*, 3–4.

Slavery and Ancient Liberty

Athens and Rome as Slave Societies: The Emergence of Freedom

Consider that, while all ancient societies "shared without exception, and throughout their history, a need for dependent, involuntary labor,"[5] it is in Athens and Rome that the relevant ideas about freedom first emerged. What set classical Athens[6] and Rome apart from their neighbors was the increasing dependence on the slave labor of noncitizens.[7] This "fundamental difference" marked by the shift "from reliance on the half-free within to reliance on chattel slaves from outside" was connected to an equally important "corollary": "the emergence of the idea of freedom."[8] The classical republics acquired their characteristically free institutions just as they became slave societies.

Slave societies in what sense? After all, most Athenians and Romans likely did not own slaves.[9] Most Athenians were in agriculture, and "the vast majority of the rural producers remained free persons in Greece."[10] There is similar evidence for the existence of hired labor, freehold farming, and independent craftsmanship in classical Rome.[11] If slaves never numbered more than one for every three free citizens, and were probably not a majority of the entire workforce, then perhaps they were not slave societies at all.[12] But it is not absolute

---

[5] Moses Finley, "Between Slavery and Freedom," *Comparative Studies in Society and History* 6, no. 3 (1964), 244.

[6] Ibid., 238–41.

[7] Ibid., 244–47.

[8] Ibid., 245, emphasis added. See also Orlando Patterson, *Freedom Vol. 1: Freedom in the Making of Western Culture* (New York: Basic Books, 1991), 1–44.

[9] Moses Finley, "Was Greek Civilization Based on Slave Labour?," in *Slavery in Classical Antiquity: Views and Controversies*, ed. M. I. Finley (Cambridge: W. Heffer & Sons Ltd., 1960); Ellen Meiksins Wood, *Peasant-Citizen and Slave: The Foundations of Athenian Democracy* (London: Verso, 1988), 42–80; Peter Garnsey, "Non-Slave Labour in the Roman World," *Cambridge Philological Society*, Supplementary Volume no. 6 (1980), 34–47; Peter Garnsey, "Peasants in Ancient Roman Society," in *Cities, Peasants and Food in Classical Antiquity*, ed. Walter Scheidel (Cambridge: Cambridge University Press, 1998), 91–106; Keith Hopkins, *Conquerors and Slaves* (Cambridge: Cambridge University Press, 1981), 99–132; Patterson, *Freedom Vol. 1*, 80–81; J. E. Skydsgaard, "The Disintegration of the Roman Labour Market and the Clientela Theory," in *Studia Romana in Honorem Petri Krarup Septuagenarii*, ed. Karen Ascani (Odense, 1976), 44–48.

[10] Patterson, *Freedom Vol. 1*, 70. Also, Finley, "Was Greek Civilization Based on Slave Labour?," 154.

[11] In addition to earlier references, see Andrew Lintott, "Citizenship," in *A Companion to Ancient History*, ed. Andrew Erskine (West Sussex: Blackwell, 2009), 515–17; Andrew Lintott, *Judicial Reform and Land Reform in the Roman Republic* (Cambridge: Cambridge University Press, 1992), 5, 34–39, 41–43; G. E. M. De Ste Croix, "Review: Slavery," *The Classical Review* 7, no. 1 (1957), 58–59; Moses Finley, *The Ancient Economy*, (Berkeley: University of California Press, 1999), 95–122; Patterson, *Freedom Vol. 1*, 212–19.

[12] Representatives of this view include Chester G. Starr, "An Overdose of Slavery," *The Journal of Economic History* 18, no. 1 (1958), 17–32; A. H. M. Jones, "Slavery in the Ancient World," in *Slavery in Classical Antiquity: Controversies and Debates*, ed. Moses Finley (Cambridge: W. Heffer & Sons Ltd., 1960), 1–16.

The Paradox of Slavery and Freedom

numbers but role and function that matter. A comparison with the American South is helpful here. In 1860, slightly less than a third of the population of the slave states were slaves, most Southerners were nonslaveholding farmers, yet "no one would think of denying that slavery was a decisive element in southern society."[13] By comparison, the use and ownership of slaves was, if anything, more widespread in Rome and Athens than in the American South.[14] Slave labor permeated, and sometimes dominated, many areas of economic activity, setting the tone for the general organization of and opinions about work.[15]

The coemergence of slavery and freedom is not accidental. It reflects a real historical process by which freedom-guaranteeing institutions were constituted in the classical republics. The rise of independent citizenship altered the balance of power between poor and rich citizens, making it difficult to compel peasants and artisans to work for others. In both Athens and Rome, "the peasantry had won their personal freedom and their tenure on the land through struggle, in which they also won citizenship, membership in the community, the polis."[16] They acquired basic legal protections, political rights, the exclusive right to own land, and the abolition of debt-slavery. This bundle of rights meant the average citizen had sufficient economic alternatives and civil power to avoid being forced to perform continuous labor for other citizens.[17] As one historian puts it, "everyone knew the impossibility of compelling the peasant- or artisan-citizens ... to become a hired labour force ... everyone knew that free men would not regularly work for another voluntarily."[18]

---

[13] Finley, "Was Greek Civilization Based on Slave Labour?," 151.

[14] See, for instance, Finley, *The Ancient Economy*, 79; Finley, "Between Slavery and Freedom," 238–39, 42–44; Michael H. Jameson, "Agriculture and Slavery in Classical Athens," *The Classical Journal* 73, no. 2 (1977–1978); Patterson, *Freedom Vol. 1*, 64–81, 203–26.

[15] Aside from the sources already cited, see also W. L. Westermann, "Slavery and the Elements of Freedom," in *Slavery in Classical Antiquity: Views and Controversies*, ed. M. I. Finley (Cambridge: W. Heffer & Sons Ltd., 1960), 17–32; Garnsey, "Non-Slave Labour in the Roman World." Nobody disputes the extensive use of slaves in mining and urban manufacturing. There is more disagreement about its role in agriculture. It appears that in Rome, slave labor on large latifundias squeezed out the independent, "free" labor of the peasants in certain areas. See Garnsey, "Non-Slave Labour in the Roman World;" Garnsey, "Peasants in Ancient Roman Society"; Lintott, *Judicial Reform and Land Reform in the Roman Republic*, 41–49, 55–58.

[16] Finley, *Ancient Slavery and Modern Ideology*, 89–90.

[17] Claude Mossé, *The Ancient World at Work*, trans. Janet Lloyd (New York: W. W. Norton & Company, 1969), 49. Finley notes that "after Solon debt-bondage and other non-slave forms of involuntary labor effectively ceased to exist in Attica." Finley, *Ancient Slavery and Modern Ideology*, 87; Josiah Ober, *Mass and Elite in Democratic Athens: Rhetoric, Ideology, and the Power of the People* (Princeton, NJ: Princeton University Press, 1990), 60–64. Likewise, in the early Roman republic, "debt-bondage was made illegal in Rome in 326 BC." Hopkins, *Conquerors and Slaves*, 22. See also Lintott, *The Constitution of the Roman Republic*, 36–37; Claude Nicolet, *The World of the Citizen in Republican Rome*, trans. P. S. Falla (Berkeley: University of California Press, 1980), 149–53, 317–24; Patterson, *Freedom Vol. 1*, 66–67, 204–09.

[18] Finley, *Ancient Slavery and Modern Ideology*, 90.

Peasant-citizen independence forced the classical economies toward other labor sources, namely slavery. As one commentator puts it, "mass chattel slavery has arisen only where there was either a shortage of a local labour force in the conquered territory, or some effective limitation on the number and degree to which conquerors could themselves be exploited; or both."[19] The "effective limitation" in the classical republics was the aforementioned economic independence of the citizen – a defining feature of both "democracy in Athens and plebeian privileges in Rome."[20] As one historian says of the peasant-citizen, "the creation of that type of free man in a low-technology, pre-industrial world led to the establishment of a slave society. There was no realistic alternative."[21] Slaves would have to work the large plantations, mines, and urban workshops that were the basis for the growing wealth of the upper classes, as well as the foundation of these states' war-making abilities.[22] Slave labor allowed upper classes to maintain and even increase their wealth without directly threatening the independence of the free laborers. The privileges of citizenship, meanwhile, wedded poor citizens to their slave society.[23] Both the leisure of the wealthy and the free labor of the poor citizen presupposed social and political privileges sustained by the dependence of slave labor.

These are general claims about the historical necessity of slavery in classical republics that promised freedom to their citizens. These claims hold despite the important institutional and social differences of the ethnically constrained, small-scale Athenian democracy and the multinational, continuously expanding Roman republic. Freedom presupposed slavery not just because the few demanded their propertied leisure. Rather, it was the preservation of that leisure together with the relative independence of poorer citizens that forced a turn to slave labor.

The interdependence of slavery and freedom was not just a sociological fact of the classical republics. It was consciously understood and formally acknowledged – a cultural feature of those republics that modern readers would have noticed. It has been noted that one of Athenian "society's most fundamental and determining ideas" was "the consciousness of the division between slaves and free men."[24] The sentiment is echoed in Rome by the well-known statement from the Digest that "the fundamental division within the law of persons is that all men are either free or are slaves," a distinction that has

---

[19] Hopkins, *Conquerors and Slaves*, 114.
[20] Ibid.
[21] Finley, *Ancient Slavery and Modern Ideology*, 90.
[22] Hopkins, *Conquerors and Slaves*, 114.
[23] As Josiah Ober puts it in the case of Athens, "by loosening the ties of birth at the top of the social order and strengthening them at the bottom, Solon could reasonably hope to achieve long-term social stability.... Defining the rights of citizenship in terms of personal freedom severed the interest of the poor from those of the foreign slaves." Ober, *Mass and Elite in Democratic Athens*, 63, generally 59–65.
[24] Fisher, *Slavery in Classical Greece*, 1.

The Paradox of Slavery and Freedom

been the touchstone not only for early moderns but also for neo-republicans.[25] Freedom and slavery were foundational classifications through which a wide variety of social relations were understood. "For social status ... and often for purposes of private law," Athenians and Romans were often willing to use the "simple antinomy, slave or free" despite awareness of "certain gradations" of social standing and especially of kinds of labor.[26]

Thus, while it is true to say that republican liberty can be understood as the "opposite" of slavery, this thought has to be managed carefully. Recall Philip Pettit's claim that the theory of republican liberty has extraordinary critical potential because it is "an idiom of freedom in which enslavement and subjection are the great ills."[27] It is evident that the sheer conceptual opposition of freedom to slavery did not, on its own, generate a criticism of slavery. Instead, the original value of freedom rested on the fact that the free were lucky or deserving enough to avoid the servitude to which others were necessarily or legitimately condemned. Freedom was the opposite of slavery because it was a negation of that condition of dependence to which various classes of humanity were still subject. Although slavery was to be abhorred, it was also accepted, even defended. There is of course no shortage of denunciations of enslavement in the ancient republics. Solon, for instance, demanded the repatriation of all Athenian slaves; Cicero objected to the "servitude" of Romans subjected to kingly power.[28] These, however, were denunciations of the enslavement of those who *ought not* to be enslaved, or criticisms of political analogues to chattel slavery.[29] There are few known ancient critics of slave labor *tout court*, and none who rejected slavery or those forms of dependent labor akin to slavery.[30] Even ancient slave revolts do not seem to have sought the abolition of the institution of slavery itself. They sought *their* freedom.[31] The aspiration of the average free citizen was to become a slave-owner himself.[32] Hence, if republican liberty is "an idiom of freedom in which enslavement and subjection are the great ills," its ideological power originally rested on the assumption that

---

[25] Quoted in Skinner, "A Third Concept of Liberty," 248. See *The Institutes of Justinian*.
[26] Finley, "Between Slavery and Freedom," 233.
[27] Pettit, *Republicanism*, 132.
[28] Cicero, *On Duties*, trans. E. M. Atkins (Cambridge: Cambridge University Press, 1991), II.63; Cicero, "On the Commonwealth," in *On the Commonwealth and on the Laws*, ed. James E. G. Zetzel (Cambridge: Cambridge University Press, 2003), I.50.
[29] E.g., examples from Cicero in Arthur Albert Rupprecht Jr., "A Study of Slavery in the Late Roman Republic from the Works of Cicero" (Dissertation, University of Pennsylvania, 1960), 173–86.
[30] Critics laid out codes of ethics for slave masters, or argued that slaves could be virtuous *despite* their servitude. Garnsey, *Ideas of Slavery from Aristotle to Augustine*, 53–63, 75–86, 237–43; Finley, "Between Slavery and Freedom," 244.
[31] Finley, *The Ancient Economy*, 80–84; Finley, "Between Slavery and Freedom," 236.
[32] On Rome, Garnsey, "Non-Slave Labour in the Roman World;" Skydsgaard, "The Disintegration of the Roman Labour Market and the Clientela Theory." On Greece, Fisher, *Slavery in Classical Greece*, 45; Jameson, "Agriculture and Slavery in Classical Athens," 139.

freedom presupposed slavery. Freedom was a privilege, not a universal right. There was little in the conceptual apparatus or in the broader set of attitudes surrounding republican liberty, however that idea was interpreted, that raised the question whether it ought to be universalized.

The main sources for modern republicanism ring out with this particularistic vision. Whether moderns looked to the leading political philosophers, Aristotle or Cicero, or to the dominant institutions and practices of Athens or Rome, they would have discovered some version of the idea that freedom presupposed slavery. To be sure, the Athenians and Romans negotiated this relationship between freedom and slavery differently. The Athenian democracy was grounded in the idea that everybody ought to rule and be ruled in turn as equals. For the Romans, the key to political liberty lay in the complex formula of the balanced constitution, which offered the plebs a certain degree of political power and civil protection in relation to the propertied senators and magistrates who ran the day-to-day state machinery. But, when it came to slavery, these were variations on a theme. Let us look briefly at Aristotle and Athens and then turn to Cicero and Rome. Although the interpretive and historiographic issues here are immense and contested, we must have at least the outlines of the dilemma facing modern republican thought in all its variations.

Freedom and Slavery I: Aristotle and the Athenians
In our time, neo-Aristotelian republicans point to the "long-standing republican conviction that economic independence is essential to citizenship."[33] Independence is a necessary condition for developing the virtues and for having the time required for participation in politics. This is a reasonable reading of Aristotle, who says that the free citizen must be capable of "participation in judgment and office."[34] This participation requires that each possess the virtue or excellence required for good citizenship, which Aristotle summarizes as "the capacity to rule and be ruled."[35] The capacity for ruling and being ruled breaks down into a natural ability and the opportunity to develop this ability. That is because, on Aristotle's account, "people become excellent because of three things ... nature, habit and reason."[36] This view of the development of virtue explains Aristotle's thinking on slavery.

There are, says Aristotle, slaves by nature.[37] A natural slave lacks deliberative reason,[38] which means he lacks the natural ability to form independent judgments about his own or the shared good. Slavery is thus of "mutual benefit and mutual friendship for ... masters and slaves" because it allows

---

[33] Sandel, *Democracy's Discontent*, 169.
[34] Aristotle, *Politics*, trans. C. D. C. Reeve (Indianapolis: Hackett, 1998), 1275a23.
[35] Ibid., 1277a25.
[36] Ibid., 1332a39–40.
[37] Ibid., 1254a6–55b15.
[38] Ibid., 1254b21–23.

the slave indirectly to participate in deliberative reason.[39] However, equally important for Aristotle is that there are those, such as craftsmen and hired laborers, who, though not natural slaves, appear to share in the essential quality of slaves: lack of deliberative reason. For instance, "a vulgar craftsman has a kind of delimited slavery."[40] Activities like craft-work are analogous to slavery because they involve dependence on another's will. "It is the mark of a free man not to live at another's beck and call"[41] because only with that kind of independence can he develop the requisite virtues. Craftsmen and hired laborers, however, are subject to a kind of "rule by a master," based on taking orders and anticipating needs, rather than "the kind of rule exercised over those who are similar in birth and free [that] we call 'political' rule."[42] These labors "debase the mind and deprive it of LEISURE,"[43] rendering "free people useless for the practices and activities of virtue."[44] In other words, the daily labor of vulgar craftsmen and hired laborers make them slaves by *habit*, not by nature. They are daily subject to orders, never give orders or assemble with free men, and never have the time or opportunity to develop their deliberative capacities. While Aristotle's theory of natural slavery draws the most attention, it is the broader theory of how virtue develops that explains what counts as independence or servitude. That is why the relevant conception of dependence is "not restricted to slaves but was extended to wage labour and to others who were economically dependent."[45]

Of course, Aristotle's view of work and citizenship is complex. He argues that, ideally, citizens should not engage in *any* work "since leisure is needed both to develop virtue and to engage in political actions."[46] Nevertheless, he also allows that self-sufficient, land-owning farmers might also enjoy adequate independence to count as not-servile.[47] Because of its self-sufficiency, this class is moderate and law-abiding, forming a stabilizing, middle element in any constitution.[48] So, for Aristotle, when the necessary forms of servitude ("hirelings" and vulgar craftsmen) intrude into the citizenry, they constitute a threat to the practices and institutions that maintain freedom. Furthermore, although the category of independent citizen *can* be extended to include peasant proprietors, it is assumed they will not participate too much,[49] and that the ideal condition

---

[39] Ibid., 1255b12–13.
[40] Ibid., 1260a42–1269ob1.
[41] Aristotle, *Rhetoric*, trans. W. Rhys Roberts (New York: Courier Dover Publications, 2004), 1367a31–32.
[42] Aristotle, *Politics*, 1277a32, 77b6–7.
[43] Ibid., 1337b13–14.
[44] Ibid., 1337b11.
[45] Finley, *The Ancient Economy*, 41; Finley, "Between Slavery and Freedom," 239.
[46] Aristotle, *Politics*, 1328b37–29a1.
[47] Ibid., 1318b6–19a19.
[48] Ibid. 1292b28, 1295a25–96b1.
[49] Fisher, *Slavery in Classical Greece*, 40–41; Jameson, "Agriculture and Slavery in Classical Athens."

of independence remains slave-supported leisure. Even on this nuanced view, Aristotle's views force a series of judgments about the way freedom presupposes a variety of servile forms of labor.

If we look past Aristotle's aristocratic views to the Athenian democracy, then the connection between freedom and slavery might appear weaker. The democracy, after all, *ennobled* labor by creating a "'radically new' phenomenon, the peasant-citizen."[50] Athenian democracy appears to teach not the exaltation of leisure, but the celebration of free labor. However, this Athenian ideal shares with Aristotle the view that not just chattel slavery but various other kinds of dependent labor are servile, especially wage-labor.[51] That is probably why, to the degree there is evidence of citizens hiring themselves out, it was to supplement their income, not as a permanent occupation, and it retained a stigma.[52] Moreover, the exclusion of dependence from production and the exaltation of "independent" labor was an ideal that held for citizens only. The rise of independent citizen-farmers went hand-in-hand with a shift to slave production in large rural estates and in urban workshops.[53] Even the peasant-citizens themselves might have held or aspired to hold a slave so as to ease work burdens and to make possible adequate leisure to participate politically.[54] After all, the democratic citizen found himself called to some public event – religious, civic, or political – almost one out of every two days.[55] Thus, even if we take the peasant-citizen, not leisured citizen, to be the thematic figure, the logic of this citizen's independence still presupposes slavery. A conclusion reinforced by the ethnic character of Athenian citizenship, which morally and politically bound even those nonslaveowning peasant-citizens to a system based on slave labor.[56]

In sum, whether modern republicans look at Aristotle or Athens, they might discover an ideal of the independent peasant-proprietor, but there is little in the theory or practice of that peasant's citizenship that suggests it was inconsistent with the institution of slavery and plenty that suggests it presupposed slavery.

---

[50] Wood, *Peasant-Citizen and Slave: The Foundations of Athenian Democracy*, 81–83.
[51] Finley, *Ancient Slavery and Modern Ideology*, 87; Ober, *Mass and Elite in Democratic Athens*, 61–62.
[52] Ober, *Mass and Elite in Democratic Athens*, 129–30; Jameson, "Agriculture and Slavery in Classical Athens," esp. 132–41; Patterson, *Freedom Vol. 1*, 72–79; Fisher, *Slavery in Classical Greece*, 100–03; Ober, *Mass and Elite in Democratic Athens*, 274–79.
[53] Compare Wood, *Peasant-Citizen and Slave: The Foundations of Athenian Democracy*, 42–80; Finley, "Was Greek Civilization Based on Slave Labour?"; Ober, *Mass and Elite in Democratic Athens*, 61–62; Patterson, *Freedom Vol. 1*, 76–81.
[54] Fisher, *Slavery in Classical Greece*, 45–46; Jameson, "Agriculture and Slavery in Classical Athens," 40–46; Finley, "Between Slavery and Freedom;" Patterson, *Freedom Vol. 1*, 64–81.
[55] Mogens Herman Hansen, *The Athenian Democracy in the Age of Demosthenes* (Oxford: Blackwell, 1991).
[56] Ober, *Mass and Elite in Democratic Athens*, 61.

Freedom and Slavery II: Cicero and the Romans

But perhaps the foregoing is only of concern for neo-Aristotelian republicans. As scholars like Quentin Skinner and Philip Pettit have argued, there is an important distinction between the Athenian and the Roman understanding of liberty. Roman *libertas* gives no special priority to political participation or to particular human capacities. Freedom is independence, regardless of any specific capacities this independence allows us to develop and exercise. As a legal status, available to all members of an expanding multiethnic republic, Roman liberty had a more universalizing character than the Athenian.[57]

The differences between Rome and Athens cannot be ignored. However, although liberty in the Roman context revolved around a theory of the balanced constitution and legal status, not equal democratic citizenship, it was still the case that freedom presupposed slavery. The Romans gave this relationship a different inflection. For instance, while the *Institutes* stated that slavery is "against nature,"[58] that just meant that slavery, like freedom, was a legal convention. The unnatural character of slavery in no way implied a rejection of it so much as a different justification. Slavery was necessary for maintaining a free republic and was thus legitimate.

Consider the following passages from two of the most influential texts in the neo-Roman tradition.[59] In the *Conspiracy of Catiline*, Sallust writes that, once out of politics, he refuses to "waste [his] valuable leisure in indolence and inactivity, or, engaging in servile occupations, to spend my time in agriculture or hunting."[60] Similarly, Cicero, in *On Duties*, says that "all those workers who are paid for their labour and not for their skill have servile and demeaning employment; for in their case the very wage is a contract to servitude."[61] He later continues that "there is no kind of gainful employment that is better, more fruitful, more pleasant and more worthy of a free man than agriculture."[62] By agriculture Cicero does not mean farming but rather landed wealth in which others till the soil.[63] Together, Cicero and Sallust present the view that some occupations are "of a menial kind"[64]; that any labor performed for a wage is

---

[57] E.g., Quentin Skinner, "The Republican Ideal of Political Liberty," in *Machiavelli and Republicanism*, ed. Quentin Skinner and Maurizio Viroli Gisela Bock (Cambridge: Cambridge University Press, 1990), 292–309; Fergus Millar, *The Roman Republic in Political Thought* (Lebanon: University Press of New England, 2002).

[58] *The Institutes of Justinian*, I.iii.2.

[59] Skinner, "Machiavelli's *Discorsi* and the Pre-Humanist Origins of Republican Ideas."

[60] Sallust, *Conspiracy of Catiline*, trans. Rev. John Selby Watson (New York and London: Harper & Brothers, 1899), I.IV. See also Cicero, *On the Ends of Good and Evil*, trans. H. Rackham (London: Loeb Classical Library, 1914), I.III.

[61] Cicero, *On Duties*, [I.150] 58.

[62] Ibid., [I.151] 58.

[63] Cicero's meaning is evident from the context, in which he says agriculture is best only after listing all other occupations from the lowest status crafts to "small scale" trading to large merchants and finally "agriculture" or landed wealth. Ibid., I.150–51.

[64] Cicero, *On the Ends of Good and Evil*, I.3.

servile; that the only real independence is that of leisured, landed wealth[65]; and any reader would have known and assumed that this land would have been worked by slaves.[66]

These different ideas are held together in the idea of the balanced constitution. The core feature of this balanced constitution is that the upper classes ruled while the plebs enjoyed certain basic protections. Cicero identifies this balance as the key to the liberty all citizens enjoy: "[T]he state, through the reasoned balance of the highest and the lowest and the intervening orders, is harmonious in the concord of very different people."[67] This "moderate and harmonious order of the state [is] maintained" by a "blending of rights" in which "the people have power and the senate has authority."[68] Crucially, the "real, not nominal, freedom" of the plebs is consistent with and dependent on the willingness "to yield to the authority of the first citizens."[69] Cicero regularly praises the "many excellent customs"[70] that produce this deference, including respect for tradition and religious authorities, not to mention private property.[71] Meanwhile, the ruling class must be "free from necessary business"[72] so that it has the leisure to acquire "the proper education and training"[73] and to discharge its duties. A life "free from necessary business" requires slaves

[65] Notably, both Sallust and Cicero are essentially apologizing for doing something (writing) that can be confused with working rather than active politics. They offer their writings as the best service they can render to the republic in its decline. Cicero, *On Duties*, II.5; Sallust, *Conspiracy of Catiline*, I.III-IV. To be sure, there are many examples of Cicero praising the manly, self-dependent, and martial, virtues of agricultural labor over commerce and urban manufacture. Cicero, "On the Commonwealth," II.7; Cicero, *The Nature of the Gods*, trans. H. Rackham (Cambridge: Harvard University Press, Loeb Classical Library, 1956), II.99. Cicero, "On Old Age," in *On Old Age, on Friendship, on Divination* (Cambridge: Harvard University Press, Loeb Classical Library, 1923), 56-61; Paul A. Brunt, "The Roman Mob," *Past & Present* 35 (1966), 24; Wood, *Cicero's Social and Political Thought*, 96-97. But when Cicero celebrates "the pastures filled with cattle, and the teeming life of the woodlands!" (*On the Nature of the Gods*) or hypothesizes that "no life can be happier than that of the farmer" (*On Old Age*), he speaks as the observer, not the worker, enjoying the "charm" of the pastoral idol, or as an old man no longer able to participate in public life.
[66] Garnsey, "Peasants in Ancient Roman Society"; Hopkins, *Conquerors and Slaves*, 109-14; Lintott, *Judicial Reform and Land Reform in the Roman Republic*, 5, 41-43.
[67] Cicero, "On the Commonwealth," II.69a.
[68] This meant the people have formal supremacy but the Senate has moral authority. Cicero, "On the Laws," in *On the Commonwealth and on the Laws*, trans. James E.G. Zetzel (Cambridge: Cambridge University Press, 2003), III.28, III.25. Lintott, *The Constitution of the Roman Republic*, 65-93, 222-23, 230-32; Malcolm Schofield, "Cicero's Definition of *Res Publica*," in *Cicero the Philosopher: Twelve Papers*, ed. J.G.F. Powell (Oxford: Clarendon Press, 1995).
[69] Cicero, "On the Laws," III.25.
[70] Ibid.
[71] Ibid., II.26 and 30, generally 19-69. For Cicero on property, see Cicero, *On Duties*, II.78-79, II.82-84, III.30-31; Nelson, *The Greek Tradition in Republican Thought*, 57-59; Lintott, *The Constitution of the Roman Republic*, 220-32; Wood, *Cicero's Social and Political Thought*, 105-19.
[72] Cicero, *On Duties*, [I.13] 6.
[73] Cicero, "On the Commonwealth," III.29.

The Paradox of Slavery and Freedom

working the plantations, not to mention managing business affairs and political correspondence, because the poor citizen cannot be made to do so and the ruling class cannot spare the time.[74] In all, Cicero's works draw a picture of a political order in which slavery was a precondition for the balanced constitution and thus for political liberty.[75]

Of course, Cicero romanticized the Roman republic, failing to concede that much of the institutional "balance" that existed was the product of violent conflicts, not everyday concord.[76] Yet if one was inclined to look to the Roman law and its political institutions, not just its most famous thinkers, one also found that freedom presupposed servitude. Studies of *libertas* as an institution find that first in importance were those rights guaranteeing that "the magistrates' coercive power was not unlimited."[77] The reason is that social status came with legal privileges, which extended from the highest public offices to the basics of criminal procedure.[78] These legal privileges "eliminated a large number of citizens" from many positions of power. There "grew up a ruling class" occupying the key political, administrative, and military offices.[79] Thus, when *libertas* was understood as a set of basic rights to limit "magistrates' coercive power," these rights presupposed that the magistrate was a member of a different class. That, in turn, is why *libertas* was spoken of as the condition of a class, not an individual: "the Plebs as a whole, and not with regard to any individual."[80] The idea of *libertas* was invoked "by the people as a whole vis a vis the dominant oligarchies (patricians and senators), and by the plebs against members of the old gentes."[81] By freedom from domination, then, the lower orders sought something more defensive than continuous participation in rule. They sought protection from the arbitrary power of a ruling class.[82]

---

[74] Susan Treggiari, "The Freedmen of Cicero," *Greece & Rome* 16, no. 2 (1969); Skydsgaard, "The Disintegration of the Roman Labour Market and the Clientela Theory," 47–48; Rupprecht, "A Study of Slavery in the Late Roman Republic from the Works of Cicero," 88–118, 188–89.

[75] See also Garnsey, *Ideas of Slavery from Aristotle to Augustine*, 40–43.

[76] Andrew Lintott, *The Constitution of the Roman Republic* (Oxford: Clarendon Press, 1999) 213–32.

[77] Nicolet, *The World of the Citizen in Republican Rome*, 320.

[78] Peter Garnsey, *Social Status and Legal Privilege in the Roman Empire* (Oxford: Oxford University Press, 1970), 263; Wirszubski, *Libertas as a Political Idea at Rome During the Late Republic and Early Principate*, 9–15; Nicolet, *The World of the Citizen in Republican Rome*, 207–324. Also Brunt, "The Roman Mob"; Patterson, *Freedom Vol. 1*, 203–26; Elizabeth Rawson, "The Ciceronian Aristocracy and Its Properties," in *Studies in Roman Property*, ed. M. I. Finley (Cambridge: Syndics of the Cambridge University Press, 1976).

[79] Nicolet, *The World of the Citizen in Republican Rome*, 318. Also Cicero, *On Duties*, xxv; Patterson, *Freedom Vol. 1*, 219–26; Wood, *Cicero's Social and Political Thought*, 22–29.

[80] Wirszubski, *Libertas as a Political Idea at Rome during the Late Republic and Early Principate*, 11.

[81] Nicolet, *The World of the Citizen in Republican Rome*, 320.

[82] See also Kapust, "Skinner, Pettit and Livy: the Conflict of the Orders and the Ambiguity of Republican Liberty," 377–401. I return to this defensive character of Roman liberty at the end of Chapter 4.

Even this more limited vision of independence gave poor Romans enough power to resist performing continuous labor for the upper classes. Their defensive rights included familiar civil and political protections, such as suffrage, right of appeal to the people's tribune,[83] and formal popular sovereignty.[84] These protections extended into the economic domain. Livy describes the abolition of debt-bondage in 326 BC as "the dawn, as it were, of a new era of liberty for the plebs,"[85] and it significantly alleviated plebeian dependence on upper classes.[86] The struggle of the plebs to free themselves from various forms of dependent labor[87] also yielded, with few exceptions, an exclusive right of land-ownership for Roman citizens.[88] Although the Roman upper classes successfully blocked most attempts to redistribute land,[89] freehold farmers nonetheless defended their ability to be self-sufficient rather than work for another, to the point of leaving Rome itself.[90] What emerges from these institutional features of Roman *libertas* is that, although defensive, plebs won enough rights against and economic alternatives to performing continuous dependent labor for the upper classes. That is why historians observe an increasing reliance on slave labor around the fourth century BC, especially after abolition of debt-bondage.[91] If the Roman, balanced constitution generated a different view of freedom from the Athenian one, both its theory and its practice still presupposed the existence of slaves as a necessary, stabilizing element.

Conclusion: Slavery and Ancient Liberty

The first and most important result of the foregoing discussion is that, in both ancient republics, liberty emerged with and presupposed slavery. Whether speaking of the leisured independence of the upper classes or of the free labor of the citizen-farmer, of the Athenian democracy or of the Roman republic, or of

---

[83] Nicolet, *The World of the Citizen in Republican Rome*, 319–24. See generally Lintott, *The Constitution of the Roman Republic*, 33–34, 152–57.

[84] Cicero, "On the Commonwealth," I.48–50; Cicero, "On the Laws," III.28; Lintott, *The Constitution of the Roman Republic*, 40–43, 63–64, 199–208; Schofield, "Cicero's Definition of *Res Publica*." Millar adds "a broader concept, the requirement of publicity, namely, that a range of public acts should be performed 'under the gaze of the *populus Romanus*.'" Millar, *The Roman Republic in Political Thought*, 6.

[85] Titus Livius, *The History of Rome*, Vol. 2, trans. Rev. Canon Roberts (London: J. M. Dent & Sons, 1905), 8.28.

[86] Finley, *Ancient Slavery and Modern Ideology*, 79; Hopkins, *Conquerors and Slaves*, 22, 114; Lintott, *The Constitution of the Roman Republic*, 36–37; Patterson, *Freedom Vol. 1*, 208–09.

[87] Lintott, *The Constitution of the Roman Republic*, 38–40, and generally 40–64, 199–213; Millar, *The Roman Republic in Political Thought*, 27–36.

[88] Lintott, "Citizenship," 515–17; Lintott, *Judicial Reform and Land Reform in the Roman Republic*, 36; Mossé, *The Ancient World at Work*, 49.

[89] Lintott, *Judicial Reform and Land Reform in the Roman Republic*, 41–43, 55–57. Cicero considered attempts to redistribute land arbitrary and tyrannical. See fn130.

[90] Garnsey, "Peasants in Ancient Roman Society," 96–105; Garnsey, "Non-Slave Labour in the Roman World," 35–40; Nicolet, *The World of the Citizen in Republican Rome*, 17–47.

[91] Finley, *Ancient Slavery and Modern Ideology*, 84; Hopkins, *Conquerors and Slaves*, 22.

The Paradox of Slavery and Freedom

natural slavery or slaves by legal convention, "there was a general acquiescence in the shift to slave labour."[92] Slavery was the condition in relation to which the free consciously recognized their freedom and it was also an organizing feature of the political sociology of the classical republics. Regardless of how a republican revival approaches the recovery of ancient liberty, the particularistic character of this ideal must be recognized. After all, as we shall see, this was just the issue that troubled many early modern republicans. For them, slavery was no mere fact or cultural assumption: it was an outright moral and political problem.

From Dilemma to Paradox: Slavery and Modern Equality

So far we have encountered at most a dilemma, but no paradox. In the classical republics, the independence of some presupposed the dependence of others, but this co-constituting relation between freedom and slavery was not itself questioned. An actual paradox only emerges in modernity, when the principle of human equality acquires political significance. Respect for equality requires that political principles be universalizable, or applicable to all. As Langdon Byllesby, an American artisan about whom we will hear more in Chapter 3, argued, it was impermissible that a social system exist in which "when one would avail himself of its attractions, he must necessarily do it by retarding or depressing his fellows who are in the same pursuit."[93] Yet this "retarding or depressing" seemed to be just what republican liberty required, producing a paradoxical commitment to mutually conflicting principles of liberty and equality. The paradox produced outbursts, such as the following from St. George Tucker, a prominent late eighteenth-century Virginian, who proposed gradual emancipation of slaves to his state's legislature:

> that a people who have declared, "That *all men are by nature equally free and independent*", and have made this declaration the first article in the foundation of their government, should in defiance of so sacred a truth, recognized by themselves in so solemn a manner, and on so important an occasion, tolerate a practice incompatible therewith, is such an evidence of the weakness and inconsistency of human nature, as every man who hath a spark of patriotic fire in his bosom must wish to see removed from his own country.[94]

The relationship between freedom and slavery had here become an active historical problem. Modern republicans attempted not just to revive the

---

[92] Finley, *Ancient Slavery and Modern Ideology*, 90. Also Garnsey, *Ideas of Slavery from Aristotle to Augustine*, 1–21, 240–43.
[93] Langdon Byllesby, *Observations on the Sources and Effects of Unequal Wealth* (New York: Lewis J. Nichols, 1826), 9.
[94] St. George Tucker, "A Dissertation on Slavery, in Blackstone's Commentaries," in *Founders' Constitution*, ed. Philip B. Kurland and Ralph Lerner (Chicago: University of Chicago Press, 1986 [1803]).

republican theory of liberty, but also attempted to make human equality an organizing principle for collective life. The principle of human equality now began to dictate the shape of new social and political institutions and to inspire new groups to action. Nowhere was this more visible than in the critique of slavery. The existence of freedom together with slavery was now a real, practical problem, spurring actors to find actual solutions and reasons for those solutions.

The American republic is the perfect terrain for understanding how important the paradox of slavery and freedom is to modern republicanism. Early America is a particularly vivid example of the re-appearance of republican ideas about liberty alongside the growth of modern slavery. In what follows, we shall first see how the paradox of slavery and freedom emerges as the founding generations of the American republic reflected on new world slavery. Although figures such as Jefferson and Madison faced this paradox unhappily and without ever fully coming to terms with it, the paradox soon sharpened into an historical conflict in which everyone had to take sides. The Southern slaveowners offered one "solution." They rejected equality in favor of republican liberty and slavery. In response, other early republicans offered an alternative: universalize independence. They did so by reinventing the latent republican ideal of free labor as peasant-proprietorship.

Greece and Rome in Virginia: Slavery as Republican Necessity

Virginia is the paradigmatic example of the "ties that bound freedom to slavery."[95] The land of Jefferson was also home to a dramatic revival of republican thinking. As Douglass Adair, one of the first modern historians to make the point, once wrote, "we dare start no later than the fourth century B.C. if we would understand the Agrarian Republic that Jefferson and Madison idealized in 1800."[96] Wealthy landowners the likes of Jefferson and Madison reproduced classical views about slavery, free labor, and independence in agrarian conditions.[97]

In words that could have been taken straight from Cicero, or Machiavelli or Algernon Sidney for that matter, Jefferson famously commented in his

---

[95] Edmund Morgan, "Slavery and Freedom: The American Paradox," *The Journal of American History* 59, no. 1 (1972), 29.

[96] Douglass G. Adair, *The Intellectual Origins of Jeffersonian Democracy: Republicanism, the Class Struggle, and the Virtuous Farmer* (Lanham, MD: Lexington Books, 1964 [1943]), 30. Although the nature of the republicanism in the early republic is complex and contested, the standard account remains Wood, *The Creation of the American Republic*. See also Joyce Appleby, *Capitalism and a New Social Order: The Republican Vision of the 1790s* (New York: New York University Press, 1984).

[97] See also Edmund Morgan, *American Slavery, American Freedom* (New York: W. W. Norton & Co., 1975), 293–387; Jameson, "Agriculture and Slavery in Classical Athens," 122fn3, 39fn84; Robert E. Shalhope, "Thomas Jefferson's Republicanism and Antebellum Southern Thought," *The Journal of Southern History* 42, no. 4 (December 10, 2007), 529–56.

The Paradox of Slavery and Freedom 33

Notes on the State of Virginia, "dependence begets subservience and venality, suffocates the germ of virtue, and prepares fit tools for the designs of ambition."[98] Dependence was a danger because "it is the manners and spirit of a people which preserve a republic in vigor."[99] Jefferson's primary concern was urban laborers who were economically dependent but had the political rights of a citizen and used them for disruptive purposes: "The mobs of great cities add just so much to the support of pure government, as sores do to the strength of the human body."[100] Madison, too, lamented the "dependence of an increasing number on the wealth of a few," especially in the expanding urban areas.[101] In particular, Madison was worried that the "freeholders, or the heirs, or aspirants to Freeholders"[102] were being replaced by these new, permanently dependent, workers with the result being that an increasingly "smaller part only can be interested in preserving the rights of property."[103] As they knew from classical sources,[104] property was the key to the independence of a free citizen, while landless wage-labor was a kind of servitude.

It was not mere romantic anti-capitalism or nostalgic agrarianism that drove Jefferson to say things like "let our workshops remain in Europe"[105] and "while we have land to labor then, let us never wish to see our citizens occupied at a workbench, or twirling a distaff."[106] After all, Jefferson embraced commercial agriculture,[107] but he was worried about the political dangers of landless workers. The "distrust of free labor amongst Revolutionary republicans"[108] stemmed from the worry that wage-laborers "could lay claim to freedom without the independence to go with it."[109] This fear of the "daily drudge[s] in agricultural or mechanical labour" dated back to the earliest

---

[98] Thomas Jefferson, *Notes on the State of Virginia* (New York: Harpers & Row, 1964), 157.
[99] Ibid., 158.
[100] Ibid.
[101] James Madison, "James Madion, Note to His Speech on the Right of Suffrage," in *The Founders' Constitution*, ed. Philip B. Kurland and Ralph Lerner (Chicago: University of Chicago Press, 1821).
[102] Ibid.
[103] Madison quoted in Adair, *The Intellectual Origins of Jeffersonian Democracy*, 159.
[104] Ibid., 39–56, 153–64, Morgan, "Slavery and Freedom: The American Paradox."
[105] Jefferson, *Notes on the State of Virginia*, 158.
[106] Ibid., 157–58.
[107] As Appleby points out, unlike the ancients, where the virtues of agrarian life were linked with self-sufficient production, Jefferson identified the free-holding, agrarian citizen with progress and production for a global market. Joyce Appleby, "The 'Agrarian Myth' In the Early Republic," in *Liberalism and Republicanism in the Historical Imagination* (Cambridge, MA: Harvard University Press, 1992); Joyce Appleby, "Republicanism in Old and New Contexts," *The William and Mary Quarterly* 43, no. 1 (1986). Contrast with Pocock's reading of Jefferson as one of the last anti-commercial virtue theorists in the civic humanist tradition. Pocock, *The Machiavellian Moment*, 529–43.
[108] Morgan, "Slavery and Freedom: The American Paradox," 14.
[109] Ibid., 10.

participation of poor workers in the revolutionary politics of the period.[110] In *Federalist 10*, Madison notoriously worried that the propertyless might use their newfound sovereignty to threaten the property of the best citizens, exercising their suffrage to satisfy their "rage for paper money, for an abolition of debts, for an equal division of property, or for any other improper or wicked project."[111]

If wage-laborers were dangerous then slavery was the only reasonable alternative. When combined with small-scale free-holding, slavery reduced to a manageable size the free but landless class that threatened property and republican liberty.[112] As the historian Edmund Morgan puts it:

> It was slavery ... more than any other single factor ... that enabled Virginia to nourish representative government in a plantation society ... slavery that made the Virginians dare to speak a political language that magnified the rights of freemen, and slavery, therefore, that brought Virginians into the same commonwealth political tradition with New Englanders. The very institution that was to divide North and South after the Revolution may have made possible their union in a republican government.[113]

Slavery was a kind of practical necessity given certain political commitments.

Slavery's stabilizing function helps explain Jefferson's somewhat inconsistent thoughts on the institution. He never abandoned the worry that slavery might be morally objectionable.[114] He also fretted that slaves might take it upon themselves to eliminate their masters and even to destroy the American republic itself in a bloody race war – "we have the wolf by the ears."[115] For much the same reason, Jefferson also thought emancipation impractical: former slaves could never be assimilated, even if they might not commit outright violence

---

[110] Alexander Graydon, upper class Philadelphia attorney, quoted in Ronald Schultz, *The Republic of Labor: Philadelphia Artisans and the Politics of Class, 1720–1830* (New York: Oxford University Press, 1993), 53.

[111] James Madison, "Federalist No. 10," in *The Essential Federalist and Anti-Federalist Papers*, ed. David Wootton (Indianapolis: Hackett, 2009), 51.

[112] Adair and Morgan point out that Jefferson and Madison, like Aristotle and Cicero, were especially concerned with the stability of their agrarian commercial republics. They saw freeholders as self-sufficient, mildly apathetic citizens, not highly active ones. Adair, *The Intellectual Origins of Jeffersonian Democracy*, 79fn16, 153–64; Morgan, *American Slavery, American Freedom*, 293–315; Morgan, "Slavery and Freedom: The American Paradox," 23–29.

[113] Morgan, "Slavery and Freedom: The American Paradox," 29. See also Morgan's fascinating account of the problem of early labor shortages and the shift from seeing Africans as rights-bearing members of a colonial society to a belief in their racial difference. Morgan, "Slavery and Freedom: The American Paradox," 15–29.

[114] Compare Thomas Jefferson, "Letter to Edward Coles," in *Thomas Jefferson: Political Writings*, ed. Joyce Appleby and Terence Ball (Cambridge: Cambridge University Press, 1999 [1814]); Jefferson, *Notes on the State of Virginia*, 132–39; Thomas Jefferson, "To Dr. Edward Bancroft, Jan. 26, 1789," in *Thomas Jefferson: Political Writings*, ed. Joyce Appleby and Terence Ball (Cambridge: Cambridge University Press, 1999 [1789]).

[115] Thomas Jefferson, "To John Holmes, April 22, 1820," in *Thomas Jefferson: Political Writings*, ed. Joyce Appleby and Terence Ball (Cambridge: Cambridge University Press, 1999 [1820]), 496.

The Paradox of Slavery and Freedom 35

once freed.[116] The upshot was that, despite the evil of the institution, slavery was necessary. At best, it could only gradually be transformed.[117] Jefferson's frequent twists and turns speak to a mind seriously, if unsatisfactorily, grappling with the paradox of slavery and freedom in an age of equality.[118] Nor was he alone in his acceptance of slavery.[119] No matter how many early figures agreed with Jefferson's statement that slavery was "a moral & political reprobation,"[120] they thought it necessary for the republic to flourish, let alone survive. The only option, as one of Jefferson's contemporaries put it, was to "bear for a time an evil with patience."[121]

The founding generation was almost Roman in its willingness to accept that, on the one hand, slavery was unnatural, but on the other hand, it was a necessary convention to uphold the common interest in republican institutions. Even those, such as George Tucker, who denounced the institution, considered all possible options – manumission, incorporation, colonization, separation – only to conclude that "human prudence forbids that we should precipitately engage in a work of such hazard as a general and simultaneous emancipation."[122] This is the same man who said that "all hearts should be united, every nerve strained, and every power exerted" to eliminate this violation of the principle that "all men are by nature equally free and independent."[123] Here is open recognition of the paradox. For those who thought slavery was an abomination, its eradication was even less imaginable because it threatened the very basis of a free political order. Awareness of this paradox produced extensive self-reflection and anxiety, but with no satisfying resolutions.[124] It appeared

---

[116] Compare Jefferson, "Letter to Edward Coles"; Jefferson, *Notes on the State of Virginia*, 132–39; Jefferson, "To Dr. Edward Bancroft, Jan. 26, 1789."

[117] See respectively Jefferson, "Letter to Edward Coles"; Jefferson, "To John Holmes, April 22, 1820"; and Jefferson, *Notes on the State of Virginia*, 139; Thomas Jefferson, "To Dr. Thomas Humphreys," in *Thomas Jefferson: Political Writings*, ed. Joyce Appleby and Terence Ball (Cambridge: Cambridge University Press, 1999 [1817]); Thomas Jefferson, "To St. George Tucker, August 28, 1797," in *Thomas Jefferson: Political Writings*, ed. Joyce Appleby and Terence Ball (Cambridge: Cambridge University Press, 1999 [1797]).

[118] That slaves might destroy republican liberty in a bloody race war was a commonly expressed anxiety among the landed gentry. Jefferson is no doubt one of the sources for Tocqueville's famous claim that "[t]he more or less distant but inevitable danger of a conflict between the blacks and whites of the South of the Union is a nightmare constantly haunting the American imagination." Alexis de Tocqueville, *Democracy in America*, trans. George Lawrence (New York: HarperCollins, 2006 [1850]), 358.

[119] E.g., James Sullivan, "James Sullivan to Jeremy Belknap," in *The Founders' Constitution*, ed. Philip B. Kurland and Ralph Lerner (Chicago: University of Chicago Press, 1986 [1795]); Tucker, "A Dissertation on Slavery, in Blackstone's Commentaries."

[120] Jefferson, "Letter to Edward Coles," 493.

[121] Sullivan, "James Sullivan to Jeremy Belknap."

[122] Tucker, "A Dissertation on Slavery, in Blackstone's Commentaries."

[123] Ibid.

[124] Notably, later defenders of slavery seized on the impracticability of various long range plans for emancipation as evidence of the earlier generation's bad faith. For example Thomas Dew,

that republican liberty could not easily be squared with emancipation. The freedom of some presupposed the enslavement of others.

Proslavery Republicanism

It is a familiar fact of American history that, by 1830, the rise of an abolitionist demand for immediate emancipation produced its opposite: a hardened and more vigorous, not to mention splenetic, proslavery ideology.[125] This reactionary attempt to argue that slavery was a permanent and "positive good" included a vigorous "proslavery republicanism."[126] Southerners increasingly "envisaged themselves before, during, and after the Civil War as the true guardians of classical republicanism in North America."[127] By upholding slavery, they defended freedom against the dangerous perversions of Northern society. Here are but a few examples from some of the most prominent proslavery figures:

I fearlessly assert that the existing relation between the two races in the South ... forms the most solid and durable foundation on which to rear free and stable political institutions. *John C. Calhoun*[128]

Every scholar whose mind is at all imbued with ancient history and literature, sees that Greece and Rome were indebted to this institution. *George Fitzhugh*[129]

We must recollect that the laws of Lycurgus were promulgated, the sublime eloquence of Demosthenes and Cicero was heard, and the glorious achievements of Epaminondas and Scipio were witnessed, in countries where slavery existed-without for one moment loosening the tie between master and slave. *Thomas Dew*[130]

"Review of the Debate in the Virginia Legislature," in *Slavery Defended: The Views of the Old South*, ed. Eric L. McKitrick (Englewood Cliffs, NJ: Prentice-Hall, 1963 [1832]).

[125] The character of pre-1830 proslavery discourse is somewhat more debated. Larry Tise's important study broke with previous scholarship by arguing that there was nothing distinctive about Southern proslavery arguments, and by finding that Northern defenders of slavery were nearly as vigorous as their Southern counterparts. Larry E. Tise, *Proslavery: A History of the Defense of Slavery in America, 1701–1840* (Athens: University of Georgia Press, 1987).

[126] Calhoun, "Speech on the Reception of Abolition Petitions," 12–16; Tise, *Proslavery: a History of the Defense of Slavery in America, 1701–1840*, 347–62.

[127] David Montgomery, *Citizen-Worker: The Experience of Workers in the United States with Democracy and the Free Market During the Nineteenth Century* (Cambridge: Cambridge University Press, 1995), 126. See also Leon Fink, "From Autonomy to Abundance: Changing Beliefs About the Free Labor System in Nineteenth-Century America," in *Terms of Labor: Slavery, Serfdom, and Free Labor*, ed. Stanley L. Engerman (Stanford, CA: Stanford University Press, 1999), 122–23. The contradiction of an agrarian republicanism mapped onto the defense of commercial farming yoked to global circuits of trade has caught the attention of a number of other critics. Louis Hartz, *The Liberal Tradition in America* (New York: Harcourt, Brace & World, Inc., 1955), 145–200; Appleby, "The 'Agrarian Myth' In the Early Republic"; 'Calhoun: Marx of the Master Class' in Richard Hofstadter, *The American Political Tradition and the Men Who Made It* (New York,: Knopf, 1973), 86–117.

[128] Calhoun, "Speech on the Reception of Abolition Petitions," 14.

[129] George Fitzhugh, "Sociology for the South," in *Slavery Defended: The Views of the Old South*, ed. Eric L. McKitrick (Englewood Cliffs, NJ: Prentice-Hall, 1963 [1854]), 43.

[130] Dew, "Review of the Debate in the Virginia Legislature," 32–33.

The Paradox of Slavery and Freedom

As George Fitzhugh, an extremist among extremists, put it, "to become independent is to be able to make other people support you, without being obliged to labor for them. Now, what man in society is not seeking to attain this situation? He who attains it is a slave owner."[131] Such arguments became part and parcel of public discourse. In 1858, James Henry Hammond, a Senator from South Carolina, famously argued on the floor of the United States Senate that, "in all social systems there must be a class to do the menial duties, to perform the drudgery of life." This "mud-sill" is required to create the surplus for "that other class which leads progress, civilization, and refinement."[132]

This proslavery republicanism included strains of *herrenvolk* populism, which defined freedom as an ethnic privilege. Planters argued that even the poor, unrefined, nonslaveowning citizen had "an interest in slavery" because it secured "the status of a white man ... not regarded as an inferior or a dependent" and held out the possibility that "he can become a slaveholder."[133] These statements found a sympathetic audience among some nonslaveowning citizens. Theophilus Fisk, a New England labor reformer, though a critic of the industrial conditions experienced by "the white slaves of the North," spent much of 1836 in the South denouncing abolition as inconsistent with labor reform.[134] Ely Moore, a labor leader and congressman of the 1830s, "denounced abolition not only as a 'blind, reckless, feverish fanaticism' but also as a plot to rob whites of their independence."[135]

Here are echoes of the ancient peasant-citizen, bound to a slave society by status and the aspiration to full independence, but now updated to address the existence of mass wage-labor. Keenly aware of class conflict in the North and in Europe,[136] slave-owners were quick to point to the social advantages of slavery.[137] They did so by seizing on Northern critiques of wage-labor. Fitzhugh characteristically took the argument to its logical conclusion: "Capital exercises a more perfect compulsion over free laborers than human masters over slaves;

---

[131] George Fitzhugh, *Cannibals All!: Or, Slaves without Masters* (Cambridge, MA: Harvard University Press, 1988), 18.

[132] James Henry Hammond, "Mudsill Speech," (The Congressional Globe, March 4, 1858), 962.

[133] J. D. B. Debow, "The Interest in Slavery of the Southern Non-Slaveholder," in *Slavery Defended: The Views of the Old South*, ed. Eric L. McKitrick (Englewood Cliffs, NJ: Prentice-Hall, 1963 [1860]), 174–5.

[134] Theophilus Fisk, *Capital Against Labor: An Address Delivered at Julien Hall, before the Mechanics of Boston, on Wednesday Evening, May 20* (Boston: Theophilus Fisk, 1835), 9; Edward Pessen, *Most Uncommon Jacksonians: The Radical Leaders of the Early Labor Movement* (Albany: State University of New York Press, 1967), 92–94.

[135] David Roediger, *The Wages of Whiteness: Race and the Making of the American Working Class* (London: Verso, 2007), 75, and 74–77.

[136] Slaveowners regularly used the writings of socialists and other labor agitators in favor of Southern slavery. Debow, "The Interest in Slavery of the Southern Non-Slaveholder," 173–74; Fitzhugh, "Sociology for the South," 42.

[137] Fitzhugh, *Cannibals All!: Or, Slaves without Masters*, 31; Calhoun, "Speech on the Reception of Abolition Petitions," 13–14.

for free laborers must at all times work or starve, and slaves are supported whether they work or not."[138] This, they said, was intolerable. Hammond, the "mud-sill" theorist, told Northern Senators, "your slaves are white.... They are your equals ... and they feel galled by their degradation.... If they knew the tremendous secret, that the ballot box is stronger than an army with bayonets.... Your society would be reconstructed ... your property divided."[139] The social dangers of wage-labor inspired George Fitzhugh's non-racial defense of "slavery in the abstract,"[140] and Calhoun said, "it is impossible with us that the conflict can take place between labor and capital, which make[s] it so difficult to establish and maintain free institutions in all wealthy and highly civilized nations where such institutions as ours do not exist."[141] Slavery was a positive good for the leisure it provided leading citizens and for the social stability it afforded republican institutions. Although in one sense reproducing a classical view, slave-owners were now in the position of reactionaries. They had to defend slavery by publicly rejecting respect for human equality – a defense they engaged in with gusto.

Resolving the Paradox in Favor of Free Labor: Lincoln and the Agrarian Ideal

Such a robust proslavery republicanism rendered the ambivalence of Jefferson's generation untenable. It defiantly asserted and defended republican liberty as a privilege, a value applicable to a particular class of persons only. Any coherent response to such an argument had to develop a language through which to express the potential universality of republican liberty. This meant resolving the paradox of slavery and freedom in a different way: by showing that independence was a condition that did not presuppose slavery. The key intellectual steps were not only to extol the virtues of a kind of free labor that all could enjoy, but also to show how the existence of slavery threatened that independence.

Abraham Lincoln's speech to Wisconsin farmers in 1859 is perhaps the most famous example of this re-articulation of republican liberty. Forged in the heat of sectional struggle, Lincoln's speech sharpens and focuses certain aspects of the free labor ideology that had remained at the level of unarticulated premise. Here the familiar agrarian ideal of freeholding independence, rattling around the Jeffersonian and in some sense Ciceronian and Aristotelian imagination, is enlisted as a universal ideal *against* slavery. Although Lincoln's immediate audience is a group of citizen-farmers in Midwest America, the relevant context is the slaveholders' defense of slavery, especially Hammond's much commented upon "mud-sill" oration from the year before.

---

[138] Fitzhugh, *Cannibals All!: Or, Slaves without Masters*, 32; Hammond, "Mudsill Speech," 962.
[139] Hammond, "Mudsill Speech," 962.
[140] On "slavery in the abstract" see Eugene D. Genovese, *The World the Slaveholders Made* (New York: Pantheon, 1969), 165–94.
[141] Calhoun, "Speech on the Importance of Domestic Slavery," 18–19.

In his speech, Lincoln rejects the "'mud-sill' theory [in which] it is assumed that labor and education are incompatible."[142] He argues that, "education – cultivated thought – can best be combined with ... any labor, on the principle of thorough work."[143] This "thorough work" is not hard work but free labor – an activity carried out under the worker's own control. By free, Lincoln clearly does not mean just "non-slave" but rather the independent, property-owning farmer: "[T]he prudent, penniless beginner in the world, labors for wages awhile, saves surplus with which to buy tools or land, for himself; then labors on his own account another while.... [This] is free labor."[144] Wage-labor is at best a temporary condition on the way to truly free labor. Lincoln continues, "if any continue through life in the condition of the hired laborer, it is not the fault of the system, but because of either a dependent nature which prefers it, or improvidence, folly, or singular misfortune."[145]

Lincoln here expresses a view that liberates independent, free labor from its association with slavery. He has in mind a republic of free producers in which the independence of each citizen is guaranteed through their own, self-developing efforts. What makes free labor consistent with the development of an independent personality is that, for the individual proprietor, "heads and hands should cooperate as friends; and that that particular head, should direct and control that particular pair of hands."[146] By emphasizing the educative effects of free labor, Lincoln self-consciously appropriates and inverts the classical, slave-holder theory of independence and virtue. The great benefit of the "agreeable combination of labor with cultivated thought"[147] is that it would produce a citizenry alert to "oppression in any of its forms."[148] Those in control of their labor will always be attentive to those who attempt to live off the dependent labor of others.

If the idea that a republic needs a class of independent proprietors is familiar from Jefferson, and before him Cicero and Aristotle, Lincoln stands out because he gave very public voice to a reinterpretation of the relationship between the free producer and republican liberty. Lincoln not only argued for the advantages of free labor, but for its incompatibility with slavery. If only the free laborer was properly independent, then slavery undermined republican liberty. Idleness corrupted the unmoored slave-holder just as much as extreme dependence oppressed the slave. The latter lacked a will of his own; the former failed to develop one. Both were dependent in their own ways. A slave society lacked independence, and hence "the most cherished values of the free labor

---

[142] Abraham Lincoln, "Address to the Wisconsin State Agricultural Society," in *The Portable Abraham Lincoln*, ed. Andrew Delbanco (New York: Penguin Books, 1992 [1859]), 159.
[143] Ibid., 161.
[144] Ibid., 158.
[145] Ibid.
[146] Ibid., 159.
[147] Ibid., 160.
[148] Ibid., 161.

outlook ... all appeared to be violated in the South."[149] This is the famous "political antislavery"[150] view, which linked the wrongs of slavery to the interests and ideals of non-slaves, especially through the argument that slavery threatened free labor everywhere.[151] Only in the nineteenth century did this ideal of property-owning free labor emerge as a separate, self-conscious ideal standing in opposition to the existence of slave labor anywhere in the political community. The struggle to articulate this way of thinking about republican liberty was the first step in overcoming the paradox of slavery and freedom.

Conclusion: Internal Contradictions of Free Labor

The Limits of Neo-Republicanism Reconsidered
Contemporary scholars have made the concept of independence central to their effort to revive a republican theory of liberty. While acknowledging the concept's origins in a slave society, these neo-republicans have left it unclear what it means to say this concept "transcends its origins."[152] They have not explained how it is that the republican theory has overcome its original, inner connection with slavery, nor accounted for the conceptual problems that arise in this process. In particular, "neo-Roman" scholars have either presented the relationship with slavery in purely conceptual terms, as a way of clarifying the meaning of liberty, or they have focused on the early modern recovery of republican liberty in disputes over political, not economic, questions.[153]

This chapter showed us the steps by which the republican theory of liberty began to "transcend its origins" in the institution of slavery. If originally the citizen's independence was conceptually the opposite of slavery because it presupposed the slavery of others, this became a paradox when moderns also wished to make political ideals consistent with human equality. In the effort to universalize republican liberty, presupposition turned into opposition. The institution of slavery went from a condition for freedom to a threat to it.

The reason for reconstructing this paradox and the various attempts at a resolution of it is that it alerts us to an important, if underappreciated, theoretical issue. Recall that one of the virtues of the republican theory of liberty is supposed to be its ability to "articulate grievances which far outrun the complaints of its founding communities,"[154] and it possesses this power because "enslavement and subjection are the great ills, and independence and status

---

[149] Eric Foner, *Free Soil, Free Labor, Free Men: The Ideology of the Republican Party before the Civil War* (London, New York: Oxford University Press, 1971), 40.
[150] Ibid., 58.
[151] Ibid., 40–72. See also Eric Foner, "Abolitionism and the Labor Movement," in *Politics and Ideology in the Age of the Civil War* (Oxford: Oxford University Press, 1980), 57–76.
[152] Pettit, *Republicanism*, 133.
[153] Skinner, *Liberty before Liberalism*, 5–6, 38–42; Skinner, "A Third Concept of Liberty," 248–51.
[154] Pettit, *Republicanism*, 133.

the supreme goods."[155] To the degree that republicanism has demonstrated this power, it has done so less because it is a "negative" or "positive" theory of liberty, as its current defenders say, but because republicans have attempted to *universalize* it. As we have seen, the "articulation of new grievances" took the form of attempting to demand independence *without* presupposing the "enslavement and subjection" of others. In those historical efforts we begin to appreciate not just the way in which republican liberty transcends its origins, but also its critical power – a power that we shall see fully coming into its own in the following chapters.

In sum, the aim of this chapter was to vindicate the claim that the paradox of freedom and slavery is unjustifiably overlooked in republican scholarship. It plays a central role in republicanism's modern ideological development and leads to a republican defense of free labor. Failing to recognize the way the principle of equality, represented in real struggles over slavery, forced republicanism to face the particularistic nature of its ideal of independence, neo-republicans have overlooked key conceptual and historical problems. They have focused too narrowly on whether a theory of liberty is negative or positive, and have said very little about the role that labor plays in republican thinking.

The Paradox's Second Moment: Wage-Labor

So far, the narrative we have told gives the impression that the paradox of slavery and freedom was exclusively concerned with chattel slavery. However, the paradox had a second iteration: the debate over wage-labor. For instance, in Lincoln's 1859 speech, the free laborer only "works for wages awhile" before becoming a small proprietor. There is a considered ambiguity in this formulation, which speaks to the way the first and second moments of the paradox overlapped. Lincoln's speech was carefully crafted to focus attention on Southern slavery. Part of this rhetorical care reflected the fact that Northern workers and land reformers had already opened a second front in the conflict over slavery, which focused on the urban workers of the industrial North and the fate of Western lands. Lincoln participated in containing this second front by emphasizing "free soil," giving legislative support to homesteading, and focusing attention on the danger of Southern slavery.[156] As we turn to the wage-labor question, it is appropriate to end this chapter with a sketch of the controversy that stood in the background of Lincoln's speech. These debates show the complexity of the paradox of slavery and freedom and set the tone for the following chapters.

On January 1, 1831, abolitionist William Lloyd Garrison published the first issue of *The Liberator*, which opened with his epoch-making demand

---

[155] Ibid., 132.
[156] On the absorption of northern criticisms of wage-labor into political antislavery in the 1850s, see Foner, "Abolitionism and the Labor Movement in Antebellum America," 57–76.

for the "immediate enfranchisement of our slave population."[157] Ever the uncompromising radical, Garrison was quick to fight on as many fronts as possible. A reader who made it to page three of the inaugural issue would have discovered an editorial entitled "WORKING MEN," in which Garrison attacked the attempt to "inflame the minds of our working classes against the more opulent ... to array them under a party banner; for it is not true, that, at any time, they have been objects of reproach."[158] Garrison was not wasting his time on side-questions pertaining to northern labor reform. Just as militant abolitionists were making the immediate eradication of Southern slavery their celebrated cause, workers across the country were forming "workingmen's parties," which attacked inequalities of wealth and industrial "wage-slavery." We shall hear much more from these "workingmen" in Chapter 3. For now what matters is that Garrison found them threatening because they too spoke the language of abolition. For some years they had been using epithets such as "bondage" and "oppression" to criticize the way northern workers were "consigned over to eternal toil and never-ending slavery."[159] Garrison was anxious to police discursive boundaries, especially when it came to the rhetoric of freedom, so as not to dilute or distract from his cause.

Later that January, a certain "W" took exception to Garrison's "WORKING MEN" editorial:

> there is a very intimate connexion between the interests of the workingmen's party and your own. You are striving to excite the attention of your countrymen to the injustice of holding their fellow men in bondage, and depriving them of the fruits of their toil. We are aiming at a similar object, only in application to another portion of our fellow men.[160]

"W" put the slavery of the workingmen in decidedly republican terms, "those working classes, which, though nominally free, still are in Europe and America, to a great extent, dependant [sic] on the power and will of the wealthy, educated and exalted."[161] A worker "dependant on the power and will" of another was *the* republican definition of a slave. Garrison quickly and vigorously rejected W's assertion that workingmen were unfree, going so far as to blame them for their poverty: "[W]here the avenues to wealth, distinction and supremacy are open to all; it must, in the nature of things, be full of inequalities.... If our

---

[157] William Lloyd Garrison, "To the Public," *The Liberator* no. I (January 1, 1831), 1.
[158] William Lloyd Garrison, "Working Men," *The Liberator* I, no. 1 (January 1, 1831).
[159] William Heighton, *An Address to the Members of Trade Societies and to the Working Classes Generally: Being an Exposition of the Relative Situation, Condition, And Future Prospects of Working People in the United States of America. Together With a Suggestion and Outlines of A Plan, By which they may gradually and indefinitely improve their condition*. (London: Sold at the Rooms of the Co-operative Society, Reprinted from Philadelphia Edition), 10. Hereafter *An Address to the Members of Trade Societies and to the Working Classes Generally*.
[160] William Lloyd Garrison, "The Working Classes," *The Liberator* 1, no. 5 (January 29, 1831).
[161] Ibid.

The Paradox of Slavery and Freedom

mechanics do not retain their due proportion of power and influence, theirs is the fault."[162] Whatever might be wrong with industrial poverty, it could not be said to flow from the workers' own unfreedom. Although over time Garrison would come to accept that there may be some injustice that poor workers faced, he consistently rejected that this injustice could be considered in any way unfreedom. Garrison's conception of freedom was voluntaristic, a matter of whether one could or could not legally consent to one's labor contract. Wage-labor was free labor because it was based in a voluntary contract. If free, then workers were as much to blame for their condition as anyone else, especially given their penchant for alcohol and the theater rather than temperance and prudence.[163]

Garrison was not alone. For many leading abolitionists, this voluntaristic conception of freedom stood in opposition to the republican view. William Jay, drafter of the constitution of the American Antislavery Society, described the prospects for an emancipated slave in the following terms:

> He is free, and his own master, and he can ask for no more. Yet he is, in fact, for a time, absolutely dependent on his late owner. He can look to no other person for food to eat, clothes to put on, or house to shelter him. His first wish therefore is, to remain where he is, and he receives as a favor, permission to labor in the service of him whom the day before he regarded as his oppressor. But labor is no longer the badge of his servitude, and the consummation of his misery: it is the evidence of his liberty, for it is voluntary. For the first time in his life, he is a party to a contract.[164]

In clear and vivid contrast to republican critics of wage-slavery, Jay thought economic dependence, even "absolute dependence," was not unfreedom. Legal self-ownership was enough to guarantee the individual's freedom, a freedom the slave would immediately value.

This early contrast between abolitionist and republican perspectives on free labor set the tone for decades to come. Although the workingmen's parties faded from the scene, the arguments over wage-slavery did not. It remained a thorn in the side of those abolitionists who attempted to police the language of freedom so that only the chattel slave could be considered a true slave. This conflict reproduced at the level of thought the tensions between working class critics of slavery and the abolitionists.[165] In the 1840s and 1850s, the National

---

[162] Ibid.
[163] E.g., Garrison, "The Working Classes"; "Wants of the Working Men," *The Liberator* 1, no. 8 (February 19, 1831).
[164] Quoted in Foner, "Abolitionism and the Labor Movement in Antebellum America," 64.
[165] On labor reform and abolition, see Foner, "Abolitionism and the Labor Movement in Antebellum America"; Eric Foner, "Workers and Slavery," in *Working for Democracy: American Workers From the Revolution to the Present*, ed. Paul Buhle and Alan Dawley (Urbana: University of Illinois Press, 1985), 21–30; Marcus Cunliffe, *Chattel Slavery and Wage Slavery: The Anglo-American Context, 1830–1860* (Athens: University of Georgia Press, 1979); Roediger, *The Wages of Whiteness*.

Reform Association (NRA)[166] demanded breaking up of land monopolies and distribution of land to all citizens to eliminate "wage-slavery," reigniting an intellectual battle that ranged across *The Liberator* and the NRA's *Young America*. The editor of *Young America*, George Henry Evans, made sure that its pages ardently and repeatedly promoted the argument that landless workers were slaves. According to one June, 1845 article, the landless worker "must ask leave to live ... he is liable to be driven away at the will of another-at the caprice of avarice, selfishness, pride, or unbridled power."[167] Another National Reformer argued that wage-workers are, "hemmed in and made dependent on the non-producing classes ... [an employer] can purchase the bones and sinews of the working men, and the laborers are practically dependent upon him."[168] Nearly every issue of *Young America* deployed the familiar republican language of economic dependence and employer "caprice" to argue that landless workers experienced a servitude as bad or even worse than the chattel slave.

Prominent abolitionists such as Garrison and Wendell Phillips were quick to attack Evans and his fellow Reformers. In September 1846, *The Liberator* reprinted a debate between Phillips and Evans from *Young America*, prefacing it with an editorial from Garrison saying "who either cannot discern, or willingly attempts to confound, the distinction between Slavery and Poverty ... shows ignorance of the first elements of natural morality."[169] Poverty was bad, but it was not *slavery*. Phillips' abolitionist remarks then followed, expressing some sympathy for the free poor, but also rejecting their republicanism. Phillips claimed that Evans was on the way to "sacrificing the rights of one race in the vain hope of more easily securing those of another."[170] In response, Evans reasserted the validity of the concept "wages slavery" on the grounds that landless workers were subject to the will of their employers. Only land redistribution could guarantee true freedom for chattel and wage-slave alike: "The National Reform measures would not merely substitute one form of slavery for another, but would replace every form of slavery by entire freedom."[171] Abolitionists and land reformers continued to spar throughout the decade. The former continued to defend their voluntarist views and to reject dependence as a badge of servitude. Unless there was active interference with a person's will, that person remained free to make a contract. "It seems to us an abuse of language to talk of the 'slavery of wages,'" Garrison wrote.[172] To which William

---

[166] We shall discuss them in greater detail in Chapter 3.
[167] "From the New England Farmer," *Young America* 2, no. 14 (June 28, 1845). *Young America* hereafter *YA*.
[168] "Great Mass Meeting of the Working Classes at National Health: Comments of Alvin Bovay," *YA* 2, no. 12 (June 14, 1845).
[169] "Wendell Phillips and 'Young America,'" *The Liberator* 16, no. 36 (September 4, 1846), 143.
[170] Ibid.
[171] Ibid.
[172] William Lloyd Garrison, "Free and Slave Labor," *The Liberator* XVII, no. 13 (March 26, 1847), 50.

The Paradox of Slavery and Freedom

West, a National Reformer, later responded, "there may be those who believe that wages slaves work when and for whom they please – make their own contracts, are protected by law, &c. You appear to. I will not question your sincerity ... [but] [i]nstead of being free to make their own contracts, they are not allowed to make any, except such as bitter necessity forces upon them."[173] These ideological differences reflected practical differences. Garrison argued for singular devotion to immediate abolition, while National Reformers and other workingmen's groups argued that because their oppression touched on them directly, it legitimately commanded their attention over that of Southern slavery.[174]

I have, of course, simplified this history considerably. Its terms shifted over time and across interlocutors. For instance, later in life Garrison eventually came to endorse some labor reform, and Wendell Phillips, after the Civil War, became an ardent labor advocate. Some of Phillips' final speeches intone in republican terms against the oppression of laborers.[175] More generally, some abolitionists *accepted* the republican theory of freedom but rejected the argument that wage-laborers were dependent in the relevant sense. Meanwhile, many workers embraced the abolitionist cause, including some of the aforementioned National Reformers.[176] Nevertheless, in the wider arc of this book's narrative my simplification of this debate serves a purpose. It helps vivify the ideological stakes of the discussion about wage-labor. As the following chapters show, both the voluntarist and the republican position eventually took on a different shape, especially once industrial wage-labor took center stage. On the one hand, as we see next chapter, it turns out that Garrisonian voluntarists were not in static opposition to the republican theory. Over time, it became possible to argue that legal self-ownership just *was* economic independence because it guaranteed that no worker was dependent on any *particular* employer. This was the laissez-faire republican theory that emerged in the late nineteenth century. On the other hand, as we see in Chapters 3 and 4, the National Reformers' critique of wage-labor turned out to be the last gasp of an agrarian republicanism that, in time, became a robust labor republicanism. What drove both of these intellectual developments was an attempt to answer whether wage-labor reconstituted the paradox of slavery and freedom or realized the promise of universal free labor. The sectional conflict over the

---

[173] William West, "Wages Slavery and Chattel Slavery: to William Lloyd Garrison," *The Liberator* XVII, no. 14 (April 2, 1847).
[174] George Henry Evans, "'Abolition at Home'," *YA* 2, no. 5 (April 26, 1845).
[175] E.g., speeches given in the early 1870s in Massachusetts on "The Labor Question" published as Wendell Phillips, *The Labor Question* (Boston, MA: Lee and Shepard, 1884).
[176] Still the best sources are Foner, "Abolitionism and the Labor Movement in Antebellum America"; Foner, *Free Soil, Free Labor, Free Men: The Ideology of the Republican Party before the Civil War*.

first moment of this paradox slavery – chattel slavery – was also the chrysalis sheltering the second moment.

By the 1850s, the hardening of ideological lines between North and South imposed a kind of truce between the abolitionists and the various land and labor reformers as they gathered under the Republican tent. Lincoln elided the dispute by accepting that wage-labor was not fully free labor, but then by focusing attention on the immediate danger to all northern workers posed by Southern slavery. Once slavery was abolished, this elision was no longer sustainable. The challenge of wage-slavery would once again take center stage.

2

"Independent Laborers by Voluntary Contract"
The Laissez-Faire Republican Turn

> Where are the slave auction-blocks ... the slave-yokes and fetters ...
> They are all gone! From chattels to human beings.... Freedmen at work
> as independent laborers by voluntary contract!
> *William Lloyd Garrison*[1]

It was 1869. The Civil War was over and Congress had ratified the Thirteenth and Fourteenth Amendments to the American Constitution, which abolished slavery and guaranteed equal protection of the laws. William Lloyd Garrison's debates with working men and national reformers were long behind him. He could finally consider his life's work accomplished. Surveying the new economy, he exulted that he saw nothing but "independent laborers by voluntary contract." It was a telling turn of phrase – "independent ... by contract." Although in the last chapter we saw how Garrison opposed his abolitionist theory of freedom to the republican emphasis on independence, in this later utterance we see a blurring of the lines. Now, for Garrison, the absence of interference with voluntary agreements just *was* independence.

Garrison might not have been running these ideas together intentionally, but it was an important feature of the postbellum ideological atmosphere. As the "labor crisis" took center stage, it became increasingly common to find economists, legal theorists, employers, and public officials arguing that wage-labor was free labor because legal self-ownership was enough to guarantee a person's economic independence. If the wage-laborer was legally "*sui iuris*," or under his own power, then that was enough to know he was independent. Legal status described economic condition. The abolition of slavery and the universal guarantee of freedom of contract eliminated chattel slavery and secured legal protection against becoming subject to any particular employer's will. Nobody could be forced to work for anyone else; each chose his employer voluntarily.

---

[1] Quoted in Stanley, *From Bondage to Contract*, 4.

This chapter reconstructs this view because it was the hegemonic idea against which labor republicans would react. This reconstruction is also important because it reminds us that the purity of two ideological traditions, represented in scholarly statements like "we have inherited two rival and incommensurable theories of negative liberty,"[2] is difficult to maintain. In fact, laissez-faire ideas arose not so much by negating the republican theory as by incorporating it into liberal thinking and practice.

As we proceed, it is important to recognize that all of the competing intellectual tendencies discussed in this and the following chapters share a theoretical commitment to the idea that independence must be universal. That is why the ensuing theoretical and political contest for the soul of modern republicanism was over whether wage-labor was a realization or violation of free labor. After all, if wage-labor was unfree, it was not unfree in the same way as chattel slavery. The nature of the wage-laborers' servitude required analysis and exposition. If the wage-laborer was free, then defenders of that position had to show why legal self-ownership was adequate to guarantee a workers' independence. In other words, the terrain of the struggle shifted from whether republican liberty could be universal to competing accounts over what counted as a relation of domination and thus what counted as a truly universalizable conception of free labor.

To understand this contested and shifting ideological terrain, this chapter begins with the prehistory of republican thinking about wage-labor. This prehistory points us to ambiguities in the theory of "dependence" or "domination" on which the republican theory of liberty rests, which in turn directs our attention to the way in which a society organized on the basis of wage-labor imposes new conceptual demands on that theory. Both the legal freedom and the complex interdependence of the workers in the emerging labor market presented important challenges to existing ways of thinking about wage-labor and economic dependence. With an appreciation of this material challenge in hand, we then move to the nineteenth-century laissez-faire republican theory itself. We see how the defense of wage labor as free labor emerged, especially in the judiciary, as a way of attempting to reconcile the republican theory to new social realities. On this view, wage-labor was free labor because the wage-laborer was sole proprietor of his own labor. In virtue of his legal self-ownership, he exercised the control over his labor that any independent property-owner exercised over property. As such, the wage-laborer was a free laborer in full possession of his republican liberty.

The Prehistory of Wage-Labor in Republicanism

Prior to the nineteenth century, there are two notable features of the republican discussion of wage-labor. The first is the near universal assumption that wage-labor is dependent and servile. As far back as Cicero, we find comments such

[2] Skinner, "A Third Concept of Liberty," 262.

as "all those workers who are paid for their labour and not for their skill have servile and demeaning employment; for in their case the very wage is a contract to servitude."[3] Kant, whose ideas about wage-labor were taken from republican sources, said a citizen "must be his own master (*sui iuris*), and must have some property.... In cases where he must earn his living from others, he must earn it only selling that which is his, and not by allowing others to make use of him; for he must in the true sense of the word serve no-one but the commonwealth."[4] Recall, too, that slavery appealed to Jefferson, Madison, and many in the Founding generation as an alternative to the dependence of wage-laborers. Even Lincoln, in the speech quoted in the previous chapter, structures his vision of social mobility around the contrast between wage-labor and free labor: "[T]he prudent, penniless beginner in the world, labors for wages awhile, saves surplus with which to buy tools or land, for himself; then labors on his own account another while.... [This] is *free labor*."[5] From Cicero to Lincoln, wage-labor is avowedly a dependent form of labor. For those, unlike Cicero but like Lincoln, willing to conceive of some forms of work as fully free, economic independence was more than a condition of self-ownership. It was also control over one's labor and property – a lack of subjection to the commands of others in how one performs one's daily activity.

If wage-labor was understood to be dependent, it nevertheless received very little direct theoretical attention by pre-nineteenth-century republicans. The quotations assembled previously are mostly offhand, throwaway comments, extraneous footnotes, and casual historical inferences. That is mainly because of the second notable feature of pre-nineteenth-century republican thinking: it was based on a social assumption that wage-labor would never be more than a passing, marginal, or seasonal fact of the economy, rather than a central and permanent way of organizing economic production. That assumption was based on a further belief about property and labor. Republicans had assumed there would always be enough land such that a citizen could acquire adequate property to be individually self-sufficient. This tacit belief is immediately evident in Lincoln's speech and undergirded the early republican ideal of individual proprietorship. The further assumption was that, to the degree that there *would* be a class of dependent laborers, they would be slaves or other kinds of legally bound workers. That thought is apparent in thinkers from Aristotle and Cicero through Jefferson, and is the reason the paradox of slavery and freedom emerges in the first place.

But these were all semi-articulated premises. They were not carefully arranged in relation to other key aspects of the republican tradition. A chain of social

---

[3] Cicero, *On Duties*, 58.
[4] Immanuel Kant, "On the Common Saying: 'This May Be True in Theory, but It Does Not Apply in Practice,'" in *Kant Political Writings*, ed. H. S. Reiss (Cambridge: Cambridge University Press, 1991), 61–92, 78.
[5] Lincoln, "Address to the Wisconsin State Agricultural Society," 158 first emphasis added.

assumptions and theoretical premises were connected in an unstable equilibrium. Wage-labor was servile; free labor was self-sufficient and autarkic; property was land; land was abundant; the state guaranteed independence by guaranteeing personal property and legal status. These positions roughly held together so long as they bore some relation to social reality and so long as challenges to them remained marginal. Because this set of theoretical positions rested on some underdeveloped social assumptions, any attempt to understand the development of republican thought must touch on the social history of the period.

The Crisis of Free Labor

The social and economic transformations of the nineteenth century undermined all of these assumptions at once. The dominant form of human labor, its interdependent organization, its legal status, and the distribution of and kinds of property, all changed rapidly. The Civil War did settle the question of whether republican thought could generate a universalizable conception of liberty, embodied in the free labor ideal. That ideal possessed some relation to social reality in antebellum United States, which "had spread self-employment remarkably widely," thus control over one's labor could still be "the moral norm, the bedrock meaning of free labor."[6] In these circumstances, it was possible to maintain something like the National Reformer conception of the free labor ideal as an individuated condition of personal dominium. The individual exercised complete, undominated control over his own personal activity. However, the rise of a permanent wage-labor force produced an intellectual crisis for this conception. As historian Leon Fink puts it, "the fact that by 1870 two-thirds of the American workforce were hirelings posed a stark ideological dilemma for a culture in which the lack of property and independence was associated with slavery or 'wage slavery.'"[7] Permanent wage-laborers were defined by the absence of any realistic chance to own productive property, be it land or tools and raw material, which appeared to mean that they could not be independent.

Permanent wage-labor went hand-in-hand with factory production. Here the problem was not just the sale of one's labor, but the fact that the labor activity itself was routinized and mechanized into a process over which workers lost control.[8] Terence Powderly, General Master Workman of the Knights of Labor, gave voice to these worries in Gothic tones:

The village blacksmith shop was abandoned, the road-side shoe shop was deserted, the tailor left his bench, and all together these mechanics turned away from their country

---

[6] Daniel T. Rodgers, *The Work Ethic in Industrial America, 1850–1920* (Chicago: University of Chicago Press, 1979), 34–35.

[7] Fink, "From Autonomy to Abundance: Changing Beliefs about the Free Labor System in Nineteenth-Century America," 116–36, 128.

[8] Rodgers, *The Work Ethic in Industrial America*, 23–26; Montgomery, "Labor and the Republic in Industrial America," 201–15, 202–4; Melvyn Dubofsky, *Industrialism and the American Worker* (Arlington Heights, IL: Harlan Davidson, Inc., 1985), 4–9.

"Independent Laborers by Voluntary Contract" 51

homes and wended their way to the cities wherein the large factories had been erected. The gates were unlocked in the morning to allow them to enter, and after their daily task was done the gates were closed after them in the evening.[9]

Here it was not just subjection to an employer but to a particular kind of process that threatened the self-directed character of free labor. The social and mechanical character of factory production appeared to mean a loss of individual productive control. The problem was not just technological, but organizational: "[N]ew techniques of organization separated specific tasks hitherto the responsibility of one artisan among teams of workers."[10] Where new skilled positions did arise, they were part of an integrated social process, unlike the autarky of the self-employed farmer or artisan.[11] The crisis of the free labor ideal was therefore the product of widespread and growing wage-labor alongside interdependent factory production. The citizen-worker faced potentially new forms of dependence in the wage-labor contract and in the labor process itself.

The crisis in the concept of free labor was registered at all levels of society, in court cases, congressional inquiries, popular presses and theoretical tracts.[12] After all, it was not merely objective social changes that challenged republican thinking. Different social actors applied republican categories to these new circumstances in ways that led to reinterpretations of its core concepts. Following William Forbath, what I call "laissez-faire republicanism"[13] interpreted the republican ideal in the direction of a classical liberal defense of freedom of contract and legal autonomy. Although evident in a number of areas of public opinion, it was perhaps most pronounced as a doctrinal strand of American state and federal Supreme Court decisions. In the hands of justices, along with legal theorists and social critics, the republican ideal became a kind of intellectual medium out of which grew a liberal jurisprudence and body of thought.

The stakes in this ideological move were high. In the late nineteenth century, various state and federal courts struck down labor laws regulating hours, wages, and work safety, as well as blocked or curtailed union organizing,

---

[9] Powderly, *Thirty Years of Labor 1859–1889*, 26. General Master Workman, originally "Grand" Master Workman, was the highest office in the Knights of Labor. See Chapters 4 and 5 for a discussion of the Knights and the relevant references.

[10] Dubofsky, *Industrialism and the American Worker*, 4.

[11] Ibid., 5.

[12] On wage-slavery, see Eric Foner, *The Story of American Freedom* (New York: W. W. Norton, 1998), 116–37; Rodgers, *The Work Ethic in Industrial America*, 30–35. On legal conceptions of free labor, see Montgomery, *Citizen-Worker*, 13–50; Robert J. Steinfeld, "Changing Legal Conceptions of Free Labor," in *Terms of Labor: Slavery, Serfdom and Free Labor*, ed. Stanley L. Engerman (Stanford, CA: Stanford University Press, 1999), 137–47. See also Forbath, "Ambiguities of Free Labor," 767; Pope, "Labor's Constitution of Freedom," 941–1031; Bernard Mandel, *Labor, Free and Slave: Workingmen and the Anti-Slavery Movement in the United States* (Champaign: University of Illinois Press, 1955); Cunliffe, *Chattel Slavery and Wage Slavery*; Roediger, *The Wages of Whiteness*.

[13] Forbath, "Ambiguities of Free Labor," 767.

strikes, and boycotts – many of which were organized or supported by the Knights of Labor and their labor republican leaders.[14] Although the "laissez-faire" character of this period can be over-stated,[15] it is true that a very influential set of ideas emerged connecting the freedom of the individual laborer to a defense of freedom of contract.[16] These ideas contributed to a rejection of many attempts to regulate or control the workplace through various types of collective action.

Laissez-Faire Republicanism and Jurisprudence: The Slaughterhouse Cases

It is important to recall that the defense of wage-labor did not begin as a straightforwardly republican one. As one historian puts it, "antislavery rendered freedom abstract by enshrining ownership of self, at the expense of an older republican emphasis on ownership of productive property."[17] We saw something of this opposition between a voluntarist and a republican conception of freedom in the previous chapter, but as a picture of history it misses the way in which many came to interpret the commodification of labor-power as the condition of republican liberty itself. Not only did Garrison and other abolitionists eventually participate in this fusion of languages,[18] but the independent citizen-worker, selling his labor for wages, was soon to become a dominant ideal of public discourse.[19]

How, then, did treating labor as a commodity that could be bought and sold come to be seen as the guarantee of republican liberty? Post–Civil War actors inherited the idea that the free laborer is independent insofar as he controls his own labor. His labor is not subject to the arbitrary will of anyone else. But

---

[14] "Boycotting May Be Illegal," *JSP* 2, no. 101 (September 13, 1885); "Law and the Boycott," *JUL* VII, no. 20 (January 29, 1887), 2268; Forbath, *Law and the Shaping of the American Labor Movement*, 37–127; Christopher L. Tomlins, *The State and the Unions: Labor Relations, Law, and the Organized Labor Movement in America, 1880–1960* (Cambridge: Cambridge University Press, 1985), 32–52.

[15] For instance, Michael Les Benedict, "Laissez-Faire and Liberty: a Re-Evaluation of the Meaning and Origins of Laissez-Faire Constitutionalism," *Law and History Review* 3, no. 2 (Autumn 1985), 293–331; William Novak, "The Legal Origins of the Modern American State," in *Looking Back at Law's Century*, ed. Robert Kagan and Austin Sarat Bryant Garth (Ithaca: Cornell University press, 2001).

[16] Montgomery, *Citizen-Worker*; Morton J. Horwitz, *Transformation of American Law, 1870–1960: The Crisis of Legal Orthodoxy* (New York: Oxford University Press, 1994), 160–210; Steinfeld, "Changing Legal Conceptions of Free Labor," 137–67; Fink, "From Autonomy to Abundance."

[17] Stanley, *From Bondage to Contract*, 23.

[18] Garrison, ed., "Free and Slave Labor"; Forbath, "Ambiguities of Free Labor," 783–84.

[19] Montgomery, *Citizen-Worker*. Montgomery argues that it was up to labor reformers to overcome the conceptual limitations on not just abolitionists but the radical Republicans. Montgomery, *Beyond Equality: Labor and the Radical Republicans, 1862–1872* (New York: Alfred A Knopf, 1967), 230–60.

what kind of control? As we have seen, republicans had always tacitly assumed that this control meant continuous control over one's labor activity. Yet the rise of a modern labor market, alongside disappearance of legally constituted master-slave relations, seemed at once to eliminate the hated form of personal dependence on a master, while increasingly putting full control over one's labor out of reach. Nineteenth-century defenders of wage-labor as free labor had to show that the wage-laborer still enjoyed the morally relevant form of control. They did so by arguing that because a wage-laborer owned his labor, he controlled it in the way any property owner controls any of his property. As an influential legal textbook of the era put it: "Every person sui juris has a right to make use of his labor in any lawful employment on his own behalf, or to hire it out in the service of others. This is one of the first and highest of civil rights."[20] So long as the individual could sell his labor on terms of his own choosing, then he controlled his labor as an independent, republican citizen. As Forbath puts it, "the worker's freedom rested simply in his ownership of his capacity to labor."[21]

This ownership of one's capacity to labor deserved to be called independence because, unlike the slave, the wage-worker was not forced to work for a particular master. He stood in an equal relationship to employers and forged only those relationships he agreed to. William Graham Sumner, an especially influential nineteenth-century social thinker, and *bête noire* for labor reformers like the Knights of Labor,[22] had no time for the "wild language about wage-slavery and capitalistic tyranny"[23] coming from the mouths of labor reformers. Contrasting feudal relations of status and dependence with the modern society of contract, Sumner argued, "a society based on contract is a society of *free and independent* men, who form ties without favor or obligation, and *cooperate without cringing or intrigue*."[24] Sumner here deployed the republican odium for servility – "cringing or intrigue" – with deliberate intent. Wage-laborers were in no way subject to an employer's will; they could leave their job if they wanted, unlike slaves and indentured servants of earlier eras. The only way to violate a worker's independence was through a law that interfered with his voluntary agreement with an employer. Such interference gave one side an unfair, coercive advantage or, like a maximum-hours law,

---

[20] Thomas McIntyre Cooley, *A Treatise on the Law of Torts, or, The Wrongs Which Arise Independently of Contract* (London: Callaghan & Company, 1888), 326.
[21] William Forbath, "Ambiguities of Free Labor," 767–817, 769.
[22] For example, a Knight of Labor in Gantt's didactic novel calls Sumner a "fossilized relic of Yale College," who is important to read to be "better able to prove the falseness of the doctrines" of labor's enemies. T. Fulton Gantt, "Breaking the Chains: A Story of the Present Industrial Struggle," in *The Knights in Fiction: Two Labor Novels of the 1880s*, ed. Mary C. Grimes (Champaign: University of Illinois Press, 1986), 68.
[23] William Graham Sumner, "The Absurd Effort to Make the World Over," *Forum*, March 1894, 95.
[24] William Graham Sumner, *What Social Classes Owe to Each Other* (New York: Harper & Brothers Publishers, 1883), 26 emphasis added.

unjustifiably limited what each side could agree to. Absent any such law, both faced each other as equally situated property-owners. They were "sui juris," possessing the ability and legal power to make rational judgments about the best use of their property.

The basic outlines of this "laissez-faire republicanism" emerge in force soon after the Civil War in a series of Supreme Court decisions commonly known as the Slaughterhouse Cases. Decided in 1873, these were the first cases to test the new Reconstruction amendments banning slavery and giving citizens equal rights.[25] After Louisiana passed a law forcing butchers to do their work in a single New Orleans slaughterhouse chartered as a private corporation, a group of white butchers appealed to the antislavery Reconstruction Amendments to raise the republican objection that the law compromised their economic independence.[26] Among other things, they argued that the Louisiana law violated the Thirteenth Amendment's ban on "slavery and involuntary servitude"[27] because it illegitimately restricted their control over their own activity. The law forced them to work according to the rules of the chartered slaughterhouse, rather than as they saw fit. This, "if not strictly a servitude" in the sense of chattel slavery, was

> certainly a servitude in a more popular sense, and, being an enforced one, it is an involuntary servitude. Men are surely subjected to a servitude when ... every man and every woman in them is compelled to refrain from the use of their own land and exercise of their own industry and the improvement of their own property, in a way confessedly lawful and necessary in itself, and made unlawful and unnecessary only because, at their cost, an exclusive privilege is granted to seventeen other persons to improve and exercise it for them. We have here the "servients" and the "dominants" and the "thraldom" of the old seignioral system.[28]

The butchers' argument was a version of the early republican idea that free labor was a matter of continuous control over one's productive activity. At the state level their argument succeeded, with one of the justices proclaiming that there is no "more sacred right of citizenship than the right to pursue unmolested a lawful employment in a lawful manner. It is nothing more nor less than the sacred right of labor."[29]

But the butchers lost at the national level. Justice Miller, writing for the majority of the Supreme Court, rejected their expansive interpretation of "involuntary servitude," saying he found it "difficult to see a justification

---

[25] "This court is thus called upon for the first time to give construction to these articles," *In Re Slaughter-House Cases*, 83 U.S. 36, 67 (1872).

[26] For an extensive history of the case, emphasizing the legislation's origins in public health concerns, see Ronald Labbé and Jonathan Lurie, *The Slaughterhouse Cases: Regulation, Reconstruction, and the Fourteenth Amendment* (Lawrence: University Press of Kansas, 2003).

[27] "Constitution of the United States of America," in *The Declaration of Independence and the Constitution of the United States* (Washington, DC: Cato Institute, 2002).

[28] *In Re Slaughter-House Cases*, 50–51.

[29] Ibid., 106.

"Independent Laborers by Voluntary Contract" 55

for the assertion that the butchers are deprived of the right to labor in their occupation."[30] Notably, the Supreme Court might have wished to avoid the free labor question altogether. The original case did not start out as a referendum on it.[31] But the butchers' broad interpretation of the Thirteenth Amendment ban on "involuntary servitude" forced the Court to define the parameters of this republican ideology and in effect to *reject* the conception of free labor as continuous productive control. On Miller's view, though involuntary "servitude is of larger meaning than slavery," that was only because "the obvious purpose [of the Reconstruction Amendments] was to forbid all shades and conditions of African slavery."[32] There were many shades of *legal* dependence to which slaves had been subject, and thus the furthest these Amendments could stretch were similarly extreme conditions of legal subjection, such as possibly "Mexican peonage or the Chinese coolie labor system."[33] Beyond that, any self-owning citizen was suitably independent to be considered a free laborer. It was almost as if a white man could not be unfree so long as he avoided one of the historical servitudes of other races.

The Slaughterhouse Cases are important because they illuminate the conceptual puzzles that faced any defender of free labor in emerging, industrial conditions. For instance, the majority decision may have rejected an expansive interpretation of free labor, but it was the pro-butcher *minority* ruling, written by Justice Field, that inspired the later strand of laissez-faire constitutionalism.[34] That is because the thrust of Field's dissent was largely about illegitimate state interference in private economic activity. Although Field approvingly quotes the lower court's proclamation about the "sacred right of labor,"[35] he does so less to accept the view of free labor as continuous control over labor and more to reject restrictions on private contracts.

Part of the reason for these peculiarities of the majority and minority decision in the *Slaughterhouse Cases* is that the plaintiffs were property-owning, skilled craftsmen, not industrial wage-laborers. The butchers' claims were still those of artisans, who conceived of free labor in the highly individuated terms of individual dominion over the labor process – precisely the kind of labor that industrialization was eliminating. Free labor was still a private activity for them, performed by individuals who were brought into relations with each other by selling the products of their labor, not their capacity to labor itself. The butchers' views therefore blurred into arguments for the sanctity of individual property rights and of freedom from interference. Moreover, the butchers defended noninterference with contracts because they thought it prevented the emergence of state-backed monopoly privileges, like the chartered

[30] Ibid., 61.
[31] Labbé and Lurie, *The Slaughterhouse Cases*.
[32] *In Re Slaughter-House Cases*, 70, also 72.
[33] Ibid., 72.
[34] See Forbath's excellent discussion Forbath, "Ambiguities of Free Labor."
[35] *In Re Slaughter-House Cases*, 106.

butcher-house, and the aristocratic class that benefited from these privileges: "It was from a country which had been thus oppressed by monopolies that our ancestors came."[36] Although the Slaughterhouse Cases might have signaled a rejection of the idea that free labor was continuous control over one's labor, it was only later decisions – which specifically dealt with wage-labor – that could address the ambiguities of applying old terms to new situations. In the *Slaughterhouse Cases*, labor and laissez-faire republican arguments remained significantly intertwined. In fact, the cases are ideologically unstable enough that a judicial path could have emerged in which free labor acquired a more expansive definition, consistent with a conception of servitude applicable to wage-labor.[37] All *Slaughterhouse* accomplished was to say that the independence of the free laborer was not *uniquely* a matter of whether each exercised continuous control over his or her own labor. Subsequent justices had to do more work to establish just how and why wage-labor was independent in the relevant sense.

From Slaughterhouse to Lochner: Ownership as Control

It did not take long for the ideological contest over the meaning of free labor to sharpen, and for various state and the federal justices to develop the laissez-faire republican view. For instance, in 1886, the Pennsylvania Supreme Court struck down an 1881 anti-truck statute, which among other things prohibited employers from paying employees in "scrip" or orders from company stores, rather than in money – the same issue that would inflame tensions in Thibodaux, Louisiana the following year.[38] The justice writing for the majority in *Godcharles v. Wigeman* argued that the anti-truck law prevented "persons who are sui juris from making their own contracts."[39] It was therefore, "an infringement alike of the rights of the employer and the employe[e]; more than this, it is an insulting attempt to put the laborer under legislative tutelage, which is not only degrading to his manhood, but subversive to his rights as a

---

[36] Ibid., 48. On the anti-monopoly strand of republican argument, see Howard Gillman, *The Constitution Besieged: The Rise and Demise of Lochner Era Police Powers Jurisprudence* (Durham: Duke University Press, 1993), 33–45; Appleby, *Capitalism and a New Social Order*; Benedict, "Laissez-Faire and Liberty."

[37] See for instance James Gray Pope's fascinating reconstruction of the labor movement's interpretation of the Thirteenth Amendment's abolition of servitude. Pope, "Labor's Constitution of Freedom," 941–1031; James Gray Pope, "The Thirteenth Amendment Versus the Commerce Clause: Labor and the Shaping of American Constitutional Law, 1921–1957," *Columbia Law Review* 102, no. 1 (January 2002), 1–122.

[38] I am indebted to Laura Phillips for illuminating conversations about *Godcharles* and the early free contract cases. See Laura Phillips Sawyer, "Contested Meanings of Freedom: Workingmen's Wages, the Company Store System, and the Godcharles v. Wigeman Decision," *The Journal of the Gilded Age and Progressive Era*, 12, no. 3 (July 2013), 285–319. On Thibodaux, see the Introduction.

[39] *Godcharles v. Wigeman*, 113 Pa. St. 431, 437.

citizen."⁴⁰ Note the republican cast of the argument. To have his freedom of contract restricted for any other purpose than for the sake of public health was to place the wage-laborer under a political "tutelage" because it substituted the judgment of a legislator for the judgment of the worker as to how to dispense with his labor. This loss of control transformed the worker into a dependent laborer. If the worker consented to being paid scrip then that was up to him, not to anyone else. Laws that restricted hours, enacted wage floors, or regulated conditions, unless they had a specific public health purpose, were understood to be a form of "class legislation," whereby one class illegitimately used the law to advance its interests by restricting the contractual freedom of both the employer and employee.⁴¹

The insistence that a person was independent so long as he remained legally *sui juris* was a consistent feature of labor cases during the period. In a case from 1895, *Ritchie v. People*, the Illinois Supreme Court struck down a law limiting the legal working day for women in various garment industries to eight hours. Here again, the majority intoned against restricting the judgments of legally independent workers:

> In this country the legislature has no power to prevent persons who are sui juris from making their own contracts, nor can it interfere with the freedom of contract between the workman and the employer. The right to labor or employ labor, and make contracts in respect thereto upon such terms as may be agreed upon between the parties, is included in the constitutional guaranty above quoted.⁴²

Recall that the phrase *sui juris* means "under one's own power" and is taken from the definition of a free person in the Roman law. It is taken from the selfsame portion of the Roman law that has served as the touchstone for the modern and neo-republican theory of liberty.⁴³ That the same idea should appear in these court cases is more than a verbal coincidence. These courts understood themselves to be identifying the conditions under which a person was truly under his own power and then to be subsuming wage-laborers under that description.

These judicial rulings found support in the wider sphere of public opinion. John Bates Clark, an important economist of the day, argued that labor could be treated as a commodity that was exchangeable like any other; while Francis Amasa Walker, another economist who was sympathetic to labor reform, said about wage-laborers that "you can control your own time, brains, and hands," which was why to sell your labor was not to "sell yourself at all."⁴⁴ Notably,

---

⁴⁰ Ibid.
⁴¹ Benedict, "Laissez-Faire and Liberty."
⁴² *Ritchie v. The People*, 155 Ill. 98.
⁴³ Skinner, "The Republican Ideal of Political Liberty."
⁴⁴ Stanley, *From Bondage to Contract*, 82. On Walker, Clark and the new economists' sympathy to the labor movement see Rosanne Currarino, *The Labor Question in America: Economic Democracy in the Gilded Age* (Urbana, Chicago, and Springfield: University of Illinois Press, 2011), 60–85.

economists such as Walker supported unionization, the need for higher wages, and the role of these reforms in protecting a certain idea of citizenship. But they stopped short of saying there was any further claim labor had to exercising control over work itself. As one historian observes, "Walker denounced workingmen for 'seeking to legislate concerning the ways in which industry shall be carried on' and [for] the 'spirit which delighted in humiliating and harassing the employer.'" Because workers had no legitimate claim to being denied their liberty, their demand to exercise control at work was just an attempt to "overbear the rightful authority of the employer."[45] Even a commentator such as E. L. Godkin, who, in a famous article for a leading magazine, expressed concern for wage-laborers' "dependence for their bread on the good-will of employers," their "long subjection to factory discipline," and their "servile tone and servile way of thinking," refused to take this republican language in radical directions. He did not argue that the relevant domination was bound up with labor contracts themselves and he rejected arguments for infringing employer's rights to rule the workplace.[46] Many important public investigations of the labor question, including a famous 1883 U.S. Senate inquiry, showed a similar willingness to consider labor's concerns while rejecting the idea that the commodification of the capacity to labor was inconsistent with the wage-laborer's independence.[47] In fact, as early as an 1866 report by a special committee of the Massachusetts House of Representatives, we find the authors arguing that maximum hours legislation was unjustifiable "legal compulsion" that interfered with the "spontaneous" agreements between "the capitalist and the laborer."[48] With a nod to the wider, post–Civil War ideological context of their report, they argued that in "the long struggle for the abolition of slavery … it was not till the capitalist was left free as the laborer, that labor was really emancipated."[49]

Leading legal treatises similarly affirmed the independence of the wage-laborer. Thomas Cooley, a law professor, Michigan Supreme Court Justice, and eventual head of the Interstate Commerce Commission, wrote in his 1878 *Treatise on the Law of Torts*, that "every person sui juris has a right to make use of his labor in any lawful employment on his own behalf, or to hire it out in the service of others. This is one of the first and highest of civil rights."[50] Another important legal scholar, Christopher Tiedeman, wrote in his *A Treatise on the Limitations of the Police Power in the United States*: "No

---

[45] Quoted ibid., 83.
[46] E. L. Godkin, "The Labor Crisis," *The North American Review* CV (July 1867), 177–213 212.
[47] *Report of the Committee of the Senate upon the Relations Between Labor and Capital, and Testimony Taken by the Committee: Volume I* (Washington, DC: Government Printing Office, 1885), 82–83.
[48] *Report of the Special Commission on the Hours of Labor and the Condition and Prospects of the Industrial Classes* (Boston: Wright & Potter, State Printers, February 1866), 30.
[49] Ibid., 31.
[50] Cooley, *A Treatise on the Law of Torts*, 326.

man's liberty is safe, if the legislature can deny him the right to engage in a harmless calling."[51] Neither Cooley nor Tiedeman were themselves particularly committed to republican ideas. Instead, they were providing the contours for thinking about the relationship between law and power in the new economy. Others took the same language and connected it more directly to republican citizenship. "To-day the labor contract is perfectly free," wrote Frederic J. Stimson in his *Labor in its Relation to Law*; "the recognition of the laborer as a free citizen, free to contract, capable of acquiring contractual rights, has been his great emancipation of the past."[52] No matter how self-consciously republican, all of these writers understood themselves to be intervening in a political debate. Tiedeman made the stakes clear in the 1886 preface to his treatise on police powers, written at the peak of Gilded Age class conflict, when the Knights of Labor had the active support of roughly a million workers and when massive strike waves roiled mines, railways, factories, and indeed whole cities[53]: "Socialism, Communism, and Anarchism are rampant throughout the civilized world. The State is called on to protect the weak against the shrewdness of the stronger, to determine what wages a workman shall receive for his labor, and how many hours daily he shall labor.... The principal object of the present work is to demonstrate ... that under the written constitutions, Federal and State, democratic absolutism is impossible in this country."[54]

Not every judge who adopted the laissez-faire republican view shared Tiedeman's revanchist spirit. But they adopted the same basic theory of power and freedom when interpreting the meaning of free labor. They knew that in doing so they were taking a position in the central political question of the time. Echoing William Lloyd Garrison's early abolitionist view that "poverty was not slavery,"[55] they adopted some version of Tiedeman's view that liberty did not require protecting "the weak against the shrewdness of the stronger." Mere "weakness" in bargaining over the terms of a contract did not count as dependence or subjection. So long as individuals owned their own labor, they were under their own power, and thus arbiters of their fate. They enjoyed the republican liberty owed to all.

The identification of individual self-ownership with republican self-government continued through the 1890s. In an 1896 California Supreme Court decision, *ex parte Jentzsch*, the court struck down a law prohibiting barbers from working on Sundays. The majority held that "our institutions are founded upon the conviction that we are not only capable of self-government as a community, but what is the logical necessity, that we are capable, to a great extent,

---

[51] Christopher Gustavus Tiedeman, *A Treatise on the Limitations of the Police Power in the United States* (St. Louis: The F. H. Thomas Law Book Co., 1886), 195.
[52] Quoted in Stanley, *From Bondage to Contract*, 74.
[53] Richard Oestreicher, "A Note on Knights of Labor Membership Statistics," *Labor History* 25, no. 1 (1984), 102–8.
[54] Tiedeman, *A Treatise on the Limitations of the Police Power in the United States*, vii.
[55] "Wendell Phillips and 'Young America'," *The Liberator* 16, no. 36 (September 4, 1846), 143.

of individual self-government."⁵⁶ Such individual self-government required permitting each individual "the utmost possible amount of personal liberty, and, with that guaranteed him, he is treated as a person of responsible judgment, not as a child in his nonage, and is left free to work out his destiny as impulse, education, training, heredity, and environment direct him."⁵⁷ Again, the main threat to this worker's independence was a law, ostensibly passed in his interest, but limiting his contractual freedom and thus his independent judgment.

As this laissez-faire republican argument developed, justices repeatedly emphasized that they were not just defending a purely negative, private liberty but a form of political freedom appropriate for self-governing individuals: "A man's constitutional liberty means more than his personal freedom. It means, with many other rights, his right freely to labor, and to own the fruits of his toil."⁵⁸ Or again, *in re Jacobs*, an 1895 New York case overturning a law prohibiting cigar rolling in tenements, stated

> Liberty, in its broad sense as understood in this country, means the right, not only of freedom from actual servitude, imprisonment or restraint, but the right of one to use his faculties in all lawful ways, to live and work where he will, to earn his livelihood in any lawful calling, and to pursue any lawful trade or avocation.⁵⁹

The making of contracts to sell property, including one's own labor, was the activity through which one reproduced and maintained one's independence as a citizen. Contracts were the central medium through which one exercised and realized one's liberty as a republican citizen because they were the most important way in which the citizen exercised control over his life. The absence of interference in contracts made possible this positive exercise of independent judgment – the kind of judgment, or "individual self-government," every citizen as a citizen was expected to be able to make.

Through the end of the century, courts regularly argued that freedom of contract was about free labor, and that free labor was a positive condition of individual self-control, not mere absence of restraint. In an important Colorado Supreme Court case from 1899, *In re Morgan*, striking down eight-hours legislation for mining and smelting, the majority drew together quotations from Cooley and Tiedeman's earlier treatises, as well as language from some of the earlier cases to pass judgment on the whole line of thinking. Justice Campbell, writing for the majority, asserted the familiar republican view that freedom is not mere absence of interference, but the positive exercise of independent judgment:

> Liberty means something more than mere freedom from physical restraint. It includes the privilege of choosing any lawful occupation for the exercise of one's physical and

---

⁵⁶ *Ez Parte Jentzsch* 112 Cal. 468, 472 (1896).
⁵⁷ Ibid., 473.
⁵⁸ Ibid.
⁵⁹ *In re Jacobs*, 2 N.Y.Crim.R. 539, 106 (1895).

mental faculties which is not injurious to others. The right to acquire and possess property includes the right to contract for one's labor. The latter is essentially a property right.[60]

For judges, it was now a settled question that the free laborer is free in virtue of the control he exercises over his labor-power as his own property, not as a form of inalienable control over the activity of work itself. To freely alienate this control over one's capacity to labor, through a labor contract, was no violation of one's independence because the individual had consented to give this control over his property to another for a specified period of time and on terms to which he had consented. Significantly, the *in re Morgan* Court was rejecting a view, expressed the year earlier by the Utah Supreme Court, in *Holden v. Hardy*, that the rise of industry had created new social inequalities and work conditions that placed individual workers in conditions of extreme disadvantage, greatly constraining their will. The *Holden* court said:

> prior to the adoption of the constitution ... we were then almost purely an agricultural people, the occasion for any special protection of a particular class did not exist ... in the vast proportions which these industries have since assumed, it has been found that they can no longer be carried on, with due regard to the safety and health of those engaged in them, without special protection against the dangers necessarily incident to these employments.[61]

For the *Holden* court, substantial regulation of the workplace did not so much violate the independence of the worker as recognize that legal status did not describe economic reality:

> the experience of legislators in many states has corroborated, that the proprietors of these establishments and their operatives do not stand upon an equality, and that their interests are, to a certain extent, conflicting. The former naturally desire to obtain as much labor as possible from their employees, while the latter are often induced by the fear of discharge to conform to regulations which their judgment, fairly exercised, would pronounce to be detrimental to their health or strength. In other words, the proprietors lay down the rules, and the laborers are practically constrained to obey them.[62]

The majority in Holden was commenting on a new kind of economic dependence, based on extremes of wealth and poverty, which gave reason to think freedom of contract did not bear as tight a relation to independent judgment "fairly exercised" as others believed. Of course, *Holden v. Hardy* only went so far as to say that workers could be treated as dependents and thus protective legislation extended to miners and smelters. It did not offer a full theory of how to eliminate the new economic dependence to which the new class of "operatives" were subject. In fact, the classification of groups such as women and veterans as "dependents" was a standard intellectual move by which

---

[60] *In re Morgan*, 26 Colo. 415, 420 (1899).
[61] *Holden v. Hardy*, 169 US 366, 392 (1898).
[62] Ibid., 397

courts permitted infringements of freedom of contract.[63] As such, even Holden backhandedly affirmed the view that, to the degree a person could be considered independent, he should be treated as a wage-laborer, in full legal possession of his labor-power. The full, laissez-faire republican view, expressed in decisions such as *in re Morgan*, simply refused to accept the social ontology of a case like Holden, which suggested that there were fewer and fewer parts of the economy in which one could realistically imagine employer and employee as similarly situated with respect to power over the terms of work and the use of property. As the *Morgan* court said,

> in a purely private, lawful business ... the carrying on of which is attended by no injury to the general public, it is beyond the power of the legislature ... to prohibit an adult man who desires to work thereat from working more than eight hours a day, on the ground that working longer may, or probably will, injure his own health.[64]

To claim that workers, despite their legal autonomy, were subject to some other kind of compulsion that forced them to take these hazardous jobs and extreme hours was not only wrong as a description of social power but indicated a failure to respect their independence. As such, it threatened core institutions: "Such legislation does not denote an advance in the law of the domestic relations. On the contrary, it is a distinct and emphatic return – a retrogression – to that period in English history ... against which our ancestors rebelled."[65] The exercise of collective power to regulate contracts and work conditions was a threat to the legal and social foundations of republican self-government.

As these ideas reached the U.S. Supreme Court, their republican roots started to fade. In 1897, the Court ruled in *Allgeyer v. Louisiana* that freedom of contract was an explicit, substantive right guaranteed under the due process clause of the Fourteenth Amendment. It thereby established a constitutional limit to various labor reform laws.[66] In *Allgeyer*, Justice Peckham argues for the unanimous Court that liberty of contract means:

> to be free in the enjoyment of all his faculties; to be free to use them in all lawful ways; to live and work where he will; to earn his livelihood by any lawful calling; to pursue any livelihood or avocation, and for that purpose to enter into all contracts which may be proper, necessary and essential to his carrying out to a successful conclusion the purposes mentioned above.[67]

The language of free labor – "free in the enjoyment of all his faculties" or "to pursue any livelihood or avocation" – is seamlessly fused with freedom of

---

[63] E.g., the "maternal welfare state" in *Protecting Soldiers and Mothers: The Political Origins of Social Policy in the United States*, ed. Theda Skocpol (Cambridge, MA: Belknap Press of Harvard University Press, 1992).
[64] *In Re Morgan*, 428.
[65] Ibid., 419.
[66] Paul Brest et al., *Processes of Constitutional Decisionmaking: Cases and Materials*, 4 ed. (Boston: Little Brown, 2003), 344–45.
[67] *Allgeyer V. Louisiana*, 165 U.S. 578, 589 (1897).

"Independent Laborers by Voluntary Contract"

contract through the prepositional clause "for that purpose." The constitutional goal remains the guarantee of free labor. Free labor is equated with legal autonomy because the law protects him from arbitrary interference both by the state and by individuals in civil society. Any interference by the state not clearly in the public interest is essentially class legislation, the arbitrary imposition of one group's will on another through the instrument of the state.[68] Only those interfering laws narrowly pertaining to "health, safety, and morals" – that is, in the public interest – are legitimate.[69] Legal autonomy, moreover, ensures no specific individual can exercise arbitrary power over the contracting individual.

By 1905, in the most famous case of the period, *Lochner v. New York*, we see liberty as noninterference fully emerging out of an earlier republican language. Lochner is regularly identified as the most important "laissez-faire" liberal case of the period,[70] which set the defining precedent for more decades of hostility to labor legislation.[71] In Lochner, which struck down a maximum-hours law for bakers, it is the same judge from *Allgeyer*, Justice Peckham, who makes the case that the bakers' liberty as citizens have been infringed:

There is no contention that bakers as a class are not equal in intelligence and capacity to men in other trades or manual occupations, or that they are not able to assert their rights and care for themselves without the protecting arm of the state, interfering with their independence of judgment and of action. They are in no sense wards of the state.[72]

To infringe on an individual's freedom of contract, for instance by limiting the hours he contracts to work, implies that the individual lacks the capacity for "independence of judgment and of action" required to pursue his own interests rationally. It marks him as a dependent or "ward of the state."[73] Moreover, independence of judgment can be exercised under nearly any economic conditions so long as the person's freedom of contract is not constrained by interfering laws. It is only the law, not anything like economic dependence, that can arbitrarily constrain a person's independence of judgment.

In Peckham's opinion, the language of "independence" remains but mostly sapped of its republican origins. It is true that the primary justification for

---

[68] Benedict, "Laissez-Faire and Liberty," 305–14; Gillman, *The Constitution Besieged*, 45–60.
[69] Horwitz, *Transformation of American Law*, 30. Gillman shows how class conflict undermined consensus understandings of 'public interest,' *The Constitution Besieged*, 93–97.
[70] See for instance ibid., 29–31; Ackerman, *We the People: Foundations*, 63–67.
[71] Forbath, *Law and the Shaping of the American Labor Movement*; Pope, "Labor's Constitution of Freedom"; Tomlins, *The State and the Unions*, 3–98.
[72] *Lochner V. People of State of New York*, 198 U.S. 45, 57 (1905).
[73] The "ward of the state" concept has its own complex history, for which there is no space here. But the protection, then loss of protection, then recovery of protection for women tracks the degree to which they were considered dependent or independent and the degree to which that remained a relevant judicial consideration. See *Muller v. Oregon* (1908, argued by later Supreme Court Justice Brandeis); *Adkins v. Children's Hospital of District of Columbia*, 261 U.S. 525 (1923); *West Coast Hotel Co. v. Parrish Et Ux.*, 300 U.S. 379 (1937).

overturning the maximum hours law was not that contractual freedom produced efficient market outcomes, as some at the time and subsequently have argued.[74] Instead, the decision was grounded in a conception of freedom.[75] Peckham's concern was with the violation of workers' independence. But the connection between independence and republican citizenship is barely mentioned, perhaps because these connections were assumed, but also because the voluntaristic emphasis on freedom of contract was reemerging as its own principle, loosening its connections to republican foundations. Independence had become non-interference, one in which private freedom was less and less connected to any wider view about self-government as a generalized experience. If at its origins the defense of contractual freedom was saturated with republican ideas about free labor, it had now acquired a classically liberal cast.

Republican Origins of Freedom as Non-Interference Reconsidered

The identification of wage-labor with free labor was a momentous shift. Once we acknowledge the republican origins of this intellectual reorientation, we are able to appreciate two important features of modern political thought. The first is that it is not quite accurate for neo-republicans such as Philip Pettit and Quentin Skinner to argue that "we have inherited two rival and incommensurable theories of negative liberty."[76] In fact, the laissez-faire republican view of free labor made a liberal and republican theory of liberty commensurable, and it did so in one of those areas – economic relations – in which neo-republicans have suggested their theory is importantly distinct from the liberal view.[77] Although they have said the liberal theory remains "tied to the sector of interest and opinion that first gave it prominence and currency," the same "sector of interest" was, in this case, able to appeal to republican ideas to defend its economic and political project.[78] Nor is the incommensurability claim made any stronger if, like Michael Sandel, one reads history through the neo-Aristotelian approach to republican liberty. Sandel contrasts those republicans who insisted "that wage labor was inconsistent with freedom, and sought to reform the economy along lines hospitable to republican ideals" and those *anti*-republicans who "sought to reconcile wage labor with freedom by revising the ideal" in the direction of "voluntary agreement."[79] As we have seen, the view of freedom as voluntary agreement or noninterference found strong support from a certain interpretation of the republican theory of liberty

---

[74] A tradition of interpretation that started with Holmes making this claim in the dissent to *Lochner*: "The 14th Amendment does not enact Mr. Herbert Spencer's Social Statics." *Lochner V. People of State of New York*, 75.
[75] Benedict, "Laissez-Faire and Liberty."
[76] Skinner, "A Third Concept of Liberty," 262.
[77] Pettit, *Republicanism*, 131–33.
[78] Ibid., 133.
[79] Sandel, *Democracy's Discontent*, 184.

itself. On this interpretation, being *sui juris* meant having a legally constituted condition of self-ownership and then being free to use that property as one saw fit. The self-owning individual exercised control over his own labor in the way that "control" could be understood in an industrial capitalist economy: the control of a property-owner. The assimilation of labor to a form of property-ownership was the conceptual move making the republican theory of free labor consistent with a condition of permanent wage-labor. This was no mere, or at least not merely, cynical appropriation of republican language. It was also a response to the need to make sense of the new relations of power in a modern labor market.

As far as the history of political thought goes, the development of laissez-faire republicanism accords better with those scholarly attempts to show the inner connections, rather than external oppositions, between republican and liberal ideas. Historians have occasionally noted ways in which the ideal of independence could be marshalled to defend liberal conceptions of freedom and equality of opportunity, especially by fusing the classical agrarian ideal of independence with a defense of commerce and natural rights.[80] As Joyce Appleby once argued, while recognizing that the republican and liberal conceptions of liberty are "distinct and potentially contradictory concepts," nevertheless, among Jeffersonians, "these two meanings could and did merge with one another."[81] Two other scholars, Andreas Kalyvas and Ira Katznelson, have forcefully advanced a "liberal beginnings" thesis, which holds that republicanism has provided fertile territory for the development of liberal theory and practice: "[L]iberalism as we know it was born from the spirit of republicanism, from attempts to adapt republicanism to the political, economic, and social revolutions of the eighteenth century and the first decades of the nineteenth."[82] Neo-republicans have failed to give the "economic, and social revolutions" their due, which is why they present the relationship between liberal and republican liberty as stark and static. They see liberal voluntarism and freedom of contract as alien to the republican view, rather than recognizing the degree to which the modern economy posed important challenges for the interpretation of republican liberty itself. If any "revision of the ideal," as Sandel puts it, was an abandonment of it, then the only option available for republicans appeared to be an increasingly romantic agrarian radicalism and a vestigial yearning for petty proprietorship.[83] This way of thinking about the relationship between republican liberty and the modern economy cedes far more than neo-republicans should, and mischaracterizes the historical challenge posed by

---

[80] Appleby, "The 'Agrarian Myth' in the Early Republic," 253–76, 51–105; Foner, *Free Soil, Free Labor, Free Men,* 29–39.
[81] Appleby, *Capitalism and a New Social Order,* 18.
[82] Ira Katznelson and Andreas Kalyvas, *Liberal Beginnings* (Cambridge: Cambridge University Press, 2008), 4.
[83] Judith Shklar, *American Citizenship: The Quest for Inclusion* (Cambridge, MA: Harvard University Press, 1991), 64–5.

the modern economy. If, as William Forbath has suggested, "Gilded Age class conflict found cultural expression in a struggle to define and claim title to the republican legacy and the republican constitution,"[84] then we must approach the intellectual creativity of this period with the same willingness to identify and appreciate those moments of conceptual change that historians of political thought have brought to bear on earlier periods.

This brings us to the second important point regarding the development of modern republicanism. Recognizing that republicanism could lend support to the development of liberal ideas is not somehow a weakness or a problem for the republican revival. Instead, that recognition is a condition of possibility for understanding the kinds of questions about power, inequality, and dependence that modern capitalism raises for the interpretation and application of republican ideals to new conditions. There was an alternative possibility for thinking about free labor and wage-labor. But this possibility lay not with the petty-proprietor ideal of the individuated, property-owning citizen, so much as with the development of a labor republican defense of the cooperative organization of work. To appreciate the full force of labor republican ideas, we have first had to reconstruct the historical conditions as well as laissez-faire republican theory to which they reacted. To argue that wage-labor was servile, labor republicans had to find a way of arguing that legal self-ownership was inadequate to prevent workers from becoming subject to their employers. Equally important and novel was their proposal for universalizing republican liberty: cooperative ownership and control of productive property. We are now in a position not only to reconstruct these ideas, but to appreciate their originality and vitality.

---

[84] Forbath, "Ambiguities of Free Labor," 769; Fink, *Workingmen's Democracy*, 8.

3

"The Sword of Want"

Free Labor against Wage Labor

> a very numerous race of poor men;
> of unfortunate human beings;
> without resources of property; and, therefore, dependent,
> even for their very existence, upon the pleasure,
> the caprice, the tyranny, or the folly of others
>
> *Thomas Skidmore*[1]

On August 14, 1828, a group of workers crowded into the first floor of Commissioner's Hall, a sturdy, two story brick building in the Southwark district of Philadelphia, to listen to a speech called, "Principles of Aristocratic Legislation."[2] The speaker, William Heighton, was a radical cordwainer, founder of the Working Men's Party of Philadelphia, and editor of the party's journal, the *Mechanics' Free Press*, the first labor press ever published in the United States.[3] In his speech, Heighton criticized the United States for living up to its revolutionary promise in political form but not economic practice:

we all acknowledge that the *foundation* of our independence was laid in the establishment, by our forefathers, of this inestimable right [of universal suffrage], and that in

---

[1] Thomas Skidmore, *The Rights of Man to Property! Being a Proposition to Make it Equal among the Adults of the Present Generation: And to Provide for its Equal Transmission to Each Individual of Each Succeeding Generation, on Arriving at the Age of Maturity* (New York: Alexander Ming, 1829), 249. Hereafter *The Rights of Man to Property!*

[2] William Heighton, *The Principles of Aristocratic Legislation Developed in an Address Delivered to the Working People of the District of Southwark, and Townships of Moyamensing and Passyunk* (Philadelphia: J. Coates Jr., 1828). Hereafter *The Principles of Aristocratic Legislation*.

[3] For biographical information on Heighton, see Schultz, *The Republic of Labor*, 224–32; Philip Sheldon Foner, *William Heighton: Pioneer Labor Leader of Jacksonian Philadelphia* (New York: International Publishers, 1991); Louis H. Arky, "The Mechanics' Union of Trade Associations and the Formation of the Philadelphia Workingmen's Movement," *The Pennsylvania Magazine of History and Biography* 76, no. 2 (April 1952), 142–76.

it we possess the *means* of ... attaining that happy state of real liberty and universal independence ... yet who will tell us, that the superstructure *itself* is yet, more than an IDEAL one? Who that is acquainted with the actual condition of society, that has visited the Plantation, the Quarry, the Workshop, the Forge and the Factory ... who, I say, that has seen these things will yet tell us, that the sacred sounds of LIBERTY and EQUALITY have any *actual* existence among us?[4]

Heighton was not alone in worrying that it was not just the slave "Plantation" but "the Workshop, the Forge and the Factory" that threatened universal independence. Heighton's Working Men's Party of Philadelphia, founded in 1827, was the first of many to crop up in the rapidly industrializing towns and cities of the late 1820s.[5] These organizations shared a common vocabulary and were driven by a sense that the American Revolution was unfinished. As Seth Luther, an important New England labor advocate of the time, put it in an 1833 speech, "as we have adverted to Bunker Hill, we remark, in passing, that the unfinished monument is a most excellent emblem of our unfinished independence."[6] Although free from external subjection to colonial overlords, internal forms of servitude remained even in the nominally "free" North.

One of the most radical of these early labor leaders, Thomas Skidmore, cofounder of the Workingmen's Party of New York, agreed. In his 1829 tract, *The Rights of Man to Property!*, Skidmore wrote that poor workers had become "dependent, even for their very existence, upon the pleasure, the caprice, the tyranny" of their employers. Like fellow labor leaders, Skidmore was using a familiar language of subjection and freedom, caprice and tyranny, to name a new and growing threat: the servitude of wage-laborers.

Although short-lived, these "workingmen's"[7] organizations marked the beginning of a different kind of answer to the paradox of slavery and freedom. They thoroughly rejected the attempt to equate wage-labor with free labor on the grounds that propertyless workers remained economically dependent in various ways. Because of their efforts, the concept "wage-slavery" exploded onto the scene. Comparisons of "wages slavery" and "chattel slavery" became

---

[4] William Heighton, *The Principles of Aristocratic Legislation*, 5–6.
[5] On the history of these workingmen's parties, see Pessen, *Most Uncommon Jacksonians*; Edward Pessen, "The Workingmen's Movement of the Jacksonian Era," *The Mississippi Valley Historical Review* 43, no. 3 (1956), 428–43; Sean Wilentz, *Chants Democratic: New York City & the Rise of the American Working Class, 1788–1850* (New York: Oxford University Press, 1984), 107–254; David Montgomery, "The Working Classes of the Pre-Industrial American City, 1780–1830," *Labor History* IX (1968), 3–22; Arky, "The Mechanics' Union of Trade Associations and the Formation of the Philadelphia Workingmen's Movement."
[6] Seth Luther, *An Address to the Working Men of New England, on the State of Education, and the Condition of the Producing Classes in Europe and America*, ed. George Evans (New York: The Office of the Working Man's Advocate, 1833), 26. Hereafter *An Address to the Working Men of New England*.
[7] The terms "working men's" and "workingmen's" were used somewhat interchangeably, both at the time, and by subsequent historians.

"The Sword of Want"

a recurring feature of public debate.[8] Over time, this critique of wage-slavery became the centerpiece of the labor republican tradition.

In fact, by the time the editors of the *Journal of United Labor*, the official journal of the Knights of Labor, published a short editorial decades later, on May 25, 1884, called "Wages Slavery and Chattel Slavery," that headline had become something of a convention in labor presses.[9] It was just that title that had gotten under William Lloyd Garrison's skin during his running battles with "working men" in the pages of the *Liberator*.[10] In their late nineteenth-century contribution to the genre, the Knights argued that the presence of "wages slavery" presented an old problem in a new form:

> the whole process of civilization has been to emancipate human beings from the condition of slavery in which they have been held by their fellow men ... civilization has not yet reached its highest point of development, nor can it develop much further without first having abolished wages slavery, for that form of slavery stands to-day as one of the greatest barriers to the progress of civilization.[11]

Unlike their predecessors, the Knights had the luxury of being able to position their project as the legitimate heir to mid-century abolitionism, not just the ideas of the Founding generation. The earlier Workyism suffered from being submerged under and challenged by the contest over chattel slavery. But the basic idea remained the same from the 1820s to 1880s. A republic could not tolerate wage-labor because it was a form of servitude, in which employees were subject to the "caprice" of their employers, just as colonists had been subject to the caprice of the Crown in Parliament, or slaves subject to the whim of their masters. The paradox of slavery was unresolved.

If the broad features of this argument remained constant throughout the nineteenth century, the late nineteenth-century Knights differed in important ways from the earlier Workies. A number of conceptual moves were required before the Knights could both give a full account of the wage-laborer's servitude and propose the "cooperative system" as a coherent account of free labor. If we are going to understand late nineteenth-century labor republicans as the culmination of their tradition, then we have to understand how that tradition developed. Therefore, this chapter reconstructs the radical agrarian origins of the republican critique of capitalism and the early-nineteenth-century Workies'

---

[8] E.g., George Henry Evans, "Negro Slavery," *The Working Man's Advocate* III, no. 7 (October 1, 1831), 1; Heighton, *The Principles of Aristocratic Legislation*, 10. *The Working Man's Advocate*, hereafter *WMA*.

[9] It appeared in a number of variations, e.g., William Heighton, "Slavery of Wages," *YA* 2, no. 46 (February 7, 1846), 1; West, "Wages Slavery and Chattel Slavery: To William Lloyd Garrison"; Evans, "'Abolition at Home'"; "Dialogue on Free and Slave Labor," *WMA* 1, no. 11 (June 8, 1844), 4.

[10] See, e.g., William West, "Reformatory: Chattel and Wages Slavery," *The Liberator* 16, no. 38 (September 25, 1846), 152; Garrison, "Free and Slave Labor," 50.

[11] "Wages Slavery and Chattel Slavery," *JUL* V, no. 2 (1884), 702.

modification of that agrarianism. These radical agrarians and early artisans laid the groundwork for the labor republican program.

Agrarian Republicanism

The Agrarian Tradition

As far back as the English Diggers and Levellers of the seventeenth century, we can find groups of farmers and artisans seeking "to abolish all arbitrary Power" and to establish an equal republican commonwealth.[12] These attempts to provide a "constitutional foundation for a republic of small producers"[13] coupled the argument for elected government and expanded suffrage with the material guarantee of a rough equality of control over property. In conditions of material equality, no citizen would be dependent on any other and no class could dominate. Perhaps the best known early modern expression of this idea is James Harrington's statement in *Oceana* that: "An equal commonwealth ... is a government established upon an equal Agrarian."[14] An "equal Agrarian" was a law distributing property relatively equally among citizens by taking special aim at primogeniture – "a flinty custom."[15] By eliminating primogeniture, large landed estates would be gradually broken up, ensuring a relatively equal distribution among all descendants, and freeing up land for those who did not have enough. Small-scale producers were free so long as they possessed enough property to remain independent from the state or the wealthy. They controlled their own labor and met their needs through the proceeds of that labor.

This radical agrarianism crossed the Atlantic, mainly through the argument that inheritance law should guarantee a relatively equal distribution of landed property. Thomas Jefferson, in his earlier, more radical phase, had famously declared that abolishing laws of primogeniture and entail in Virginia laid the foundation

---

[12] Several Hands, "An Agreement of the People for a Firm and Present Peace upon Grounds of Common Right and Freedom," in *The English Levellers*, ed. Andrew Sharp (Cambridge: Cambridge University Press, 1998), 92–101. Arbitrating the complexities of the Diggers' and Levellers' views of property is well beyond the scope of this book. But see the excellent John Gurney, *Gerrard Winstanley: The Digger's Life and Legacy* (London: Pluto Press, 2012).

[13] Ronald Schultz, "The Small-Producer Tradition and the Moral Origins of Artisan Radicalism in Philadelphia 1720–1810," *Past & Present* no. 127 (May 1990), 92. For a more extended discussion see Schultz, *The Republic of Labor*, 3–35.

[14] James Harrington, *The Commonwealth of Oceana and a System of Politics* (Cambridge: Cambridge University Press, 1992), 34. For competing views of Harrington, republicanism, and property, see Pocock, *The Machiavellian Moment*, 423–61; Nelson, *The Greek Tradition in Republican Thought*, 87–126; John F. H. New, "Harrington, a Realist?," *Past & Present* 24 (1963), 75–81; John F. H. New, "The Meaning of Harrington's Agrarian," *Past & Present* 25 (1963), 94–95; C. B. Macpherson, "Harrington as Realist: A Rejoinder," *Past & Present* 24 (April 1963), 82–85. On Harrington's influence on later agrarianism, see Robbins, *The Eighteenth Century Commonwealthman*, 22–55; Adair, *The Intellectual Origins of Jeffersonian Democracy*, 79.

[15] New, "The Meaning of Harrington's Agrarian," 94.

by which every fibre would be eradicated of antient [sic] or future aristocracy; and a foundation laid for a government truly republican. The repeal of the laws of entail would prevent the accumulation and perpetuation of wealth in select families ... the abolition of primogeniture, and equal partition of inheritances removed the feudal and unnatural distinctions which made one member of every family rich, and all the rest poor, substituting equal partition, the best of all Agrarian laws.[16]

Many of Jefferson's contemporaries agreed with this agrarian vision. A 1784 North Carolina law revising colonial inheritance law pronounced that "it will tend to promote that equality of property which is of the spirit and principle of a genuine republic, that the real estates of persons dying intestate should undergo a more general and equal distribution than has hitherto prevailed in this state." A similar Delaware statute from 1794 stated "it is the duty and policy of every republican government to preserve equality amongst its citizens, by maintaining the balance of property as far as it is consistent with the rights of individuals."[17] Characteristically, Thomas Paine carried the thought further than his contemporaries. In his final pamphlet, *Agrarian Justice*, published in 1797, he argued that, "despotic government supports itself by abject civilization.... Such governments ... politically depend more upon breaking the spirit of the people by poverty, than they fear enraging it by desperation."[18] Although in *Rights of Man* Paine had already argued that a true republic would abolish "the unjust and unnatural law of primogeniture,"[19] *Agrarian Justice* took the more radical step of arguing for, among other things, capital grants to all citizens upon reaching maturity to help finance the purchase of land or tools.

If Paine's argument for active redistribution was a bridge too far for many of his contemporaries, who were content to attack feudal inheritance law, it resonated with the conventions of the many small farmers and petty producers of early America. The "homestead ethic,"[20] which linked land ownership to the elimination of dependence on wealthy landlords and creditors, not only spurred the participation of small farmers and artisans in the American Revolution, but also inspired the various "Regulations" and tax revolts of the late eighteenth

---

[16] Thomas Jefferson, "Autobiography," in *Writings*, ed. Merrill D. Peterson (New York: The Library of America, 1984); 1–101, 44.
[17] Stanley N. Katz, "Republicanism and the Law of Inheritance in the American Revolutionary Era," *Michigan Law Review* 76, no. 1 (November 1977), 1–29, 14.
[18] Thomas Paine, "Agrarian Justice," in *Thomas Paine: Common Sense and Other Writings*, ed. Joyce Appleby (New York: Barnes & Noble, 2005), 323–45, 343.
[19] Thomas Paine, *Rights of Man* (New York: Citadel Press, 1991), 245. On Paine and the first generation of republican critics of economic exploitation, see Gregory Claeys, "The Origins of the Rights of Labor: Republicanism, Commerce, and the Construction of Modern Social Theory in Britain, 1796–1805," *The Journal of Modern History* 66, no. 2 (June 1994), 249–90.
[20] Robert Maxwell Brown, "Back Country Rebellions and the Homestead Ethic in America, 1749–1799," in *Tradition, Conflict, and Modernization: Perspectives on the American Revolution*, ed. Richard Maxwell Brown and Don Fehrenbacher (New York: Academic Press, 1977), 73–99.

century.[21] These revolts marked the pivotal moment in which a small producer *tradition* became an active *ideology*.[22] It served as the basis of political action by those small producers now seeking to put inherited meanings to use amidst increasing commercialization of agriculture, expansion of federal debt, and incipient industrialization. Their ideology developed into a republican critique of capitalism in general and wage-labor in particular.

The Early Republican Critique of Economic Dependence

The American Revolution politicized a class of farmers and artisans who interpreted its republican ideals to include the promise of political and economic independence. As historian Leon Fink observes, "the revolutionary mobilization itself added to the ranks of those who felt a direct stake not only in the infant nation's political freedoms but also in the protection, if not extension, of control over one's own property and one's own labor."[23] By the end of the war, these small producers saw themselves as authoritative interpreters of revolutionary republicanism and pushed these ideas beyond where their originators had intended. In 1783, for instance, one "Brother Mechanick" wrote a message in the Independent Gazetteer "to the MECHANICKS of PHILADELPHIA" in which he warned that both of the city's political parties "consider you as a useless set of beings, who ought to be fed with 'butter-milk and potatoes,' while the darling objects of their attention and pursuit, are '*the flesh pots and onions.*'" Better, he said, to "establish a Society of Mechanics" for the advancement of their interests.[24] After Paine's *The Rights of Man* exploded onto the American scene in 1791, there was a marked increase in this kind of "plebeian" appropriation of republican ideas. As Seth Cotlar shows in his remarkable study of this

---

[21] Richard L. Bushman, "Massachusetts Farmers and the Revolution," in *Society, Freedom, and Conscience: The American Revolution in Virginia, Massachusetts, and New York*, ed. Richard M. Jellison (New York: W. W. Norton & Company, 1976), 77–124; Joseph A. Ernst, "Shays's Rebellion in Long Perspective: the Merchants and the 'Money Question,'" in *In Debt to Shays: The Bicentennial of an Agrarian Rebellion*, ed. Robert A. Gross (The Colonial Society of Massachusetts, 1993), 57–80; W. J. Rorabaugh, "'I Thought I Shall Liberate Myself From the Thraldom of Others': Apprentices, Masters, and the Revolution," in *Beyond the American Revolution: Explorations in the History of American Radicalism*, ed. Alfred F. Young (Dekalb: Northern Illinois University Press, 1993), 185–217; Alan Taylor, "Agrarian Independence: Northern Land Rioters After the Revolution," in *Beyond the American Revolution: Explorations in the History of American Radicalism*, ed. Alfred F. Young (DeKalb: Northern Illinois University Press, 1993), 221–45.

[22] Schultz, "The Small-Producer Tradition and the Moral Origins of Artisan Radicalism in Philadelphia 1720–1810."

[23] Fink, "From Autonomy to Abundance," 119. On revolutionary popular mobilization, see Wood, *The Creation of the American Republic, 1776–1787*, 257–343; Larry Kramer, *The People Themselves: Popular Constitutionalism and Judicial Review* (New York: Oxford University Press, 2004), 73–144; Seth Cotlar, *Tom Paine's America: the Rise and Fall of Transatlantic Radicalism in the Early Republic* (Charlottesville: University of Virginia Press, 2011), 13–48.

[24] A Brother Mechanick, "To the MECHANICKS of PHILADELPHIA," *The INDEPENDENT GAZETTEER; or the CHRONICLE of FREEDOM*, October 11, 1783.

democratic moment, radical editors such as Robert Coram, Thomas Lloyd, and Benjamin Franklin Bache, along with anonymous readers of and contributors to the new popular press, began making novel arguments against the unequal distribution of property. They argued that the government should "make disappear the great inequalities of fortune" and that "in such a republic as this, men should by every fair means by legally prevented from becoming exorbitantly rich."[25] In the name of keeping the republic consistent with "agrarian principles," some proposed selling public lands cheaply to all settlers, with maximum allowable landholdings.[26]

These thoughts persisted through the end of the century. In 1797, William Manning, a self-educated farmer and former revolutionary soldier from Massachusetts, wrote that "the few" use their superior wealth, especially control over money and credit, to keep "the many" in "a state of dependance on the few."[27] Manning's two essays, the first an attack on Hamilton's credit proposal and the second, the *Key of Liberty*, a longer, more general statement of republican theory addressed to "farmers, mechanicks, & labourers,"[28] made the same basic political point.[29] The few "are ever hankering & striving after Monerca and Aristocracy" because they live off the dependent labor of the "many." The many, on the other hand, constantly strive for economic independence, putting them in direct conflict with the few.

Like "Brother Mechanick" in Philadelphia, Manning not only worried that the new aristocracy of wealth used its control over credit and land to keep laborers in a "state of dependence," he also felt that the mechanics and petty producers should organize themselves into a "Sociaty of Labourers"[30] to influence economic policy and change the distribution of wealth. Manning's fellow Massachusetts radical, David Brown, an itinerant laborer jailed in 1798 for "seditious" writings and public speeches against the John Adams' Federalist

[25] Quoted in Cotlar, *Tom Paine's America*, 130.
[26] Ibid., 156.
[27] William Manning, "The Key of Liberty," *The William and Mary Quarterly* 13, no. 2 (1956), 219.
[28] Ibid., 209.
[29] For the credit proposal, see Manning's William Manning, "Some Proposals for Making Restitution to the Original Creditors of Government," *William & Mary Quarterly* 46, no. 2 (1989), 320–31. The cited edition of Manning's Key of Liberty is 1798 but he wrote the first draft in 1797. On Manning, see Ruth Bogin, "Petitioning and the New Moral Economy of Post-Revolutionary America," *The William and Mary Quarterly* 45, no. 3 (July 1988), 392–425; Michael Merrill and Sean Wilentz, "William Manning and the Invention of American Politics," in *The Key of Liberty: the Life and Writings of William Manning, "A Laborer," 1747–1814*, eds. Michael Merril and Sean Wilentz (Cambridge, MA: Harvard University Press, 1993), 1–86. For a rejection of Manning as a critic of early capitalism, see Gordon Wood, "The Enemy Is Us: Democratic Capitalism in the Early Republic," *Journal of the Early Republic* 16, no. 2 (Summer 1996), 293–308. For my contrasting view, see Alex Gourevitch, "William Manning and the Political Theory of the Dependent Classes," *Modern Intellectual History* 9, no. 2 (2012), 331–60.
[30] Manning, "The Key of Liberty," 248.

administration, made clear the connection between economic inequality and republican liberty: "[F]ive hundred out of the union of five million receive all the benefit of public property and live upon the ruins of the rest of the community. Yet we ... sit still and see our fellow Citizens coming into a state of abject slavery."[31] Here we see the republican language of servitude self-consciously mobilized against a new aristocracy of wealth. These turn of the century writings are the product of small producers and democratic editors seizing on the revolutionary republicanism of their "fathers."[32] They took the early agrarian arguments directed at inheritance law and broadened them into a general critique of economic dependence.

If these were the basic features of the late eighteenth-century republican critique of capitalism, the theory was still significantly underdeveloped.[33] To be sure, there were a few inklings of how wage-laborers might pick up on these ideas. For instance, when a group of striking journeymen shoemakers were arrested and tried in 1805–1806, one of their defenders, William Duane, condemned the way a "breed of *white slaves* may be nursed up in poverty to take the place of the *blacks* upon their emancipation." In an address to the public, the shoemakers said, "the name of freedom is but a shadow ... if for doing what ... the laws of our country authorize, we are to have taskmasters to measure out our pittance of subsistence."[34] After their conviction, Duane said the shoemakers should tell their employers "you are entitled to independence as well as themselves."[35]

Despite these intimations of the future, the early republican critique of inequality remained agrarian in nature. In fact, "agrarianism" was the allegation most frequently leveled at these republican radicals by their opponents.[36] Early republicanism mainly operated with a pre-modern conception of class – mainly based on "orders" and "professions" – rather than with the modern distinction between "propertied" and "propertyless."[37] "The few" were identified

---

[31] David Brown, "Seditious Writings," in *The Faith of Our Fathers: An Anthology Expressing the Aspirations of the American Common Man 1790–1860*, ed. Irving Mark and Eugene L Schwab (New York: Alfred A. Knopf, 1952), 44; Cotlar, *Tom Paine's America*, 30–31; Geoffrey R. Stone, *Perilous Times: Free Speech in Wartime From the Sedition Act of 1798 to the War on Terrorism* (New York: W. W. Norton & Co., 2004), 64.

[32] Cotlar, *Tom Paine's America*, 13–48.

[33] See Claeys and Cotlar's important work Claeys, "The Origins of the Rights of Labor: Republicanism, Commerce, and the Construction of Modern Social Theory in Britain, 1796–1805"; Gregory Claeys, "Introduction," in *The Politics of English Jacobinism: Writings of John Thelwall*, ed. Gregory Claeys (University Park: Pennsylvania State University Press, 1995), xiii-lviii; Cotlar, *Tom Paine's America*, 115–60.

[34] Schultz, *The Republic of Labor*, 160–61.

[35] Ibid., 162.

[36] On the use of the term "agrarian" in this period, see A E Bestor Jr., "The Evolution of the Socialist Vocabulary," *Journal of the History of Ideas* (1948), 259–302.

[37] Martin J. Burke, *The Conundrum of Class: Public Discourse on the Social Order in America* (Chicago: University of Chicago Press, 1995), 32.

as holders of credit and monopolizers of land. Small producers never singled out wage-labor for special criticism, as it was collapsed together with the dependence of the heavily indebted small farmer or the economically precarious artisan. Furthermore, the discussion of economic dependence was often overshadowed by the early-nineteenth-century battles over property requirements for suffrage. As one set of Virginia suffragists put it: "We have been taught by our fathers, that all power is vested in, and derived from, the people; not the freeholders: that the majority of the community, in whom abides the physical force, have also the political right of creating and remoulding at will their civil institutions."[38] Alongside the problem of chattel slavery, the republican aim of eliminating *political* dependence still weighed on public debate. As states eliminated these property requirements in the early nineteenth century, attention focused on economic questions, and especially on conditions in the rapidly industrializing towns and cities.

Wage-Labor and The Workingmen's Parties

Political and Social Background

By the 1820s, the United States was beginning to transform into a different country from its agrarian capitalist origins. When, in 1782, Jefferson penned his famous quip "let our workshops remain in Europe,"[39] there was one large-scale use of the spinning jenny, that famous technology of the early industrial revolution. Three decades later, there were eighty-seven.[40] By 1816, Jefferson himself was compelled to exclaim, "within the thirty years which have since elapsed, how are circumstances changed!"[41] He even reversed his earlier proclamations, "experience has taught me that manufactures are now as necessary to our independence as to our comfort."[42] Just a year prior, Francis Lowell had founded the first modern American factory in Waltham, Massachusetts and the organization of textile manufacturing under one roof quickly spread throughout New England.[43] By the 1820s, the transformation of male artisans, women, and children into wage-laborers was sufficiently pronounced that, "the urban working classes comprised recognizable and self-conscious elements of urban society."[44]

[38] Irving Mark and Eugene L. Schwab, eds., "The Memorial of the Non-Freeholders of Richmond, Virginian [1829]," in *The Faith of Our Fathers: An Anthology Expressing the Aspirations of the American Common Man 1790–1860* (New York: Alfred A. Knopf, 1952), 22.
[39] Jefferson, *Notes on the State of Virginia*, 158.
[40] Montgomery, "The Working Classes of the Pre-Industrial American City," 18.
[41] Thomas Jefferson, "To Benjamin Austin, January 9, 1816," in *Thomas Jefferson: Writings*, ed. Merrill D. Peterson, (New York: The Library of America, 1984), 1370.
[42] Ibid., 1371.
[43] Philip Sheldon Foner, *History of the Labor Movement in the United States, Volume 1: From Colonial Times to the Founding of the American Federation of Labor* (New York: International Publishers, 1982), 54.
[44] Montgomery, "The Working Classes of the Pre-Industrial American City," 7.

Beyond the emergence of permanent wage-labor, two additional developments contributed to the rise of a republican critique of industrial capitalism. One, the Panic of 1819, was the first recession to affect the national economy as a whole. It raised questions about the desirability of this newly emerging social order, especially by illuminating inequalities that until then had been associated with despotic Europe. At one end, there was severe urban poverty and homelessness: "In Philadelphia three out of four workers were reported idle, and 1808 were jailed for unpaid debts."[45] At the other end, there was a dramatic increase in wealth: "According to the best estimates, the share of national wealth held by the richest 10 percent jumped, mainly after 1820, from the 49.6 percent of 1774 to reach 73 percent by 1860."[46] After the Panic subsided, another decade of dramatic industrial growth marked by periodic crises drove critics to make the comparison with Europe explicit, "American Citizens! Will you longer submit to worse tyranny than the enslaved brethren in the 'old world'?"[47]

The second development was the decision to eliminate nearly all property requirements for suffrage. In these state constitutional conventions,[48] those opposed to eliminating property requirements had expressed the familiar Madisonian worry that workers would use their political liberty to expropriate owners. As General Renssalaer, a major figure in New York politics, put it during the suffrage debates at the 1821 New York state constitutional convention, "the property of the rich has always been, and always will be, an object of desire on the part of the poor, and whenever they possess the power they will gratify their desires by its distribution."[49] Figures such as Renssalaer also worried that, because workers were dependent on their employers, they would be an extension of that person's will, thereby undermining the political equality required for a free republic. A man "constantly and uniformly dependant [sic] for his subsistence on the owner of the establishment, soon looses [sic] all independence of mind, and yields himself to the views, the wishes, and desires of the individual from whom he receives his bread."[50] The suffragists rejected these concerns as alarmist and countered that a republic was based on the political independence of citizens, not property: "Our community is an association of persons-of human beings-not a partnership founded on property."[51]

---

[45] Foner, *History of the Labor Movement in the United States, Volume 1*, 137.
[46] Charles Sellers, *The Market Revolution: Jacksonian America, 1815–1846* (Oxford: Oxford University Press, 1994), 238.
[47] Luther, *An Address to the Working Men of New England*, 21.
[48] Alexander Keyssar, *The Right to Vote: The Contested History of Democracy in the United States* (New York: Basic Books, 2000), 26–52.
[49] See the objection to eliminating suffrage by General Renssalaer in Nathaniel H. Carter, William L. Stone, and Marcus T. C. Gould, *Reports of the Proceedings and Debates of the New York Constitutional Convention 1821* (Albany: E. and E. Hosford, 1821), 360–63.
[50] Ibid., 363.
[51] See the remark by Mr. Buel, ibid., 243.

What neither side expected was the emergence of a group of self-organized mechanics and wage-laborers that *accepted* the anti-suffrage argument that they were dependent, but sought to overcome it through public policy. Seizing on their newly won political liberty,[52] and responding to a form of economic dependence that emerged from within a market society itself, poor artisans and wage-laborers organized themselves into the workingmen's parties of the late 1820s and early 1830s. The leading figures of these parties produced the first sustained republican engagement with the problem of wage-labor that went beyond either relegating wage-laborers to a class of political dependents or arguing for their enfranchisement *despite* their economic dependence.

Dependency and "the Force of Necessitous Circumstances"

The Workingmen's Parties, like all social movements, appealed to a number of different intellectual traditions, including natural rights and native Christian Socialism.[53] But the republican trope of slavery and dependence ran like a red thread through their arguments against the developing market in "free" labor. For instance, in his 1827 address to "working classes generally," William Heighton intoned that for "the working classes ... the system of profit is ... an iron chain of bondage. A system of unjust abstraction, oppression, and legal fraud, by which the most useful classes of society are drained of their wealth, and consigned over to eternal toil and never-ending slavery."[54] In a speech given to workingmen from across New England, another labor advocate, Seth Luther, denounced the "tens of thousands under the *tyrannical government* of the mills."[55] "Cotton mills are called 'Republican Institutions,'" Luther continued, yet they are defined by "one sided and arbitrary rule. The hands are compelled to work ... [and] are liable to be discharged at any moment."[56] Luther dubbed these workshops "Slave Mills"[57] that, as another New Englander put it, housed "the white slaves of the North."[58] Such statements were more than mere emotional appeals, opportunistically appropriating the condition of Black slavery for rhetorical effect. For these reformers, there was a real equivalence, not just analogy, between chattel slavery and wage-labor because both forms of labor denied workers full economic independence. Yet if these workingmen wanted to argue that the wage-laborer was dependent, and thus that the industrial system compromised their republican liberty, they knew that wage-labor

---

[52] A few states, such as Pennsylvania, had eliminated property requirements earlier than the rest, but most did so only in the early nineteenth century. Keyssar, *The Right to Vote*, 26–52.
[53] Subheading quotation from Skidmore, *The Rights of Man to Property!*, 288. On Christian Socialism, see for instance, Cornelius C. Blatchly, *Some Causes of Popular Poverty*, 1818.
[54] Heighton, *An Address to the Members of Trade Societies and to the Working Classes Generally*, 10.
[55] Luther, *An Address to the Working Men of New England*, 22.
[56] Ibid., 24.
[57] Ibid., 26.
[58] Fisk, *Capital against Labor*, 9.

was different from chattel slavery. They needed new tools of social analysis and criticism that could give an account of how a wage-laborer, though making a contract, was still subject to another's will.

The individuals who went on to develop the argument were an unusual group.[59] One of these intellectual lights was Philadelphia native, Langdon Byllesby, a printer and journeyman proofreader,[60] whose 1826 *Observations on the Sources and Effects of Unequal Wealth* was the first full-length treatise written for and directed to workingmen.[61] Other Philadelphians included the aforementioned William Heighton and his fellow party-member Stephen Simpson. Simpson was a banker-cum-labor reformer, eventual congressional candidate on the Philadelphia Working Men's ticket, and author of *A Working Man's Manual: A New Theory of Political Economy* (1831), the most systematic of the various treatises of the period.[62] In New York, Thomas Skidmore's *The Rights of Man to Property!* (1829) was a similarly lengthy, if more radical, attempt to criticize the new aristocracy of wealth. Skidmore was the son of Connecticut farmers, an itinerant mechanic and inventor.[63] Along with George Henry Evans, Skidmore also cofounded the Workingmen's Party of New York and its magazine, the *Working Man's Advocate*. The *Working Man's Advocate* (New York) and *Mechanics' Free Press* (Philadelphia) were the most important labor presses of the time, transmitting the ideas of these early artisan republicans to their readership.

Mostly self-taught and drawing on wide-ranging sources of inspiration, this group settled on a consistent analysis of wage-labor. They started by identifying slavery with a specific kind of dependence: being economically vulnerable to compulsion to labor. As Byllesby put it, "the very essence of slavery is in being compelled to labour, while the proceeds of that labour is taken and enjoyed by another."[64] Although it might seem like a straightforward definition, this way of defining the "essence" of slavery had a specific conceptual purpose. It left

[59] See Pessen, *Most Uncommon Jacksonians*. For historical background on the parties, see Montgomery, "The Working Classes of the Pre-Industrial American City, 1780–1830"; Arky, "The Mechanics' Union of Trade Associations and the Formation of the Philadelphia Workingmen's Movement"; Schultz, *The Republic of Labor*; Bruce Laurie, *Working People of Philadelphia, 1800–1850*; Wilentz, *Chants Democratic*; David Anthony Harris, *Socialist Origins in the United States. American Forerunners of Marx, 1817–1832* (Assen: Van Gorcum & Comp., 1966).
[60] Not much is known about Byllesby's life. For accounts, see Wilentz, *Chants Democratic*, 164–7; Harris, *Socialist Origins in the United States*, 34–53.
[61] For the intellectual prehistory of these works, see Ronald Schultz, *The Republic of Labor*; Harris, *Socialist Origins in the United States*, 1–33.
[62] Edward Pessen, "The Ideology of Stephen Simpson, Upperclass Champion of the Early Philadelphia Workingmen's Movement," *Pennsylvania History* 22, no. 4 (October 1955), 328–40.
[63] Mark Lause's annotated edition of a biography written by one of Skidmore's contemporaries, Amos Gilbert, is still the best. Amos Gilbert, *The Life of Thomas Skidmore* (Chicago: Charles H. Kerr Publishing Company, 1984). Other good sources are Wilentz, *Chants Democratic*, 182–88; Edward Pessen, "Thomas Skidmore, Agrarian Reformer in the Early American Labor Movement," *New York History* 35, no. 3 (1954), 280–96.
[64] Byllesby, *Observations on the Sources and Effects of Unequal Wealth*, 33.

open the possibility that there were multiple ways in which a "slave" could be compelled to labor for another. The *legal* subjection of the chattel slave as the master's physical property was but one form that dependence could take. It was the original, but not the sole, defining *form* of dependence. Moreover, the artisans used their definition of slavery as a way of describing a concrete social relation that defines a wider political economy of production and exchange. Slavery, here, is not any old condition of unequal dependence, but one that has a particular social function and purpose for the employer and his society: the production and accumulation of wealth. This way of defining slavery was not a departure from republican thinking so much as a deepening of the analytics of compulsion, dependence, and law. This analysis would have staying power. Recall from the beginning of this chapter that, fifty years later, the Knights of Labor understood servitude in nearly the same terms: "[W]hen a man is placed in a position where he is compelled to give the benefit of his labor to another, he is in a condition of slavery."[65]

Defining slavery as "being compelled to labour, while the proceeds of that labour is taken" opened the conceptual space to assert the moral priority of republican liberty over and against the prevailing defense of property rights. Thomas Skidmore argued that property owners

> have no just right to use [property] in such a manner, as to extract from others, the result of their labors, for the purpose of exempting themselves from the necessity of laboring as much as others must labor.... The moment that any possessor of property, makes such use of it, I care not how, nor under the sanction of what law, or system of laws, as to live in idleness, partial or total, thus supporting himself, more or less, on the labors of others; that moment he contravenes and invades the rights of others; and has placed himself in the condition which would justify the party injured, in dispossessing the aggressor, of the instrument of his aggression.[66]

Skidmore's extraordinary thesis was that *even if* all existing property rights had their origin in perfectly just acts of acquisition and exchange, they would be illegitimate if they produce a distribution of property that made some economically dependent on others. Of course Skidmore and others were quick to note that the history of property was *not* a sequence of perfectly just acts of acquisition and exchange. They extended a tradition, begun some decades earlier by radicals such as Robert Coram and Thomas Lloyd, of rejecting Blackstone's injunction not to look too carefully into the historical origins of actually existing property rights.[67] It turned out actual history was a series of violent, unjust expropriations, now reproduced and given sanction in law.[68] The purpose of

[65] Unsigned, "Wages Slavery and Chattel Slavery," 702.
[66] Skidmore, *The Rights of Man to Property!*, 4–5.
[67] See Cotlar's fascinating reconstruction of this important moment, Cotlar, *Tom Paine's America*, 115–26.
[68] Skidmore, *The Rights of Man to Property!*, 1–76; Byllesby, *Observations on the Sources and Effects of Unequal Wealth*, 14–41.

the workingmen's theory of slavery and their history of property rights was to identify the liberty of the citizen as prior to and defining of the legitimacy of property rights. The independence of each citizen was a constraint on the accumulation of property and property rights derived their legitimacy from the inalienability of each person's independence.

This critique of property rights was more than a general moral claim. It was a piece of social analysis aimed at refuting the argument that a wage-laborer was free. As we saw in the previous chapter, this argument was already a significant feature of antebellum political discourse, especially among abolitionists. These workingmen intellectuals observed that the institution of property could produce dependence even where chattel slavery did not exist. Specifically, the legal protection of the unequal ownership of property was the means by which wage-laborers were made dependent upon employers. Although wage-laborers were formally self-owning, unequal ownership of the "means of employment"[69] meant they had no reasonable alternative to selling their labor. Stephen Simpson, for instance, lamented the condition of the "mere operative, who lives from hand to mouth, and who must sell, because he must eat."[70] The basic compulsion here was not the lash of the master but the spur of economic necessity. As Skidmore put it in a message to New York workingmen,

> thousands of our people of the present day in deep distress and poverty, *dependent* for their daily subsistence upon a few among us whom the unnatural operation of our own free and republican institutions, as we are pleased to call them, has thus arbitrarily and barbarously made enormously rich.[71]

In a slightly more philosophical vein, Heighton drew the same connection between economic need and compulsion:

> Necessity compels us to work for such prices as are offered, and pay such prices are demanded for every thing we need; we must either do this-resort to fraud or theft, or perish by hunger and nakedness.[72]

Inequality in the ownership of property made "operatives" or the "working classes" dependent on employers for jobs and therefore livelihoods. This dependence had its source in a particular kind of compulsion: the compulsion

---

[69] Skidmore, *The Rights of Man to Property!*, 240.

[70] Stephen Simpson, *The Working Man's Manual: A New Theory of Political Economy, on the Principle of Production the Source of Wealth* (Philadelphia: Thomas L. Bonsal, 1831), 70. Hereafter *The Working Man's Manual*.

[71] Thomas Skidmore, "Working Men's Meeting: Report of the Committee of Fifty," ed. George Henry Evans, *WMA* (New York, October 31, 1829), 1.

[72] William Heighton, *An Address Delivered before the Mechanics and Working Classes Generally, of the City and County of Philadelphia. At the Universalist Church, in Callowhill Street, on Wednesday Evening, November 21, 1827, by the "Unlettered Mechanic"* (Philadelphia: The Office of the Mechanics Gazette, 1828), 8–9. Hereafter *An Address Delivered before the Mechanics and Working Classes Generally*.

"*The Sword of Want*" 81

not of direct legal coercion to work for a master, like the chattel slave, but the compulsion of economic need or "necessitous circumstances."⁷³ As Skidmore summarized the view:

> if you dispossess them of their equal right, you place them in circumstances of dependence, such that others, who, thereby, will have, of course, more than they are entitled to, will exercise over them the means of reducing them to slavery.⁷⁴

Economic need compelled them to labor for others and those employers received most of the benefits of that labor. The inability of workers to accumulate property kept workers dependent on employers. They were, thereby, slaves in the republican sense. They lived at the mercy of another: "He who can feed me, or starve me; give me employment, or bid me wander about in idleness; is my master; and it is the utmost folly for me to boast of being any thing but a slave."⁷⁵

The challenge of applying inherited republican ideas to new realities was most vivid in the attempt to formulate a political program. In 1829, Thomas Skidmore headed a Committee of Fifty, whose purpose was to write a report and draft the platform for the newly created New York Workingmen's Party. The final report, published in the first issue of the *Working Man's Advocate*, reproduced almost word for word Skidmore's critique of wage-labor in *The Rights of Man To Property!*:

> For he, in all countries is a slave, who must work more for another than that other must work for him. It does not matter how this state of things is brought about; whether the sword of victory hew down the liberty of the captive, and thus compel him to labor for his conqueror, or whether the sword of want extort our consent, as it were, to a voluntary slavery, through a denial to us of the materials of nature.⁷⁶

"Sword of want," "compel him to labor," and "voluntary slavery," were turns of phrase whose purpose was both to establish the continuity with earlier, agrarian critiques of dependence and to mark the difference in social circumstances. The wage-laborer was neither chattel slave nor debtor-farmer;⁷⁷ he was dependent on more than a particular master or creditor. And to the degree he was dependent on a particular employer or creditor, this was attributed to a general economic dependence. He was dependent simply in virtue of his legally enforced propertylessness, a dependence of which employers regularly took advantage. In this political economy, the protection of property rights subverted rather than guaranteed the independence of citizens.

---

⁷³ Skidmore, *The Rights of Man to Property!*, 288.
⁷⁴ Ibid., 341.
⁷⁵ Ibid., 388.
⁷⁶ Skidmore, "Working Men's Meeting: Report of the Committee of Fifty," 1.
⁷⁷ However, it must be noted that debtors' prisons and punitive debt collection were a major concern for poor workers. Two recurring demands were abolition of debtors' prison and a "mechanics lien law." "Imprisonment for Debt," *WMA*, March 6, 1830, 3.

The Labor Theory of Value

Two further features of this early republican critique of wage-labor mark its difference from earlier agrarianism. First we have to recall that their thinking about slavery revolved not only around the fact that the wage-labor was compelled to work for others but that "the proceeds of that labour is taken and enjoyed by another."[78] In the classic case of the chattel slave, this exploitative element was evident because the slave had no formal legal claim to receiving anything in return for his labor. But these artisan republicans were well aware that wage-laborers *did* get compensated. Furthermore, they knew that the argument defending wage-labor as free labor hinged on the belief that, as one 1836 employers' association put it, "labour, like every other commodity, will seek its own level, and its own true value, in an open and unfettered market."[79] There was, on this alternate view, no measure of the value of that labor-commodity independent of the one agreed to by the commodity's owner. Its value was in some sense arbitrarily defined by the subjective appraisals of the two contracting parties. As we saw previous chapter, laissez-faire republicans thought that to assert a quasi-objective basis for value, which one might use to criticize the labor contract, would contravene the will of the laborer, thus compromising his independence. Earning wages just *was* the mark of freedom, and as such, the market wage expressed the true value of that labor. Realized value was real value. This position presented workingmen with a theoretical challenge. If the labor market compensated workers for their labor, and they consented to that compensation, it was harder to argue they were nonetheless unfree. They, not masters, determined the value of their labor. These workingmen had to give some account of how the wage-laborer was not only economically dependent but in fact exploited – that they were, in fact, compelled to labor for others in a way that allowed those others to benefit from that compulsion.

Heighton, Skidmore, and company found the tools they needed in the new science of political economy, especially in the labor theory of value. Although a labor theory of *property* had been around for centuries, in canonical figures such as John Locke and as part of a moral common sense,[80] the labor theory of value was newer. The basic premise was that the value of all objects could be measured by the one thing they had in common, they were products of labor. Labor was measured by time, or by the number of man-hours it took to produce the object. Benjamin Franklin appears to have been the first to make it part of American conversations, especially, and not surprisingly, in the early manufacturing city of Philadelphia.[81] But it was Smith and Ricardo

---

[78] Byllesby, *Observations on the Sources and Effects of Unequal Wealth*, 33.
[79] Quoted in Sean Wilentz, "Against Exceptionalism: Class Consciousness and the American Labor Movement, 1790–1920," *International Labor and Working Class History* 26 (Autumn 1984), 11. Also Garrison, "Free and Slave Labor."
[80] Schultz, *The Republic of Labor*, 25–26. Also Wilentz, "Against Exceptionalism."
[81] Franklin is credited as one of the first ever to have discussed the labor theory of value: "By Labour may the Value of Silver be measured as well as all other Things." Benjamin Franklin,

who were the first to fully develop the labor theory of value into a theory of political economy. Their ideas, as interpreted by the so-called British Ricardian Socialists, especially William Thompson and John Gray,[82] blended effortlessly with early republican concerns to produce a "scientific" critique of the labor contract. The basic thought was that only labor creates value. If a fair contract was defined as a free exchange of equivalents, it was possible to evaluate independently whether there had been real equivalence, and thus truly free exchange. If a worker received a lower wage than the value he created, the employer unfairly acquired the "proceeds" or value of that worker's labor. As Heighton put it,

ALL WEALTH is the PRODUCT of HUMAN LABOUR: he therefore, who accumulates in a given time more than can be produced in an equal time, must accumulate that which has been produced by others, and for which he cannot have received an equivalent from him.[83]

If, for instance, a worker spent twelve hours working, but received wages that could only buy goods that it takes four hours to produce, then the worker was giving up the products of an extra eight hours of labor for nothing. Byllesby summarized the view, "there can be no natural or moral justice in a system that takes from one man the products of two days' labour, and gives him in compensation of only day of another, when the ability ... of those men are equal ... yet ... this fact is the whole of the present mode of the arts of life.[84] Insofar as nearly every actual wage contract took this exploitative form, there was reason to believe the worker was not, in fact, free despite giving his consent to the contract's terms.

"A Modest Enquiry Into the Nature and Necessity of a Paper Currency," in *The Works of Benjamin Franklin, Vol. I Autobiography, Letters and Misc. Writings 1725–1734*, ed. John Bigelow (New York: G. P. Putnam's Sons, 1904). Franklin's essay was significant enough that Karl Marx said "one of the first economists ... to have seen through the nature of value, [was] the famous Franklin." Karl Marx, *Capital: Volume 1*, trans. Ben Fowkes, (New York: Penguin Classics, 1990). On Franklin in Philadelphia, see Schultz, *The Republic of Labor*, 25.

[82] On the Ricardian Socialists, see Esther Lowenthal, "The Ricardian Socialists," *Studies in History, Economics and Public Law* XLVI, no. 1 (1911), 5–105; Anton Menger, *The Right to the Whole Produce of Labour*, ed. H. S. Foxwell, trans. M. E. Tanner (London: Macmillan and Co., 1899); J. E. King, "Utopian or Scientific? A Reconsideration of the Ricardian Socialists," *History of Political Economy* 15, no. 3 (1983), 345–73. See especially H. S. Foxwell's extensive introduction to Menger, which served as the basis and inspiration for Lowenthal's more detailed account of the Ricardian Socialists. H. S. Foxwell, "Introduction," in *The Right to the Whole Produce of Labor*, ed. H. S. Foxwell (New York: Macmillan and Co., Limited, 1899), v–cx. On Lowenthal's account, the Ricardian Socialists – so called because of the way they used Ricardo's labor theory of value to develop a set of scientific arguments parallel to the moral arguments for Socialism – consist primarily of William Thompson, John Gray, Thomas Hodgskin, and John Francis Bray. The label "Ricardian Socialist" remains disputed, especially because someone like Thomas Hodgskin was not a socialist. However, its use here introduces no major confusions into our narrative because only Thompson and Gray play a role.

[83] William Heighton, *The Principles of Aristocratic Legislation*, 3. Although many were a bit fuzzy about distinguishing between value and wealth, they all gravitated toward an interpretation that identified value with labor time.

[84] Byllesby, *Observations on the Sources and Effects of Unequal Wealth*, 42.

Whether early workingmen arrived at this thought independently, as Byllesby claimed,[85] or embraced it after reading Thompson and Gray, as Heighton claimed,[86] is of less moment than that they all immediately saw the ideological value of this new political economy. It gave them a response to opponents like the aforementioned employer's association that argued labor should "seek its own level, and its own true value, in an open and unfettered market." When Heighton quoted Thompson and Gray in his own speeches[87] or excerpted them in the *Mechanics' Free Press*, and when Byllesby and Skidmore referred to them in their writings,[88] it was because these early labor theorists' analysis of wage-labor revealed the underlying inequality and exploitation of otherwise formally free and equal economic relations. The following lines from Thompson's *Labour Rewarded*, excerpted in Heighton's *Mechanics Free Press*, are a case in point: "*Free, voluntary,* exchanges … no where prevail." These "unjust *exchanges,*" in which "the products of the labor of the industrious classes [are] taken out of their hands," are caused either "by direct operation of law, or by indirect operation of unwise social arrangements." These "unwise social arrangements" were defined by the lack of "equal command of means of production."[89] The last line completed the analysis, explaining how even without direct legal coercion, a formally free worker could be made dependent on employers, thereby turning the contract into an unfree, exploitative arrangement in which workers were forced to give up the lion's share of the value they produced.

The labor theory of value made economic dependence quantifiable. For instance, Langdon Byllesby quotes a calculation by the Benthamite reformer Patrick Colquhoun, who used the labor theory of value to calculate the first national income statistics of the British Empire, that in 1812 the laboring classes received "but *one fifth*" of the total annual product with "the rest being absorbed by the idle and unproductive classes."[90] Here was scientific proof that workers were getting far less value than they were producing and were doing

---

[85] Ibid., 105.

[86] Heighton, *An Address to the Members of Trade Societies and to the Working Classes Generally*, 12.

[87] See, for instance, the block quotation of Gray's *Lectures on Human Happiness* in Heighton, *An Address to the Members of Trade Societies and to the Working Classes Generally*, 12–15.

[88] For instance, see the Thompson citations in Byllesby, *Observations on the Sources and Effects of Unequal Wealth*, 105–13.

[89] "Thompson's Labour Rewarded," *Mechanics' Free Press* 98 (November 21, 1829), 1.

[90] Byllesby, *Observations on the Sources and Effects of Unequal Wealth*, 57. These figures were taken from Patrick Colquhoun's *A Treatise on the Wealth, Power, and Resources of the British Empire* (1814). To my knowledge, it is the first attempt in English of a complete gross national accounting, proudly advertising "copious statistical tables" on its title page. Patrick Colquhoun, *A Treatise on the Wealth, Power, and Resources of the British Empire* (London: Joseph Mawman, 1814). Other Ricardian Socialists were also quite taken with Colquhoun's statistics, using them to calculate exploitation rates according to the labor theory of value. Foxwell, "Introduction," lxvii.

so because, despite their legal freedom to make labor contracts, they were still compelled to labor for others. Their economic dependence on others left them vulnerable to exploitation. Of course, for these worker-activists, the dramatic increase in material wealth alongside urban poverty and homelessness was evidence enough that workers enjoyed very little of the fruits of their labors. They did not *need* strictly quantifiable, scientific proof to make their point, and often they simply observed the general fact of inequality to make their point about wage-labor and dependence.

But their use of political economy was no superfluity. The analytic power of the labor theory of value allowed figures such as Byllesby and Skidmore to develop a discourse appropriate to the new form of social domination they wished to criticize. Generalized market relations – defined centrally by the commodification of labor – meant that calculations were possible in a way not true of previous economies. The labor theory of value also made possible the articulation of a long-standing anxiety about dependent labor in a form specific to market relations. Note, for instance, that it allowed someone such as Skidmore to translate a general definition of slavery – being compelled to work for another who receives the benefits of that labor – into specifically modern terms. The wage-laborer is "in such necessitous condition, that he must work or die; and work, too, *on such terms, that a very great share of the value of his labor must go to the employer,* or to him, who, no matter how, affords the means of employment."[91] After all, in the case of the chattel slave, it was immediately obvious that he had no choice but to work for a master and that the master took everything that the slave produced. But in the case of the labor contract, because the worker received wages in return, the exploitative element was not immediately visible. The material expression of his dependence had to take the form of a calculation of values, of the difference between what he was paid and what he produced. If in one sense the poverty of workers made their cause seem obvious, in another sense, the formal freedom of the labor market disrupted republican common sense, calling for further tools of social analysis. The labor theory of value grounded a form of social analysis that made visible relations of power and dependence that the voluntary labor contract concealed. Using the labor theory of value as an instrument of social analysis revealed the way in which the labor market was not defined by relations of equal independence but rather by relations of unequal dependence and thus domination. The employers' regular extraction of profits was a sign of their arbitrary power over employees.

Above all, the labor theory of value was important because it described the social function of economic dependence. Economic dependence was not just a generic evil; it was the core institution by which society reproduced itself. That is to say, it was not just that this republican society happened to permit, on its peripheries or in its interstices, an objectionable but marginal form of

---

[91] Skidmore, *The Rights of Man to Property!*, 240.

subjection. Instead, economic servitude was a central fact of this society. If employers relied on the economic dependence of a class of propertyless workers, then it was clear why owners of productive property "conceive it their interest to keep us in a state of humble dependence."[92] Workers could only be paid less value than they produced if they remained dependent on some employer or another. This dependence was a product of unequal property ownership, which was reproduced by the fact that low wages, and the scarcity of productive property and credit, made it impossible for most to work their way out of wage-labor. This logic of reproduction meant their subjection was permanent, not temporary.[93] The natural conclusion, according to workingmen, was that the employers were hostile to the very idea of universalizing republican liberty. The labor theory of value gave scientific expression to the wage-laborer's exploitation, whereas the republican understanding of dependence explained the ability to exploit in the first place. Workingmen were propelled into this fusion of political economy with republican theory by the fact that the dependence they experienced was not personal and direct in the way classical slavery had been.

"The Equalization of Property"

Besides the labor theory of value, the second idea that these workingmen adapted to their purposes was the concept of cooperation. Here again the 1820s was a propitious decade for conceptual innovation. Robert Owen, founder of the cooperative movement, first known for his socialist experiment in New Lanark, traveled to the United States in 1824–25 to survey his new communitarian venture, New Harmony. Owen's *New View of Society* had been published in the United States as early as 1817 and by the time of his trip he was so well known that he was invited to give a two-part, six-hour speech on utopian socialism to a private dinner that included members of Congress, outgoing President James Monroe, and President-elect John Quincy Adams.[94] Owen commissioned an architectural model for his ideal community that stood on display at the White House for six weeks[95] and his ideas quickly became part of social discussion. Although he avoided meeting with any organized workers, preferring instead to rub elbows with middle class reformers and free thinkers when passing through Philadelphia,[96] figures such as Heighton and Byllesby

---

[92] Heighton, *An Address Delivered before the Mechanics and Working Classes Generally*, 10.
[93] Luther, *An Address to the Working Men of New England*, 22–6.
[94] Robert Owen, *Two Discourses on a New System of Society as Delivered in the Hall of Representatives at Washington* (London: Whiting & Branston, 1825).
[95] Owen commissioned the plan from one Stedman Whitwell. Stedman Whitwell, "Description of an Architectural Model From a Design by Stedman Whitwell, Esq. for a Community upon a Principle of United Interests, as Advocated by Robert Owen, Esq.," in *Cooperative Communities: Plans and Descriptions*, ed. Kenneth E. Carpenter (New York: Arno Press, 1972).
[96] Arky, "The Mechanics' Union of Trade Associations and the Formation of the Philadelphia Workingmen's Movement," 151; Schultz, *The Republic of Labor*, 212–14.

were acquainted with his ideas through the popular presses, from circulating copies of *New View of Society*, and through references to cooperation by figures including Thompson and Gray.[97]

Cooperation was broadly understood as a form of associated production in which property was held in common, all able-bodied members of the community worked, in exchange for which they received a guarantee that they would be provided all necessities, after which owners of shares in the community would be paid dividends. But whereas for Owen cooperation was a solution to the social problems of poverty and crime, for workingmen it became the guarantee of personal freedom – the practical solution to the problem of universalizing republican liberty. The workingmen's interest in cooperation flowed directly from their analysis of dependence. If unequal control of productive property, especially land and factories, made wage-laborers dependent on owners, then it followed that the way to eliminate this dependence was by giving everyone some control over productive property. Liberty appeared to require a rough equality of property; and, indeed, Skidmore, Byllesby, Heighton, and Simpson all made some version of the argument that "the principles of equal distribution [be] everywhere adopted"[98] or to "equalize property."[99] Through this "equalization" of property, workers would "no longer suffer ourselves to be the slaves of the useless few."[100]

The concrete form that this equal right should take varied with each thinker. They all shared an ambivalence toward Owenite socialism insofar as it seemed to mean the creation of cooperative communities *separate* from society. For instance, Byllesby argued against the Owenites, "we do not perceive how the means they propose, to wit, the erection of limited and independent villages … are to include the immense and important interests, with valuable uses, embraced in the composition of large cities."[101] These "limited and independent villages" could not possibly address the widespread dependence of all workers, especially in factories, and it left the existing distribution of property more or less untouched. Moreover, they thought Owen's appeal to the philanthropic impulses of the wealthy to fund these communities was unrealistic and failed to grasp the republican point that the aim was *independence*, and thus achieving these conditions through their own efforts, not another. "Allowing Mr. Owen's system to be good; where shall we find more men like Mr. Owen?" asked Skidmore, after which he said "Besides, there is something uncongenial

---

[97] The New Harmony Gazette circulated widely, as did Owen's writings. For references the Gazette and ideas about Owen's New Lanark, see, e.g., Byllesby, *Observations on the Sources and Effects of Unequal Wealth*, 120–36.
[98] Heighton, *An Address to the Members of Trade Societies and to the Working Classes Generally*, 35.
[99] Simpson, *The Working Man's Manual*, 9.
[100] Heighton, *An Address to the Members of Trade Societies and to the Working Classes Generally*, 35.
[101] Byllesby, *Observations on the Sources and Effects of Unequal Wealth*, 90.

with the best feelings of the heart ... when it is compelled to contemplate the happiness it enjoys ... as flowing from another.... It subtracts half the value of such happiness, to feel that it is dependent on another for it."[102] What stronger expression of the desire for independence than the demand to use one's own power to eliminate economic dependence?

Some, such as Simpson, broadly appealed to the idea of equalizing property, but stopped short of demanding full redistribution of land or machines, let alone the formation of workers cooperatives.[103] Others, however, identified cooperation as a necessary ingredient for managing the integrated work processes of a modern, factory economy in ways that eliminated dependent wage-labor. Byllesby called for "equalization of the advantages of industry and labour"[104] through inheritance taxes and for the redistribution of property to fund producer cooperatives – appending a plan for the formation of a cooperative to his *Observations*. Others, such as Heighton, imagined that "all the producers dwelling within the limits of each district or township" would "combine and co-operate," hire a few "agents" to manage distribution, and establish "exchanges" based on labor notes to facilitate commerce among the different worker cooperatives.[105] These proposals groped toward the image of a national community of free producers, comprising independent property-owners exchanging their individual or collective products on the basis of labor notes. Another Philadelphian fellow-traveler, Josiah Warren, founded one of the first labor note exchanges in 1828.[106] Heighton's *Mechanics' Free Press* also regularly contained excerpts from early British writings on cooperatives, as well as editorials from various local reformers proposing to set up labor exchanges and cooperatives for the purposes of "diminishing the number of dependent producers."[107]

Skidmore's proposal was the most systematic and far-reaching. His *Rights of Man to Property!* shows us not so much the majority opinion but just how

[102] Skidmore, *The Rights of Man to Property!*, 386.
[103] Simpson ran on the more "conservative" demand for free public education. On Simpson, see Pessen, "The Ideology of Stephen Simpson, Upperclass Champion of the Early Philadelphia Workingmen's Movement."
[104] Byllesby, *Observations on the Sources and Effects of Unequal Wealth*, 116.
[105] Heighton, *An Address to the Members of Trade Societies and to the Working Classes Generally*, 11. See also Arky "The Mechanics' Union of Trade Associations and the Formation of the Philadelphia Workingmen's Movement," 147–51.
[106] Josiah Warren, "Letter From Josiah Warren," in *A Documentary History of American Industrial Society Volume v: The Labor Movement*, ed. John R. Commons et al. (Cleveland: The Arthur H. Clark Company, 1910), 133–37; John R. Commons et al., eds., "Constitution of the Philadelphia Labour for Labour Association," in *A Documentary History of American Industrial Society Volume v: The Labor Movement* (Cleveland: The Arthur H. Clark Company, 1910), 129–33. Warren was probably also the author of some of the pseudonymous articles in *Mechanics' Free Press* on labor exchanges, particularly those extolling the virtues of those recently established in the Philadelphia area.
[107] Cosmopolite, "(Labor Exchange)," ed. William Heighton, *Mechanics' Free Press* (Philadelphia, October 25, 1828).

far this logic of universalizing liberty and eliminating economic dependence could go. Echoing a plan that Thomas Paine first put forward in *Agrarian Justice*, but which Skidmore appears not to have known about,[108] Skidmore felt the logical step would be a "system that should have given *each individual* as he arrived at the age of maturity, as much of the property of the world, as any contemporary of his, was allowed to possess at a similar age."[109] Each person "has an equal right with any and every other man, to an equal share of the common property; or its undoubted equivalent."[110] Skidmore did not simply try to acquire funds and land through estate taxes, but through expropriation and redistribution of existing property. His plan for an "equal division of property" involved holding a "State-convention" in which the state would conduct a property census, "claim all property within the State, both real and personal, of whatever kind it may be … [and] order an equal division of all this property among the citizens."[111] Each person would acquire credits, and upon reaching the age maturity, would be free to bid for a share of public property – mainly land – of their own, or pool those claims to form associations of workers.[112] They would be free to work their property and keep the products for as long as they lived. But their property could not be inherited; instead, it would return to the common fund to be distributed again on the principle of equal rights. Not only would this respect equal rights, but this system would eliminate the incentive to "seek to acquire property for the purpose of making it an instrument (to be placed in the hands of children), of domination over the children of other parents."[113] The analogy with that decade's state conventions, which eliminated property restrictions on the suffrage, was explicit and intentional. Here was the completion of the revolutionary republican project through one of its most characteristic acts of popular sovereignty – the constitutional convention. The equalization of property, through an act of higher law, secured universal independence.

Remarkably, this proposal for a state convention was a concession to necessity, not a sign of agrarian parochialism. Skidmore felt the *logic* of his argument was universal and thus global in scope. In principle, the ideal redistribution of land would be international, not state-level or national.[114]

---

[108] Paine, "Agrarian Justice." The edition of Paine's writings available to and quoted by Skidmore, published in 1797, did not include *Agrarian Justice*, which had just been published that year. The edition Skidmore used was Thomas Paine, *The Works of Thomas Paine, Secretary for Foreign Affairs, to the Congress of the United States, in the Late War: In Two Volumes*, Vols. 1–2, ed. James Carey (Philadelphia: James Carey, 1797). Cited at Skidmore, *The Rights of Man to Property!*, 6. However, the historian Mark Lause told me that copies of *Agrarian Justice* circulated among Skidmore and his associates, which raises questions as to why Skidmore never mentions it.
[109] Skidmore, *The Rights of Man to Property!*, 126.
[110] Ibid., 243.
[111] Ibid., 137.
[112] See Skidmore's proposal ibid., 137–44.
[113] Ibid., 120.
[114] Ibid., 48–52.

Moreover, it would include every adult individual – man and woman, enslaved black and colonized Native American. In fact, Skidmore was careful to note that blacks, women, and Native Americans had suffered especially badly at the hands of the monopolizers of wealth.[115] In an additional original step, Skidmore extended his argument for eliminating economic dependence to the domain of family relations. He thought the dependence of children on their parents for their education and inheritance corrupted family love, allowed parents to tyrannize children, and forced children into flattery – rather like attendants to monarchs. Skidmore therefore argued for free public education, state provided guarantee of means of subsistence, and a capital grant upon reaching maturity that was unlinked to the parents' economic fortunes. Their economic independence secured, children's relations with their parents would be characterized by true mutuality and love, rather than slavish obedience and flattery.[116]

As Skidmore noted, those original agrarians, the Roman Gracchi,[117] may well have blushed at the radical nature of his proposal.[118] As far-reaching as they were, Skidmore's ideas were not merely the loopy utopian musings of an isolated critic. The Report of the Committee of Fifty, the official platform of the New York Workingmen's Party, included a demand for "AN EQUAL AMOUNT OF PROPERTY ON ARRIVING AT THE AGE OF MATURITY, and *previous* thereto, EQUAL FOOD, CLOTHING, AND INSTRUCTION AT THE PUBLIC EXPENSE."[119] For a brief time, then, the argument for dividing property equally among citizens in the name of republican liberty was the official platform of an actual political party.[120] Skidmore's views were long recognized as influential and of critical importance to the debates of the period, not just among workers but in Jacksonian America.[121]

---

[115] Ibid., 158–60. He also wrote: "I would give the same rights of suffrage to the red man, the black man, and the white man." Ibid., 146. And later, "it is no more consistent with *right*, that the slaves should be subservient to [the white man], than it is for the poor white man, to be subservient to the rich one." Ibid., 270.

[116] Ibid., 262–66. For Skidmore's views of children, see Joshua R. Greenberg, "'Powerful – Very Powerful Is the Parental Feeling': Fatherhood, Domestic Politics, and the New York City Working Men's Party," *Early American Studies: an Interdisciplinary Journal* 2, no. 1 (2004), 192–227.

[117] On the Gracchi in republican mythology, see Nelson, *The Greek Tradition in Republican Thought*, 49–86.

[118] Skidmore, *The Rights of Man to Property!*, 29–30.

[119] Skidmore, "Working Men's Meeting: Report of the Committee of Fifty," 1.

[120] On Skidmore's loss of control of the party to already organized and powerful Whigs allying with Wright and Owen, see Gilbert, *The Life of Thomas Skidmore*; Pessen, "Thomas Skidmore, Agrarian Reformer in the Early American Labor Movement"; Wilentz, *Chants Democratic*, 182–88.

[121] "Agrarianism," *The Atlantic Monthly* III, no. XVIII (April 1859), 393–403. See also discussion in Pessen, "Thomas Skidmore, Agrarian Reformer in the Early American Labor Movement."

Back to the Land: The Ambivalence of Early Republicanism

Skidmore and his fellow-travelers were attacked as dangerous "agrarians."[122] A contributor to Philadelphia's *Mechanics' Free Press* proudly notes that the Roman tribunes were "working men's representatives" and that "among other names of reproach, they were called *Agrarians*; and in this city, also, the same word has been applied reproachfully to us."[123] But as we have seen, these labor advocates are more notable for the way in which they pushed the agrarian radicalism of the small producer tradition in new directions. In place of an exclusive concern with landlessness and indebtedness, these workers made wage-labor the central object of criticism. To deliver this critique in republican terms, they used the tools of modern political economy to expose the relations of dependence underlying the formal independence of "free" workers. Even more provocatively, they followed this critique of the wage-laborer's dependence with the radical demand to make control over property equal.

To be sure, they were ambiguous about what equal property meant. They found the cooperative idea attractive but many of their proposals were vague and somewhat individualistic – workers' cooperatives were but one, still relatively marginal, option. In the 1830s and 1840s, the few cooperatives established were a response to local conditions, showing little coordinated effort or even common ideological basis.[124] The workingmen were, moreover, uncertain in their thinking about the relationship between private property, collective property, and state-owned property. They uniformly avoided or explicitly rejected state-owned enterprises.[125] However, they went significantly beyond the small producer tradition in their willingness to use the state for redistributive purposes. More significant was their understanding that any attempt truly to universalize republican liberty would require not just redistribution of land, but the reorganization of industrial relationships. On this point, the idea of cooperation had a crucial, if still vaguely formulated, role to play: to recover control over one's labor required exercising that control continuously, during work itself. That control could only be achieved in a modern, industrial setting through shared, equal control, not individuated production. This was the reason why they were no longer content merely to eliminate primogeniture and entail. It was increasingly unlikely that those laws alone would guarantee property distributions that secured each citizen's independence. There was not enough land, and the nature of productive property had changed. Instead, these early republicans challenged inherited property itself and attempted to guarantee each person at least adequate ownership of productive resources so that nobody would be forced to sell his labor to another. Only this egalitarian

---

[122] E.g., "The Agrarian Party," *Ithaca Journal*, May 5, 1830; Simon Clannon, "To the Public," *The Daily Advertiser*, March 2, 1830.
[123] "Agrarians," *Mechanics' Free Press* II, no. 99 (November 28, 1829), 3.
[124] Leikin, *The Practical Utopians*, 25–52; Horner, *Producers' Co-Operatives in the United States, 1865–1890*, 42–50.
[125] E.g., Skidmore, *The Rights of Man to Property!*, 156.

distribution of property, and thus control over labor, would eliminate the "slavery of wages." No wonder that, alongside "agrarians," their critics invented another term of abuse: "Workies."

By the mid-1830s, the workingmen's parties had dissolved. The radical moment in the republican critique of capitalism subsided but did not by any stretch disappear. Citywide labor councils, such as New York's General Trades Union, protested attempts by employers' associations to suppress union activity by saying such actions would "make dark the republican atmosphere of this boasted land of liberty, for a long and wicked reign of anarchy and despotism."[126] Some Workies found their way into the radical "Locofoco" faction of the Democratic Party. One of their most notorious spokesmen, Orestes Brownson, wrote in his extraordinary 1840 essay "The Laboring Classes" that "there is a class of our fellow citizens, who stare at us as if we were out of our wits ... when we represent the workingman as still a slave.... In their estimation he is already enfranchised, already a free man ... and no more dependent on the capitalist, than the capitalist is on him."[127] But, said Brownson, this dependence was not mutual. "Which is the more urgent necessity, that of growing rich, or that of guarding against hunger? You can live, though you do not employ the laborer; but, if he find not employment, he must die. He is then at your mercy."[128] The only reasonable thing, Brownson mockingly said to an imagined audience of employers, was to "set yourselves at work in earnest to remodel the institution of property, so that all shall be proprietors, and you be relieved from paying wages, and the proletary from the necessity of receiving them."[129] The Worky critique of wage-labor continued to resonate.

Nevertheless, if the argument that the wage-laborer was dependent persisted, by the 1840s some of the latent individualistic and agrarian tendencies of the small producer tradition resurfaced. The National Reform Association (NRA), the largest mid-century reform movement in the country, preserved the republican critique of wage-labor, often self-consciously referring to the Workingmen's Parties as their predecessors.[130] There were both intellectual and biographical reasons for them to claim a Worky heritage. The NRA's originator, George Henry Evans, had edited the *The Working Man's Advocate* for the New York Workingmen's Party, and many ex-Workies ended up passing over to the NRA. However, the NRA made its emphasis not the reorganization of industrial production but rather the redistribution of land. Its basic aim was agrarian: to eliminate economic dependence by eradicating private land monopolies and

---

[126] Kim Voss, *The Making of American Exceptionalism*, 32. See also the "Ten-Hour Circular" written by the Boston Trades' Union and discussion thereof in Pessen, *Most Uncommon Jacksonians*, 43.

[127] Orestes A Brownson, "The Laboring Classes," *The Boston Quarterly Review* 3 (July 1840), 42.

[128] Ibid., 48.

[129] Ibid., 49.

[130] See for instance George Henry Evans, "Rise and Progress of Agrarianism," *YA*, September 20, 1845.

by making public lands available to all landless citizens for personal settlement and cultivation.[131] The historian Mark Lause, in his superb history of the NRA, shows how the organization's focus on land transformed the republican critique of wage-labor into a national, rather than just urban, political movement. The association succeeded in influencing mainstream political parties, eventually contributing to passage of two bills in 1862, the Homestead Act and the Morrill Land Grant Act.[132] The first dramatically expanded low-cost access to land and the second created the famous land-grant colleges to "promote the liberal and practical education of the industrial classes."[133]

For our purposes, it is worth noting only a few points to set the stage for the late-century labor republicans. Like the workingmen, the land reformers thought the United States enjoyed a republican form of government but a despotic social condition that had unthinkingly adopted feudal English property arrangements:

> The laws relative to property were adopted with no essential modification from such as prevail in Great Britain, and they have the effect of creating an aristocracy of wealth which must prove as fatal to liberty as the worst form of despotism.[134]

This is almost exactly the same language as Skidmore used in the Report of the Committee of Fifty.[135] The creation of a landless class, dependent on the monopolists of land and factory property, produced a new kind of slavery. As John Pickering, prominent National Reformer and author of *The Working Man's Political Economy*, put it: "A capitalist finds a thing called a poor man without a home, deprived of his birthright in the soil, reduced to want and destitution."[136] This landless person "would be glad to labor, but is denied the privilege" unless the capitalist hires him. In the absence of employment, "he is turned into the street to *starve, to beg, or to steal*; he must do one or the other, there is no alternative; or *die. (These are the privileges of the Free Laborer.)*"[137]

But a "man who is obliged, by his destitution, to sell himself for wages," was, on Pickering's view, treated as nothing more "than as convenient and

---

[131] The NRA's constitution was published in the inaugural issue of the revived *WMA*. George Henry Evans, "National Reform Association Constitution," eds. George Henry Evans and John Windt, *WMA*, April 6, 1844. See also George Henry Evans and John Windt, "Our Principles," *WMA*, April 6, 1844.

[132] Mark Lause, *Young America: Land, Labor, and the Republican Community* (Springfield: University of Illinois Press, 2005).

[133] The language of the Morrill Act is available at the Library of Congress website, http://www.loc.gov/rr/program/bib/ourdocs/Morrill.html. Lause shows that the NRA became a home for the interpenetration of agrarian, labor republican, and socialist views. Lause, *Young America*, 35–59.

[134] Unsigned, "Address of Mr. Wait of Ill.," *YA*, October 25, 1845.

[135] Skidmore, "Working Men's Meeting: Report of the Committee of Fifty."

[136] John Pickering, *The Working Man's Political Economy* (Cincinnati, OH: Thomas Varney, 1847), 34.

[137] Ibid., 3.

useful materials and instruments."¹³⁸ He was, in virtue of this dependence, a slave:

> Now, this human machine is virtually and positively as much a slave to the capitalist, as any chattel slave is to his master; in either case, they are controlled by the will of their masters, in all their actions, with this difference: the hired slave can leave his master; but, if he does, he runs the risk of finding another, which is often very difficult to accomplish … so that the servitude, as far as effects are involved, are alike compulsory in both cases.… In neither case would the victims consent to part with the produce of their own labor, if they could help it.¹³⁹

So far, this is boilerplate republicanism, condemning wage-labor as a species of slavery in exactly the language of Pickering's Worky predecessors. In fact, it was this kind of language that informed the land reformer's running debates with the abolitionists, which we discussed in Chapter 2. Think, for instance, of the following lines uttered by Horace Greeley and reprinted with favorable commentary in the NRA's journal, *Young America*:

> What is Slavery? You will probably answer "The legal subjection of one human being to the will and power of another." But this definition appears to me inaccurate … it excludes the subjection founded in other necessities not less stringent than those imposed by statute.¹⁴⁰

A "subjection founded in other necessities" than law was precisely what lay at the heart of the republican critique of the formally free labor contract. Yet if the land reformers sounded Worky themes, a glance at the NRA's founding "Principles" reveals a narrower train of analysis: the "traffic in the soil … we discover to be the *root* of the evil, the cause of that vast inequality of condition now existing among us."¹⁴¹ Although critical of "wage-slavery," they did not see the ownership of productive property *in general* as the problem, so much as the unequal ownership of land in particular. Their "leading measure" was "*the Equal Right of every man to the free use of a sufficient portion of the Earth to till for his subsistence.*"¹⁴² With adequate availability of land, each person would have a reasonable alternative of real economic independence available to him. For example, when George Henry Evans revived the *Working Man's Advocate* in 1844, now dedicating it to National Reform, he included in the first three issues a series of articles on the "Equal Right to Land." The first proclaimed:

> If the whole people had free access to the land, the laborer would not be *dependant* [sic] on the employer.… He would receive the full value of his labor, because he would have the ready alternative of laboring for himself.¹⁴³

---

¹³⁸ Ibid., 37.
¹³⁹ Ibid., 43–44.
¹⁴⁰ "'What Is Slavery' from the Cincinnati Morning Herald: Letter from Horace Greeley to the Anti-Slavery Convention at Cincinnati," *YA* 2, no. 14 (June 28, 1845).
¹⁴¹ Evans and Windt, "Our Principles."
¹⁴² "Equal Right to Land I," *WMA*, March 16, 1844.
¹⁴³ Ibid.

"The Sword of Want"

This comparison between "hired laborer with the farm settler" was supposed to communicate the full range alternatives available for creating a "Republican Community."[144] Tellingly, some National Reformers went so far as to *condemn* the earlier Worky demand for equal control of industrial property or "value" instead of land. As a leading Reformer from New York put it,

> the Working Men of this city (adopting the error of Thomas Skidmore) proposed an equal amount of property on coming of age in *lieu* of the right to land. This I opposed as soon as I reflected upon the proposition … and contented that the Land itself should be restored to the people, and not merely an equivalent for it.[145]

The author no doubt had in mind passages from Skidmore such as the following: "I am not to be understood as meaning anything by equality, other than that the *value* of the effects of our citizens, whether it be lands, or ships, or goods, or whatever else it may be, would be apportioned equally among us all.[146] For Skidmore and other Workies receiving value as opposed to land was what made possible pooling resources to form cooperatives and thus the running of the factory system on the basis of equal interdependence, rather than unequal dependence. It also was a tacit recognition that the land could not absorb all surplus labor – there was no purely agrarian path to universal republican liberty in an industrial society.

National Reformers formally rejected that view. They identified a concrete *form* of labor, agrarian self-sufficiency, with free labor in general.[147] As George Henry Evans put it, "it needs that the lands should be *free* … [because] many of the employed laborers … would gladly exchange their life of servitude for one of independence."[148] Here the republican critique of wage-labor was accompanied by a retreat from thinking about how industrial production itself could be made free. Redistribution of land might empty the factories, but not reorganize them. Up until the end of the Civil War, the dominant hope for universalizing republican liberty in a modern commercial republic was to return to the heroic independence of the small farmer and to identify the "Republican Community" with the republic of small producers. This view found its final and most famous exponent in Henry George, author of the immensely popular late nineteenth-century book, *Progress and Poverty*. But there is no need to trace out this line of thinking any further.[149] We follow a different path in the development of

---

[144] "Equal Right to Land III," *WMA*, April 6, 1844.
[145] "Explanation," *Subterranean, United with the Workingman's Advocate*, 1, no. 34 (1844).
[146] Skidmore, *The Rights of Man to Property!*, 248.
[147] Recall that, from Jefferson onward, agrarian "self-sufficiency" was not anti-market but rather about growing crops for the global market and combining these earnings with whatever one consumed oneself. Appleby, *Capitalism and a New Social Order*, 253–76; Allan Kulikoff, *The Agrarian Origins of American Capitalism* (Charlottesville: University Press of Virginia, 1992), 34–59, 127–51.
[148] "Equal Right to Land I."
[149] George was one of the Knights' favored political economists, and they considered him to have solved the "land question." However, as becomes clear next chapter, labor republicans thought the land question did not exhaust the labor question. On George's complex political

republican thinking about free labor. After the Civil War, that path leads back to the heart of the industrial world – "the Quarry, the Workshop, the Forge and the Factory" that William Heighton condemned in 1827 as sites of human bondage.[150] In the postbellum period, we find the redoubling of efforts to eliminate wage-labor, and thus to resolve the paradox of slavery and freedom, by transforming control over industrial property itself.

and intellectual connection to the Knights, see Robert E. Weir, "A Fragile Alliance," *American Journal of Economics and Sociology* 56, no. 4 (1997), 421–39.
[150] William Heighton, *The Principles of Aristocratic Legislation*, 5–6.

4

Labor Republicanism and the Cooperative Commonwealth

> *There is an inevitable and irresistible conflict*
> *between the wage-system of labor*
> *and the republican system of government*[1]
> George McNeill

On January 9, 1865, an iron-molder named William H. Sylvis traveled to Chicago to address the national convention of the Iron-Molders' International Union (IMIU). Sylvis, then president of the IMIU, gave a two-hour address to what was later described as the "largest Convention of Workingmen of one craft ever held on this continent."[2] The climactic end of the Civil War was still months away, and the House of Representatives had not yet ratified the Thirteenth Amendment to the U.S. Constitution, which abolished slavery and "involuntary servitude." Yet, according to Sylvis, history was already in the process of jumping over its own shadow. Even as a momentous "political revolution … has left its trail of blood upon the sky.… The year … has witnessed a social revolution such as the world has never known."[3] Sylvis described this "social revolution" as a "collision between classes," which had its origins in the industrial relationships of the North, not the slave labor of the South. These new "relations are, for the most part, that of master and slave, and are totally at variance with the spirit of the institutions of a free people, and the relations that should exist between equals."[4] In Sylvis's mind, the Civil War was "merely" a political revolution because no government could legitimately call

[1] McNeill, *The Labor Movement*, 459.
[2] Jonathan Grossman, *William Sylvis, Pioneer of American Labor* (New York: Hippocrene Books, 1973), 78.
[3] William H. Sylvis, "Address Delivered at Chicago, January 9, 1865," in *The Life, Speeches, Labors and Essays of William H. Sylvis*, ed. James C. Sylvis (Philadelphia: Claxton, Remsen & Haffelfinger, 1872), 128.
[4] Ibid., 130.

itself republican while permitting chattel slavery. But the concomitant social revolution meant that this external opposition between republican government and chattel slavery had now become an internal conflict between political form and social content. "What would it profit us as a nation," Sylvis asked, were

> all the forms of our republican institutions to remain on the statute-books ... with the wealth of the nation concentrated in the hands of the few, and the toiling many reduced to squalid poverty and utter dependence on the lords of the land.... Again, allow me to ask, what would it profit us if the forms of our institutions were preserved and all else lost.[5]

With this defense of the "toiling many" against "utter dependence" the republican critique of wage-labor reared its head once more.

Sylvis's speech, delivered from the belly of the Yankee Leviathan, was a sign of things to come. The near certainty of Northern victory had opened up the ideological space at the national level into which radical labor leaders like Sylvis rushed. In Sylvis's case, he rushed a bit too quickly. Although he succeeded in building the first international craft union (of iron-molders), the initial efforts at postwar national organizations of labor ended in failure. In 1866, Sylvis spear-headed the formation of the National Labor Union and the National Labor Party, both of which, along with their successor organization, the Industrial Congress, quickly collapsed without attracting many members.[6] Their major significance lay in the intellectual recovery of an earlier language of critique and, perhaps more importantly, in the attempt to present "cooperation" as a solution to the problem of guaranteeing all workers their economic independence.[7]

In 1869, as the first organizational efforts disintegrated, a small group of garment workers, led by a tailor and labor reformer named Uriah Stephens,[8] formed a secret organization called the Knights of Labor. Drawing on language from the National Labor Union, the Knights' Constitution said they wanted to organize "every department of productive industry and [to make] industrial, moral and social worth – not wealth – the true standard of individual and national greatness."[9] The Knights were the first post–Civil War labor organization open to nearly all workers, including unskilled, black and women workers, but excepting Chinese.[10] They remained secret for about a

---

[5] Ibid., 129.
[6] Ware, *The Labor Movement in the United States*, 1–22; Montgomery, *Beyond Equality*, 170–96.
[7] On the revival of cooperative ideology and actual cooperatives by these groups, see Leikin, *The Practical Utopians*, 5–24; Horner, "Producers' Co-Operatives in the United States, 1865–1890," 46–52.
[8] To my knowledge there is no full biography of Stephens. For a brief sketch by one of the Knights, see "Our Past Grand Master Workman," *JUL* II, no. 4 (August 15, 1881), 1–2. See also Ware, *The Labor Movement in the United States*, 26–28.
[9] Powderly, ed., "Knights of Labor Platform – Preamble and Declaration of Principles," 30.
[10] On their greater openness, especially to women and blacks, than their immediate predecessors, see Leikin, *The Practical Utopians,* 33–35, 45–46. On the history of the Knights of Labor, see the sources mentioned in footnote 25 of the Introduction.

Labor Republicanism and the Cooperative Commonwealth 99

decade out of the reasonable fear that they would be blacklisted, infiltrated by Pinkerton agents, and otherwise persecuted.[11] By 1880, their growth to nearly 30,000 members convinced them to flex their muscles publicly. Some successful strikes and labor actions in the early 1880s earned them enormous national popularity. Their official membership peaked in 1886 at a bit more than 700,000, with probably more than a million when unofficial members are included.[12] These numbers would not be matched by a national organization of labor for decades. Internal chaos and external repression in the late 1880s led to rapid decline.[13] By the mid-1890s, they were spent as a national political force, having been displaced by Samuel Gompers' American Federation of Labor.[14] But for more than a decade, the Knights of Labor was the most powerful national organization of labor of the century and was a major player in the defining events of the day.[15] Most importantly for us, the Knights as an organization, and especially its better-known leaders, were self-consciously republican, seeing themselves as keepers of the flame in the post–Civil War environment.[16]

Although the group I am here calling labor republicans were mostly concentrated around the Knights of Labor, they did not all belong to a single organization or agree on every issue of the day. They were instead united by their use of republican ideas to criticize wage-labor and to present cooperation as an alternative. The main figures all came out of a nineteenth-century tradition of independent, working class agitation.[17] William H. Sylvis (1828–1869), the son of a wagon-maker, became an iron-molder and founded the Iron-Molders'

---

[11] On their secret rituals, see Weir, *Beyond Labor's Veil*, 19–66. Blacklists against Knights were very common as was the use of Pinkertons. McNeill, *The Labor Movement*, 138; "Making War on This Paper," *JSP* II, no. 69 (February 1, 1885); Levine, *Labor's True Woman*, 56–59, 66–68, 73–81. Violence, legal and illegal, against the Knights and labor generally was a major part of the literature of the time and of labor historiography. Terence V. Powderly, *Labor: Its Rights and Wrongs* (Westport, CT: Hyperion Press, 1886); Karl Liebknecht, *Militarism* (New York: B. W. Huebsch, 1917) 140–141; Adamic, *Dynamite; The Story of Class Violence in America*; Taft and Ross, "American Labor Violence: Its Causes, Character, and Outcome"; Forbath, *Law and the Shaping of the American Labor Movement*; Tomlins, *The State and the Unions*, 3–98; Pope, "Labor's Constitution of Freedom."

[12] Oestreicher, "A Note on Knights of Labor Membership Statistics," 102–08. See also Weir's calculation: Weir, *Beyond Labor's Veil*, 16.

[13] On the internal sources of their decline, see the excellent Robert E. Weir, *Knights Unhorsed* (Detroit, MI: Wayne State University Press, 2000).

[14] However, see Oestreicher's comments that even through the 1890s their membership competed with that of the AF of L. Oestreicher, "A Note on Knights of Labor Membership Statistics."

[15] On Labor Day, see Weir, *Beyond Labor's Veil*, 308–13.

[16] Fink, *Workingmen's Democracy*; David Montgomery, "Labor and the Republic in Industrial America: 1860–1920," 201–15; Richard Oestreicher, "Terence v. Powderly, the Knights of Labor, and Artisanal Republicanism," in *Labor Leaders in America*, ed. Warren Van Tine and Melvyn Dubofsky (Urbana and Chicago: University of Illinois Press, 1987), 30–61.

[17] On the difference between these figures and the Radical Republicans, see Montgomery, *Beyond Equality: Labor and the Radical Republicans 1862–1872*, 260.

International Union before turning his attention to national labor organizing.[18] Ira Steward (1837–1883), the son of abolitionists, was a machinist and self-educated labor reformer. He was most famous as a tireless eight-hours campaigner, founder of Boston's Eight Hour League, and a major influence in the creation of the Massachusetts Bureau of Labor Statistics.[19] Steward's friend and protégé, George McNeill (1836–1907), was a labor editor, a leading member of the Knights, active in Boston labor politics and author of one of that era's most influential accounts of the labor movement.[20] After the Knights' decline he joined the American Federation of Labor. The other central figure is Terence Powderly. The son of Irish immigrants, he was a machinist who served as General Master Workman (leader) of the Knights of Labor during its heyday, from 1879 to 1893, and who also served as mayor of Scranton, Pennsylvania from 1878 to 1884. After being pushed out of the Knights in the 1890s, he later served as an official in the Bureau of Immigration and in the Labor Department.[21]

These were the major players, but labor republicanism was more than the "cranky notions"[22] of a few leading lights. As we shall see, the core thinking appeared in the pages of the *Journal of United Labor* and developed in relation to the experiences and activities of the Knights. These experiences included the rapid rise of permanent, industrial wage-labor, judicial and political hostility to organized labor, strikes and boycotts, fluctuating living standards, and the reorganization of work. In some sense, the Knights were *forced* by circumstance to

---

[18] For biographical information, see James C. Sylvis, "Biography of William H. Sylvis," in *The Life, Speeches, Labors and Essays of William H. Sylvis*, ed. James C. Sylvis (Philadelphia: Claxton, Remsen & Haffelfinger, 1872); David Montgomery, "William H. Sylvis and the Search for Working-Class Citizenship," in *Labor Leaders in America*, ed. Warren Van Tine Melvyn Dubofsky (Urbana and Chicago: University of Illinois Press, 1987), 3–29; Montgomery, *Beyond Equality: Labor and the Radical Republicans 1862–1872*, 223–229; Grossman, *William Sylvis, Pioneer of American Labor*. On the NLU and its connection to the Knights, see Ware, *The Labor Movement in the United States*, 22–55.

[19] There is no full biography of Steward, who remains an enigma among a class of enigmatic nineteenth-century labor agitators. See David R. Roediger, "Ira Steward and the Anti-Slavery Origins of American Eight-Hour Theory," *Labor History* 27, no. 3 (1986), 410–26; Dorothy W. Douglas, "Ira Steward on Consumption and Unemployment," *The Journal of Political Economy* 40, no. 4 (1932), 532–43; Montgomery, *Beyond Equality: Labor and the Radical Republicans 1862–1872*, 249–60; Stanley, *From Bondage to Contract*, 90–96; Ken Fones-Wolf, *The Boston Eight-Hour Men and the Emergence of American Trade Union Principles, 1863–1891*.

[20] McNeill, *The Labor Movement*.

[21] Terence V. Powderly, *The Path I Trod: The Autobiography of Terence v. Powderly* (New York: Columbia University Press, 1940); Powderly, *Thirty Years of Labor 1859–1889*; Oestreicher, "Terence v. Powderly, the Knights of Labor, and Artisanal Republicanism"; Weir, *Knights Unhorsed*, 9–22, 161–78.

[22] "Cranky Notions" is the name of a column that Joseph Labadie wrote in the *Labor Leaf*, the local Detroit paper of the Knights. Labadie was the paper's editor, a Knight and one-time member of the Socialist Labor Party. See Oestreicher, *Solidarity and Fragmentation: Working People and Class Consciousness in Detroit, 1875–1900* (Urbana: University of Illinois Press, 1986), 79–96.

articulate their own understanding of the republican tradition. Court cases not only served to overturn pro-labor laws and limit union activity, in explicit and implicit ways they also gave constitutional sanction to sometimes quite violent repression of labor activities.[23] The "struggle to define and claim title to the republican legacy and the republican constitution" was an unavoidable fact of post–Civil War political life.[24] Any attempt to organize workers compelled labor republicans to give their own account of the ideology of free labor that informed public discourse and constitutional interpretation.[25] The heterogeneous origins and diverse cultures of the workers they organized further compelled the Knights to articulate what was universal about the republican language in which they made their appeals.

The end of the Civil War gave labor republicans one advantage over their predecessors. Postwar reformers could not easily be accused of putting the concerns of wage-laborers ahead of black slaves. In fact, labor republicans could now present themselves as the true torchbearers of the revolutionary republicanism that the Civil War and its ideology of free labor had revived. For instance, when George McNeill wrote, "there is an inevitable and irresistible conflict between the wage-system of labor and the republican system of government,"[26] his use of the phrase "inevitable and irresistible conflict" rhetorically linked his cause to the Civil War's antislavery mission. William H. Seward, Secretary of State during the Civil War, had coined the phrase "irrepressible conflict" when arguing that chattel slavery was incompatible with republican government.[27] Like Sylvis before him, McNeill borrowed that language to argue that the freedom of a republican community had not yet been achieved.

What makes reconstructing these views difficult is that they were not articulated as a systematic whole, laid down in the philosophical form of a formal treatise. Labor republican arguments appear in books and pamphlets, novels and speeches, essays and editorials. They emerge as an interlocking sequence of partial responses to the overall challenge of defining freedom and slavery in a modern context. Often, by addressing themselves to one end of the intellectual

[23] See footnote 11, this chapter.
[24] Forbath, "The Ambiguities of Free Labor: Labor and the Law in the Gilded Age," 769. Also Fink, *Workingmen's Democracy*, 8.
[25] See especially James Gray Pope and William Forbath's excellent, if slightly differing, work on the subject. Pope, "Labor's Constitution of Freedom." Pope, "The Thirteenth Amendment Versus the Commerce Clause: Labor and the Shaping of American Constitutional Law, 1921–1957." Forbath, "Caste, Class, and Equal Citizenship." Forbath, "The Ambiguities of Free Labor: Labor and the Law in the Gilded Age"; Gillman, *The Constitution Besieged*, 61–100; Tomlins, *The State and the Unions*, 3–9, 32–59.
[26] McNeill, *The Labor Movement*, 459.
[27] Although McNeill is invoking Seward, he has the language slightly off. Seward's famous phrase was that there was an "irrepressible conflict" between the slave and non-slave states. See Foner, *Free Soil, Free Labor, Free Men: the Ideology of the Republican Party before the Civil War*, 69–72.

puzzle, they unintentionally redefined or significantly altered another related concept. It is therefore helpful to sketch the general outlines of this labor republican view before going more deeply into each of its conceptual elements.

"Away the False Idea of Liberty": Labor Republicanism as a Whole

In the heady ideological environment of post–Civil War America, labor republicans returned to first principles. Against laissez-faire republicanism, labor republicans argued both that the prevailing conception of freedom was false and that servitude persisted. For instance, in a series of twelve lectures published in the *Journal of United Labor* under the title "Chapters on Labor," one Knight argued that

> liberty signifies the moral and material possibility for each citizen, the individual, to perform his duty in all security and without being under the authority of anybody. It signifies for the people the collectivity, the certainty that their industrial relations shall serve to equitably balance the services and products of men between themselves ... away the false idea of liberty being defended by the governing classes![28]

Any reader of the *Journal* would have instantly recognized the "false idea of liberty" of the "governing classes" as the one standing behind the political treatises and anti-labor court decisions we discussed in Chapter 2. The author of "Chapters on Labor" nodded in that direction when saying,

> Are the governing classes really serious when they tell us that it is out of respect and love for liberty that they do nothing to emancipate labor from its condition of misery? ... How can they love or believe in liberty? it [sic] is the total negation of their presumptuous authority.[29]

The governing classes' "presumptuous authority" was housed in the rights of property and contract, and the claims about legal independence that stood behind them. The "false idea" resided in the fact that these legal institutions failed to prevent the laborer from, in that telling republican phrase, coming "under the authority of anybody."

This return to first principles, however, was no mere repetition. Just *saying* that wage-labor was servile, and that cooperative production was free, did not make it so. It required argument. The labor republican project therefore necessarily involved a clarification and elaboration of the meaning of both republican liberty and domination. After all, the new social conditions of industrial capitalism, just as much as the new ideological context of a post-emancipation society, forced them to say something about what free labor could mean in the mechanized and collective conditions of modern production. They had no choice but to find a way to remain true to their intellectual

---

[28] Unsigned, "Chapters on Labor: Chapter V (Continued)," *JUL*, September 25, 1885, 1082.
[29] "Chapters on Labor: Chapter V (Continued)," 1082.

tradition while expounding on the ambiguities of its basic concepts. Otherwise the labor republican critique of the new forms of slavery would collapse back into intransigent agrarianism. This, no doubt, is why they found Algernon Sidney's words, which we touched on in the introduction, so appealing. Recall that in June, 1882, the *Journal* published these lines from Sidney's *Discourses on Government*:

SLAVERY – The weight of chains, number of stripes, hardness of labor, and other effects of a master's cruelty, may make one servitude more miserable than another; but he is a slave who serves the gentlest man in the world, as well as he who serves the worst; and he does serve him if he *must* obey his commands and depend upon his will.[30]

This passage was important because it distinguished the *condition* of subjection from its original defining *instance* – chattel slavery. Whether one man's subjection to another was legal or economic, and however that domination was exercised, was a separate question from whether it counted as servitude in the first place. It opened up the conceptual space to criticize wage-labor so long as it could be shown that analogous forms of subjection existed. That the Knights do not cite Sidney as the author of these words only reinforces the sense that they cared about basic meanings, not the moral authority behind the concept. Restating the meaning of slavery in these terms was the other side of attacking the "false idea of liberty." It was not just that the hegemonic view of freedom was wrong, but that nominally free labor concealed the new forms of subjection that wage-labor introduced.

In general, then, we can say that the labor republicans did not just return to first principles, they also added content to the central concepts of slavery and of freedom. As the next four sections show in greater detail, they gave the concept of slavery more precise meaning by developing an account of the overlapping forms of structural and personal domination to which a modern wage-laborer was subject. Their domination was structural insofar as each worker was, owing to his lack of property ownership, dependent on some employer or another for a job. Their domination was personal insofar as the labor contract gave the employer a substantial amount of arbitrary power over the employee. The wage-laborer was forced to sell his labor, which meant he was forced to make a contract that left him subject to the will of his employer. All in all, the labor republican critique amounted not just to an indictment of the corrupting effects of inequality, but to an argument that a society based on labor contracts had simply replaced old forms of servitude with new ones.

The final three sections of the chapter show how, alongside this analysis of wage-slavery, labor republicans gave new content both to the *meaning* and *value* of republican liberty. Their proposal "to abolish as rapidly as possible, the wage system, substituting co-operation therefore"[31] is the most important of

---

[30] "Slavery." It comes from Sidney, *Discourses Concerning Government*, [II:21] p. 181.
[31] Jelley, *The Voice of Labor*, 203.

their modifications to the small producer tradition. The "Republic of Labor"[32] could now be described as a cooperative commonwealth, comprising interlocking producer and consumer cooperatives, rather than a body of separate free producers. Labor republicans further understood this economic independence to be a condition not just of free production but also of increased leisure, a condition of freedom in *and* from work. From this account of the meaning of independence they then moved to a new account of its value. Republican liberty, they argued, was important because it was a necessary condition for the development and enjoyment of an individual's abilities. What mattered was not the glory of the republic, the virtues of political participation, nor the priority of any particular domain of life, but the opportunity for self-cultivation.

Political Liberty and the Corruptions of Wealth

In 1890, General Master Workman Terence Powderly addressed a Knights of Labor picnic with the following question:

how it comes that the indictment drawn up against the English king applies with such startling force to the agencies we now find usurping the "divine right of kings" and making slaves of men who proudly, but thoughtlessly, boast of their freedom – that freedom which they claim came down to us from revolutionary sires as a heritage.... Are we the free people that we imagine we are?[33]

Speeches like Powderly's were a regular feature at Knights of Labor picnics, which were the central recreational institution through which the Knights developed their own political culture.[34] On this occasion, Powderly had an old republican concern in mind: corruption. The modern wage-labor system undermined republican liberty by generating extreme economic inequalities that translated into political inequalities. The wealthy wielded disproportionate influence over politics and especially the administration of justice, such that "courts are administrators of estates, and not of justice."[35] Powderly's fellow agitator, George McNeill, often sounded a similar theme: "[I]t is imperative, if we desire to enjoy the full blessings of life, that a check be placed upon unjust accumulation, and the power for evil of aggregated wealth."[36]

What made this more than a moralistic critique of luxury was the concern that inequality subverted the formal independence of citizens. If employers controlled the apparatus of the state then the legal autonomy of the free laborer

---

[32] A slogan prominently displayed at various Knight-sponsored picnics and parades. See Weir, *Beyond Labor's Veil*, 305–13.

[33] Quoted in Leon Fink, "The New Labor History and the Powers of Historical Pessimism: Consensus, Hegemony and the Case of the Knights of Labor" 115.

[34] Weir, *Beyond Labor's Veil*, 282–88.

[35] McNeill, *The Labor Movement*, 456. "Exclusion of lawyers-the technicians of American politics-from membership in the Knights of Labor in part reflected a desired distance from the contaminated machinery of the state." Fink, *Workingmen's Democracy*, 24.

[36] McNeill, *The Labor Movement*, 197.

was a sham: "[W]e are wholly in the hands of our employers ... subjects of the railroad kings and cotton lords."[37] Much like the British commonwealthsmen of the seventeenth century, or the American revolutionaries of the eighteenth, editorialists in the *Journal* regularly worried about the loss of political independence to the wealthy and well-connected:

> Corporations of capitalists ... are slowly but surely crushing out the manhood and liberties of the poor laborer, guaranteed by the Constitution and laws of the land, by creating immense fortunes which enable them to buy up legislatures, sway judges and communities as they please.[38]

Whether or not a proper labor contract guaranteed a worker's independence was immaterial if the law would not be enforced fairly in the first place.

Following a convention dating back to the American Revolution, labor republicans often drew negative comparisons with European despotism.[39] John Swinton, a famous labor journalist and Knight supporter, warned darkly of creeping "Bonapartism in America."[40] The Knights' local paper in Detroit attacked the "industrial oligarchy" for wanting to "establish a strong military government to keep [workers] in subjection and in slavery"[41] and it lauded thousands of Philadelphia workers marching "against the conduct of the police force of Philadelphia towards strikers."[42] In Chicago, the Knights' local paper noted that the city council had given police permission to revoke their "right of free assemblage," giving them "discretionary powers as to whether they will allow the people to exercise their constitution rights or not." They continued, "add to this the statement of Mayor Harrison, that he has authorized his police to do things in Chicago 'which if done in London would overturn the throne of Victoria,' and it really does not seem as if American liberty amounted to very much."[43] Inability to control legislatures, arbitrary treatment by courts, and violent conduct by police and private forces seemed to confirm that there was not one law protecting equal citizenship but two systems of law for two different classes. The law prevented boycotts but permitted blacklists, inhibited labor organizations but promoted business corporations, enjoined strikes but respected lockouts.[44]

---

[37] Ibid., 456.
[38] William McKee, "Co-Operative Shoe Factory," *JUL*, September 25, 1884, 797.
[39] On the role of these comparisons as they first appear in debates about wage-slavery, see Cunliffe, *Chattel Slavery and Wage Slavery*.
[40] Swinton, "Bonapartism in America."
[41] "Our Bitter Foes! True Sentiments of Our Industrial Oligarchy," *Labor Leaf* I, no. 48 (October 7, 1885), 3.
[42] "A Union Protest: Against Police Ruffianism in Philadelphia," *Labor Leaf* I, no. 48 (October 7, 1885).
[43] "(Right of Free Assemblage)," *Knights of Labor* 1, no. 27 (October 9, 1886), 8. See also "Fate Marked the Cards before the Game Began," *Knights of Labor* 1, no. 32 (November 13, 1886). *Knights of Labor* hereafter *KoL*.
[44] "Law and the Boycott," *JUL* VII, no. 20 (January 29, 1887), 2268; "Boycotting May Be Illegal"; L. W. Richter, "Discharge of a Mechanic," *JUL* VII, no. 2 (May 25, 1886), 2077; "Rumblings All Over," *JSP* 2, no. 93 (July 19, 1885).

Yet, if political and administrative corruption were deeply important to labor republicans, it was not the issue that set them apart from other critics of the new industrial system. Although many were willing to argue that extreme wealth corrupted political liberty, fewer were willing to drive the analysis into the heart of the labor contract and the industrial workplace. Labor republicans distinguished themselves by arguing that *even if* the law were created and enforced fairly, it would still operate in a way that left workers dependent on employers. Here labor republicans made three overlapping arguments about the structural and personal dimensions of modern wage-slavery. They argued there was domination *prior to* the making of the contract, *in the making* of the contract itself, and then *in the workplace* itself. The purpose of criticizing these three "moments" of domination was to rebut the basic laissez-faire republican proposition that the capacity to labor was a commodity like any other, and that a worker could be protected from the arbitrary will of an employer by guaranteeing the worker's property right in his own labor and freedom to make a labor contract. Let us take each of these three moments in turn.

The First Moment of Wage-Slavery: Structural Domination and "Seeming Free"

One of the most consistent arguments labor republicans made was that just because a contract was voluntary did not mean it was made freely. The workers "*assent* but they do not consent, they submit but do not agree,"[45] said George McNeill. Or, as one "Meddlesome" put it, "freedom of contract is not free, but only seeming free."[46] The labor contract was a "seeming freedom" because the worker, though legally free to sell or not sell his labor, was nonetheless compelled to sell his labor. As one Knight put it, "the producers are slaves.... Even the children and women of the American laborer are driven, *from necessity* ... to toil from dawn till night, that others may luxuriate in overabundance."[47] In one sense, this was the identical argument of the earlier Workies and National Reformers, who condemned the "necessitous circumstances" that made wage-laborers into slaves.[48] But the later labor republicans refined the argument through an analysis of the labor commodity. As owners of their labor, wage-laborers were compelled to sell their labor-commodity, because they could not withhold it from the market: "[I]f, in the place where the laborer lives, the demand for his commodity falls or ceases altogether, he cannot, like the employer, stop offering his goods and wait for a better time."[49]

---

[45] Quoted in Oestreicher, "Terence V. Powderly, the Knights of Labor, and Artisanal Republicanism," 42.
[46] Voss, *The Making of American Exceptionalism*, 94.
[47] Jelley, *The Voice of Labor*, 279.
[48] See Chapter 3.
[49] "Review of Cherouny," *JSP* 2, no. 87 (June 7, 1885).

The worker had to eat. He thus had to sell his labor at whatever price the current market offered.

At one level, this was not an argument against labor contracts themselves, but rather about the special character of the capacity to labor as a commodity. Since it was inextricable from the physical person of the worker, workers had to have some economic means to withhold that commodity from the market, otherwise their property rights in their labor were a sham: "[T]he anti-slavery *idea* was, that every man had the right to come and go at will. The labor movement asks how much this abstract right is actually worth, without the power to exercise it."[50] The labor republican argument for unions, which can bargain collectively and can use membership dues to pay their members to withhold their labor until a better deal is struck, derived from this view of the labor market. As George McNeill put it in congressional testimony,

> The fact is, there is no such thing as liberty of contract between a wage worker and an employer.... A starving man cannot contract with a man of wealth; a man that is compelled to sell his labor or starve can not make a contract. A man that is not removed from starvation by at least two or three months is not in a condition to make a contract.... [T]he union is to the wage laborer what the republican form of government is to the citizen of the union.[51]

For true freedom of contract to exist, workers had to be able to control their commodity, with its special characteristics, the way other property-owners controlled theirs. They needed some degree of *material* independence, allowing them to withhold their commodity from the market for a time, so they could meet as equals in the bargaining relationship.

But labor republicans were not just interested in making labor contracts "truly free" because, at least in the mass labor market, they thought that was not possible.[52] Although a union might temporarily alleviate the pressure on workers, it could not eliminate the basic compulsion he faced. Support from a union might allow him to temporarily withhold his labor, but he could not permanently do so. He still had no reasonable alternative to selling his labor. Here the labor republican analysis of power and dependence pushed past the dominant metaphor of property-ownership itself. As an article from the *Journal of United Labor* put it:

> A considerable percentage of those who are wage laborers to-day owe to the change in methods of production the fact that they are such, and their condition should be

---

[50] Steward, "Poverty," 412.
[51] *Report of the Industrial Commission on the Relations and Conditions of Capital and Labor Employed in Manufactures and General Business, Including Testimony So Far as Taken November 1, 1900, and Digest of Testimony Vol. 7* (Washington DC: Government Printing Office, 1901), 115. Hereafter *Report of the Industrial Commission Vol. 7*.
[52] McNeill himself makes this clear in his testimony: "Before I get through, perhaps, you will understand that I do not believe in the wage system: but as long as it continues we will simply modify and improve it until we get out of it." *Report of the Industrial Commission Vol. 7*, 118.

compared not with that of the wage laborers of fifty years ago, but with that of the independent, self-employing artisan of that time.[53]

Whether a wage-laborer today had more bargaining power or earned more than the wage-laborer from the past was not the relevant question because it failed to capture a crucial transformation in power relationships. An independent producer, working his own tools or land, could meet his own needs without selling his labor at all. He only sold his labor occasionally, to augment his income, or purchase some luxury, but he met his basic needs by consuming or selling the products of his labor. Since he could support himself and his family without selling his labor-power, he was not forced to sell his labor-power. Importantly, the point was not that the independent producer was free from economic need itself, but that he had a way of satisfying those basic needs without entering the labor market. The existence of this alternative meant that, when making a labor contract, he did so as one economically independent actor making an agreement with another. But if that really became the case, then labor contracts would become irregular features of the economy, not the core institution organizing productive activity. In Ira Steward's pithy summation: "If laborers were sufficiently free to make contracts ... they would be too free to need contracts."[54]

The current distribution of property, however, left most wage-laborers with no such alternative to selling their labor. They *needed* to make contracts because they were "dependent on wages received from a separate capitalist class"[55] for their survival. As the author of "Industrial Ideas," a series of lectures serialized in the *Journal*, put it, since this wage-dependence came not from nature but human law, it counted as a form of subjection:

> The land, the tools and materials of labor are still the exclusive property of the privileged few, and the worker cannot produce without giving himself a boss or master. It must not be supposed that the proclamation of emancipation liberated mankind from slavery. The most odious, because the most subtle form of slavery – wages slavery – remains to be abolished.[56]

Again, the problem was not that a person had to work, but that he "cannot produce without giving himself a boss or master." The laws protecting the current distribution of property arbitrarily removed the one reasonable alternative to working for another person. That, in itself, was a form of domination, exercised by the entire class of property owners and the state agents protecting them. It did not matter that the laws no longer specified which master controlled which slave because the prevailing distribution of property guaranteed that workers would have to work under some "boss or master." The

---

[53] "Some Economic and Social Effects of Machinery," *JUL* VI, no. 20 (February 25, 1886), 2011.
[54] Quoted in Stanley, *From Bondage to Contract*, 96.
[55] "Some Economic and Social Effects of Machinery."
[56] "Industrial Ideas Chapter II," *JUL* VII, no. 4 (June 25, 1886), 2097–99, 2098.

especially bitter feature of this form of subjection was that the individual's consent was mobilized against him, he "*gave himself*" a master rather than had the master directly imposed on him.

Labor republicans could criticize this form of structural domination without denying that wage-labor was relatively freer than chattel slavery. Henry Sharpe, a leading theorist of cooperation for the Knights, drew attention to this point:

> In slavery the slave was totally dependent on a force outside himself; he was driven to work, and had no interest in the affairs of life other than to keep the lash off his back. In the wage-system there are, it is true, some prizes, nay, many prizes, and many objects of interest, and many avenues for independent action, yet the condition of the man is largely still one of dependence; they are forced to work.[57]

There may be "many prizes" and it might even be possible for some wage-workers to become business owners, but most could not, and they could not *all* become property-owners in this economy.[58] The majority of propertyless workers would always be dependent on wages. They were free to "give themselves a master," but they could not choose not to have one.

Although labor republicans did not call this "structural domination," I use that phrase to distinguish this argument from other elements of their social analysis. Structural is the appropriate word because it was a form of domination arising from the background structure of property ownership and because the compulsion they felt did not force them to work for a specific individual. It is not that the "structure" was somehow an "agent," nor that there were no dominating agents. There were, in this case, many dominating agents – all those who defended property distributions that left the majority propertyless.[59] Through human design and institution, workers were left with no reasonable alternative but to sell their labor.

However, even if we can distinguish conceptually between this form of structural domination and other, more personal forms, in practice labor republicans thought the moments ran together. The full extent of wage-slavery could only be appreciated by understanding how structural domination connected up with a particular employer's power over his employee's when it came to specifying the terms of the contract and, after that, controlling the workplace itself.

The Second Moment of Wage-Slavery: The Terms of Labor

Although the structural element of wage-slavery might seem abstract and impersonal, it quickly became concrete and personal when employers exploited a

---

[57] Henry E. Sharpe, "Co-Operation," *JUL*, November 1883, 597.
[58] See also "Industrial Ideas Chapter IV," *JUL* VII, no. 7 (August 10, 1886), 2133–35, 2134.
[59] I have analyzed this conceptual issue in greater detail in Gourevitch, "Labor Republicanism and the Transformation of Work," 591–617.

worker's structural disadvantages. The following passage describes an employer taking advantage of that dependence:

> The absence of actual equality between the two parties to the labor contract make the terms of the sale unavoidably one of compulsion. Nor can the laborer, like other commodities, seek a distant market or hold himself aloof until better terms are offered ... Moreover, labor, besides accepting compulsory rates, must also labor under such conditions as the employer may impose. These may, of themselves, be destructive to health, and thus lessen the value of the commodity itself.[60]

Insofar as the employer was able to arbitrarily extract as much value from the worker as he could manage, without consideration for the worker, this amounted to a kind of servitude:

> when a man is placed in a position where he is compelled to give the benefit of his labor to another, he is in a condition of slavery, whether the slave is held in chattel bondage or in wages bondage, he is equally a slave.[61]

This was, in one sense, just a revival of the earlier Worky argument that the function of economic dependence was to get some to work for others, in exchange for only an arbitrary fraction of the amount of value they themselves produce. This argument was meant to demonstrate that economic dependence was central to the way society reproduced itself; it was not just the occasional objectionable instance but a systemic form that made the profits of the idle possible.

However, labor republicans further developed this argument by using the dominant language of property-ownership. Enjoying property rights in their capacity to labor gave workers nominal, not full control, over their labor. They were compelled to agree to the terms of its sale and to lose control over the fruits of their labor:

> We obtain in exchange for the most severe labor a salary which hardly prevents us from dying of hunger; in fear that at each moment dull times may drive us into forced idlesness ... we forego, in exchange for a stipulated salary – pittance – all claims or right to the fruits of our labor.[62]

Labor republicans even believed that employers were well aware of the function of poverty and unemployment in augmenting the employer's power over the contract. One Knight criticized

> the employers, who would not have been sorry to see the poverty of their hands augmented temporarily so that their dependence in the future might have been made more certain, at the same time their boldness in striking was being rebuked. There *are* such

---

[60] "Labor's Disadvantage," *JUL* VIII, no. 27 (January 7, 1888), 2554.
[61] "Wages Slavery and Chattel Slavery," 702.
[62] "Industrial Ideas Chapter I," *JUL* VII, no. 3 (June 10, 1886), 2085–88, 2085. "Chapters on Labor: Chapter v (Continued)"; "A Sketch of Political Economy Chapter I"; Egbert Hasard, "Our Full Fruition," *JUL*, August 15, 1880.

manufacturers, wise, farseeing business men-who [thereby] ... gain undisputed control over their workers.⁶³

The more extreme the economic need and the greater the competition among workers, the greater the latter's dependence on an employer. The more intense the dependence, the more the employer could impose his will on the terms to which a worker consented. "No amount of sophistry will ever make him regard such a life as aught else than slavery," wrote one local Master Workman; "[s]ociety makes labor terrible to him, and circumstances place other means of winning bread beyond his reach."⁶⁴ Low wages, long hours, though better than unemployment, were hardly the terms of a contract to which properly independent economic actors would agree. In fact, as we have seen, a major argument not just for unionization and collective action, but for labor regulations – such as banning payment in script, abolishing convict and child labor, and instituting maximum hours laws – was that they reduced the kinds of terms that employers were able to impose at their own discretion.⁶⁵ Although these regulations could not abolish the dependence of the wage-laborer on the employer, they could at least limit the kinds of arbitrary power he could exercise over the terms of contract. More generally, this analysis of the contract helped explain *why* employers sought dependence. Insofar as structural domination translated into personal domination in the setting of terms, employers enjoyed an arbitrary superiority in the ability to extract concessions from the workers.

The Third Moment of Wage-Slavery: "The Caprice of he who Pays the Wages"

The ability to impose terms on the contract easily slid into an even more objectionable form of domination in the workplace itself. In fact, we can only fully appreciate the intellectual debt these critics owed to specifically republican thinking when we consider their description of life after the contract is made and once the worker entered the workplace. Here is where the subjection became most "classically republican" in the sense of one individual being under the power of another specific will. Labor republicans' most deeply felt grievances were often not just with what the contract said –long hours and low pay – but with what it left unsaid – everything else. With respect to the million and one conditions of work not spelled out in the initial agreement, the silence of the contract really expressed the muteness of the worker and the voice of the employer. Both as a matter of legal right and of cultural assumption, it was expected that once the contract was made the worker would passively obey the commands of the employer.

---

⁶³ Robert D. Layton, "Salutatory," *JUL*, October 15, 1881.
⁶⁴ The Master Workman of L A 1573, "An Essay on the 'Evils Resulting From Long Hours and Exhaustive Toil,'" *JUL*, October 15, 1881, 159–60.
⁶⁵ Richter, "Discharge of a Mechanic," 2077.

Consider the four following passages. They are a small selection among dozens of similarly worded complaints, each oozing with that familiar republican contempt for servility and dependence:

> Is there a workshop where obedience is not demanded – not to the difficulties or qualities of the labor to be performed – but to the caprice of he who pays the wages of his servants?[66]

> Thus is sycophancy deified in our workshops ... thus is abject servility ennobled, as it were, by bosses and foremen.... He who is a thorough, quiet, firm and independent [worker], the boss looks on as his most dangerous enemy, for he cannot be changed or put down; but he who is the most sycophantic, pandering to all the whims of his boss, the boss looks upon as his ideal workman, to be raised above his fellows as an example for them to look up to, watch and imitate.[67]

> Liberty consists in being able to satisfy all one's wants, to develop all one's faculties, without in any way depending upon the caprice of one's fellow-beings, which is impossible if man cannot produce upon his own responsibility. So long as the workman works for a boss, a master, he is not free. "You must obey," the master will say, "for since I assume the responsibility of the undertaking, I alone have the right to its direction."[68]

> the degrading influence of the wages-slavery system.... To be dependent upon an employer who frequently merits disdain and inspires disgust, and yet be compelled to execute his commands and submit to his caprice; to have no thought but that which is filtered through the brain – less powerful than his own – of a boss, an employer, a master.[69]

This language is so familiar that, if we changed just a few words, we could easily imagine these were the grievances of American colonists or early British parliamentarians condemning the arbitrary power of colonial governors and the absolute monarch. Yet these words now described the world of the voluntary labor contract. They were directed at a new relationship, one in many ways much more pervasive, because of its immediacy and daily regularity, than that of a people subject to their arbitrary magistrate. A worker spent many hours of a day, for most of his life, working for a boss.

It is important to observe that these critics of workplace domination were not (just) indicting the bad character of a few employers. Instead, the "caprice" here referred to the objective features of the labor contract as a sale of the labor commodity. Their claim was that a contract *necessarily* involved subjection of the worker to the employer regardless of how that employer then used his power. A labor contract, said one Knight, "assumes that labor shall not be a party to the sale of itself beyond rejecting or accepting the terms offered. This purchase of labor gives control over the laborer-his physical intellectual, social and moral existence. The conditions of the contract determine the degree of

---

[66] Unsigned, "Chapters on Labor: Chapter VIII (Continued)," *JUL*, December 25, 1885 1153.
[67] "Hard Words of 'Nobody,'" *JSP* 2, no. 71 (February 15, 1885).
[68] "Industrial Ideas Chapter III," *JUL* VII, no. 5 (July 10, 1886), 2109–11, 2010.
[69] "Industrial Ideas Chapter VI," *JUL* VII, no. 10 (October 25, 1886), 2169–70.

Labor Republicanism and the Cooperative Commonwealth

this rulership."[70] It was a mockery of the idea of consent to say that the worker, by agreeing to sell his labor, had thereby consented to every command of the boss, and thus followed only his own will. The actual contract was exactly the opposite, an agreement *not* to control those decisions – an agreement of subjection.

In fact, to labor republicans, the whole point of the contract was that the worker had consented to evacuate his will, to suspend its exercise for the period of employment. Outside violating the very general terms of the contract, the employer was at liberty to do what he liked. Here was where labor republicans drove home their argument against the laissez-faire republicans. The basic logic of any contract to sell property was that sale of a commodity involves giving over ownership and control rights of that commodity to the buyer. But the special character of the labor commodity – as a physical commodity (the body) inseparable from the seller's person – meant the labor contract was necessarily an agreement to give up control over the seller's *will* for the duration of the working day. That, said George McNeill, was why the contract was by definition an instrument of subjection:

> Labor is more than a commodity in that he who sells his labor sells himself. The present system is in conflict with republican institutions.... Man should sell the product of his labor, and there can be no liberty until man has restored his right and power to sell the product of his time, skill, and endurance.[71]

A labor contract is necessarily a kind of "sale of oneself." It would not be a sale of labor if the purchaser, namely the employer, were denied the right to do with it as he pleases. It was therefore an inescapable aspect of the contract that the worker would, while at work, have to substitute the employer's will for his own. Any good republican knew that being subject to the will of another was the definition of servitude:

> We have a market for labor which is a slave market.... Labor is activity of the various mental and physical powers which are inseparably connected with the person who sells it. A sale of labor is a transfer of the use of this bodily and mental activity during the hours of labor, and consequently a dominion over it during that time.[72]

Here was why they said the labor contract was inextricably tied to making the worker live by the "caprice" of another. Whether the employer ruled benevolently or cruelly, it was still the case that the worker was under the arbitrary power of the employer – a power defended in law.

Of course, labor republicans were quick to add that, although wage-labor would still be servile if the employer was benevolent, the great evil of this condition was to be found in the way in which employers actually tended to use their power. After all, the employer's aim was to extract as much work as

---

[70] "Labor's Disadvantage," 2554.
[71] *Report of the Industrial Commission Vol. 7*, 115.
[72] "Review of Cherouny."

possible for as little pay. That is to say, employers did not possess some irrational will to dominate, or at least not all of them; instead, they materially benefited from their relationship of domination and thus exercised their power in ways that maintained that authority and worked against the interests of workers. During a famous 1883 inquiry into labor relations by the U.S. Senate, one Senator asked a witness, "well, what is the nature of the intercourse between the superintendent and the employes [sic] generally?" The witness, Secretary of the Executive Board of the Knights of Labor, John McLelland, answered, "generally the superintendent is overbearing – orders on one side and submission on the other."[73] Their examples of this overbearing use of power included "abolition of the luncheon privilege,"[74] being fired for reading a labor paper or expressing political views,[75] sexual harassment,[76] arbitrary penalties and wage-deductions,[77] and unnecessarily dangerous workplaces.[78] Many strikes of the period were sparked by the desire to eradicate these practices and more generally to demand greater worker control over the activity work.[79] Workers were at once deprived of the fruits of their labor and denied control over that labor.

The labor republican analysis of the labor contract helps us understand their view of machinery. Labor republicans, as we shall see later, were not luddites who viewed technology itself with suspicion, but they did object to the way in which it became part of the employer's apparatus of control. If workers were expected to be spontaneously and seamlessly obedient to the commands of bosses, then machines presented a terrifying, modern image of the perfection of this servitude. The automatic and inhuman capacity to serve the commands of the employer without resistance became a nightmarish ideal. A characteristic version of the complaint began: "[M]en are made to work harder than they used to, many employers attempting to run their productive capacity up to near that of machinery." It continued, "thus, while machinery is itself the product of labor, it is used to rob and enslave labor."[80] The Senate testimony

---

[73] *Report of the Committee of the Senate upon the Relations between Labor and Capital*, 219.
[74] *Report of the Industrial Commission Vol. 7*, 116.
[75] Swinton, "Making War on This Paper."
[76] "The Present Need of Woman," *JUL* VII, no. 14 (November 25, 1886), 2211; Susan Levine, "Labor's True Woman: Domesticity and Equal Rights in the Knights of Labor," *The Journal of American History* 70, no. 2 (1983), 323–39.
[77] "The Yonkers Strike," *JSP* 2, no. 73 (March 1, 1885).
[78] "Some Economic and Social Effects of Machinery"; "Labor's Disadvantage."
[79] For examples that include loss of the lunch hour, employer rape and arbitrary fining of female garment-workers, and loss of the comfort of sitting on stools see (Testimony of George McNeill), *Report of the Industrial Commission Vol. 7*, 116; Paul Buhle, "The Republic of Labor: The Knights in Rhode Island," in *From the Knights of Labor to the New World Order: Essay on Labor and Culture* (New York: Garland Publishing, Inc., 1997), 20; Levine, *Labor's True Woman*, 56–59.
[80] "The Thing in a Nutshell," *JUL* I, no. 7 (November 15, 1880), 67.

Labor Republicanism and the Cooperative Commonwealth 115

of a Knight gave the same account of machines mediating the enslavement of worker to employer:

> We find in many of those large institutions that the men are looked upon as nothing more than parts of the machinery that they work. They are labeled and tagged, as the parts of a machine would be, and are only taken into account as a part of the machinery used for the profit of the manufacturer or employer.... The working people feel that they are under a system of forced slavery.[81]

Machines, on this account, increased productivity not just by simplifying tasks but by breaking down the worker's will into a more easily employed, less resistant apparatus. As another Knight put it, "the employer exercises over labor an influence that can scarcely be given a name, but it is potent and is felt by labor in all his affairs. His opinions are not his own but belong to his master."[82] Here was a further reason why labor republicans thought that, "the wage-labor system ... makes the employer a despot, and the employee a slave."[83] Having given up control over his activity, the worker was then made to conform his activity to inhuman standards of behavior.

It is worth pausing to note how far the republican theory of liberty has traveled here. Recall that the early English republican, Algernon Sidney, despite writing words that the Knights found so inspiring, was author of such statements as "if there be a contest between me and my servant concerning my service, I only am to decide it: He must serve me in my own way, or be gone if I think fit, tho he serve me never so well; and I do him no wrong in putting him away."[84] In those lines, Sidney sounds more like a forefather of the labor republicans' worst enemies. During a Knight-led strike of carpet-weavers, the employer's journal complained of the way organized Knights "attempt to dictate to the proprietors of mills with regard to management of their business." They worried that the strike, if successful, would leave them "nominal owners of the mills, but practical control ... would have been vested in the Knights of Labor."[85] In fact, those nineteenth-century figures who objected to workers "seeking to legislate concerning the ways in which industry shall be carried on" and accused them of trying to "overbear the rightful authority of the employer"[86] could very well have laid more direct claim to being Sidney's intellectual progeny than the Knights. To argue that labor contracts and the workplace were sites of domination was no simple, straightforward extension of the republican concept of liberty. It required careful analysis of

---

[81] *Report of the Committee of the Senate upon the Relations between Labor and Capital*, 218–19.
[82] "Labor's Disadvantage."
[83] McNeill, *The Labor Movement*, 454–5.
[84] Algernon Sidney, *Discourses Concerning Government Vol II* (Edinburgh: G. Hamilton and J. Balfour, 1750), 339.
[85] Quoted in Levine, *Labor's True Woman*, 86.
[86] Francis Amasa Walker quoted Stanley, *From Bondage to Contract*, 83.

the dynamics of a labor contract and the wider consequences of property rights. Perhaps the most innovative element of this analysis was the critique of the commodification of labor and its relation to domination in the workplace. While the labor republicans gave a coherent account of wage-labor as wage-slavery, it was at war with a certain common sense, not to mention with a prevailing interest in an alternative and narrower interpretation of the republican theory.

"To Engraft Republican Principles into Our Industrial System"

By now it should be clear what labor republicans meant when they said "our rulers, statesmen and orators have not attempted to engraft republican principles into our industrial system, and have forgotten or denied its underlying principles."[87] They meant that the paradox of slavery was unresolved. Workers still experienced various forms of servitude. For one, the formal apparatus of the state was corrupt, undermining the legal independence of the citizen. And even if the rule of law were universally effective, the three interconnected forms of domination would remain. The propertyless worker was structurally dominated prior to the contract, and personally dominated in the making of the contract and once at work. The logical thrust of this critique was to say that slavery would remain so long as the labor contract was the basis for organizing the distribution of and control over work.

But what, then, could it mean to "engraft republican principles on [the] industrial system?" The answer to that question required more than critique. After all, the "industrial system" referred to more than the relationships between workers and employers. It also comprised a changed relation *among* workers and changes in the nature of work itself. Perhaps the defining feature of this new organization was its collective character. Labor republicans frequently observed that the ostensibly atomistic features of this system, based on individual effort, private profits, and "competition,"[88] were in fact reorganizing themselves on a cooperative basis. This reorganization of work was already visible in the "combination of employers" into a "union whose object was to make profit from the sale of their product, and to secure from other men as much labor as possible, at the lowest rate of compensation."[89] The tendency toward combination was no accident. It was the natural consequence of a society based on the pursuit of self-interest: "America is at the front of the forward line of evolution. It has taken the lead in developing competition to the extreme form in which it destroys competition."[90] Although it currently

---

[87] McNeill, *The Labor Movement*, 456.
[88] Powderly, *Thirty Years of Labor 1859–1889*, 30.
[89] Ibid.
[90] Henry Demarest Lloyd, *Wealth against Commonwealth* (Englewood Cliffs, NJ: Prentice Hall, Inc., 1963 [1894]), 180.

Labor Republicanism and the Cooperative Commonwealth

served the interests of the few, that was not a necessary consequence of this organizational trend:

no fault should be found with this tendency to combine. It is the natural tendency of organic life.... The system by which a *few* combine to enrich themselves at the expense of the many, is the very system by which the *many* can protect themselves against the few and secure an independence and happiness now unknown.[91]

Competition had produced monopoly, cartelization, and other large corporations.[92] Individualism had turned into its opposite.

The isolated, industrious competitor had only a spectator's role to play in this world. As Powderly put it, "we may boast of the individual enterprise of the American people as much as we please, but it has NO CHANCE when thrown into competition with the combination and the pool."[93] When competing against a massive supply of labor and large corporations, it was nearly impossible for the individual, on his own, to exercise much control over the terms of his contract. This was true not just in the labor market but inside the workplace. Workers were brought together in factories, their individual activities joined together as part of a shared process, and the regulation of tasks brought under the unified control of the manager.[94] We shall return to the labor republican response to the technical side of industrial production, but the point here regards the social aspect. Labor was now inescapably organized on a collective basis, as an integrated activity requiring conscious coordination among workers.

It was evident from this consolidation of productive activities that the time when each worker might individually control his activity, as a matter of personal dominion, was receding. There was no turning this aspect of production back to the days of the small producer. According to Powderly,

Once it was deemed a healthy sign to have different lines of railway running through a town. Cheap freight rates and easy transportation could be expected then but to-day that hope is dead, and combination of interests will stand between the town and prosperity if the railways will it so.[95]

What mattered to Powderly here was not just high prices, but the way in which the competitive process tended toward its opposite. In an inversion of the (increasingly mythological) Lincolnian story about the temporary wage-laborer earning enough to buy his own plot or tools, Powderly relates the story of a man who bought land with his small, 50-dollar savings, and then watched

---

[91] Mrs. Imogene C. Fales, "The Organization of Labor," *JUL* IV, no. 5 (September 15, 1883), 557.
[92] This is a fact that registered across the economy and culture of the United States at the time. See Trachtenberg, *The Incorporation of America: Culture and Society in the Gilded Age*.
[93] Powderly, *Thirty Years of Labor 1859–1889*, 462, capitalization in original.
[94] For a description of the reorganization of work see Dubofsky, *Industrialism and the American Worker*, 1–9.
[95] Powderly, *Thirty Years of Labor 1859–1889*, 462.

the value of that land increase over time to 25,000 dollars because of social changes beyond the man's control.⁹⁶ For Powderly, "labor ... increased the price of his land until he pompously asserts to-day that his own habits of thrift have won for him such large gains. His thrift was but an insignificant factor to the enterprise; it was co-operation that made him rich, but all co-operators did not share the profits of the labor done."⁹⁷ In this passage, the concept of "labor" is linked to the concept of "co-operation" in a new and significant way. Labor is no longer just the concrete, particular process by which specific articles are produced – the cobbler and his shoes, the tailor and his shirts – but an abstract, collective or "co-operative" process. The various activities, by which railroad track was laid, agriculture produced, iron manufactured, and workers clothed and fed, had all contributed to turning a 50-dollar piece of land into a 25,000-dollar boon. The value of the individual piece of property was, in a sense, a collective product.⁹⁸

The puzzle that labor republicans had to sort out was how, exactly, it would be possible to make the idea of independence consistent with these inescapable collective or "cooperative" features of modern labor. After all, the original vision of free labor had assumed that the citizen-worker would enjoy the kind of mastery associated with pure dominion. By their own analysis, later labor republicans appeared to inherit a choice between unattractive alternatives: nostalgia for the days of artisanal production, or, what amounted to almost the same thing, giving up on the republican theory altogether. If their critique of wage-labor was accurate, it nonetheless appeared to be a further implication of their social analysis that there was no forward looking project to be offered in republican terms.

"Abolish as Rapidly as Possible, the Wage System, Substituting Co-operation Therefore": Cooperation and Independence

The labor republicans responded to the historical challenge by arguing, with the consistency of a party line, that the principle of cooperative production could resolve the dilemma of how to universalize republican liberty in an industrial economy.⁹⁹ An economy of interdependent producer and consumer cooperatives, collectively owned and managed by workers, could eliminate the forms of subjection that arose in the labor market. As famously stated in

---

⁹⁶ Ibid., 455–59.
⁹⁷ Ibid., 462–63.
⁹⁸ Ibid., 456.
⁹⁹ See the defense of cooperation in just about every representative text of the time. Jelley, *The Voice of Labor*, 253–74; McNeill, *The Labor Movement*, 508–31; Powderly, *Thirty Years of Labor 1859–1889*, 452–70; Sharpe, "Co-Operation"; William H. Sylvis, "Co-Operation," in *The Life, Speeches, Labors and Essays of William H. Sylvis*, ed. James C. Sylvis (Philadelphia: Claxton, Remsen &Haffelfinger, 1872). Also Horner, "Producers' Co-Operatives in the United States, 1865–1890," 1–52; Leikin, *The Practical Utopians*, 41–46.

the Declaration of Principles of the Knights of Labor, and repeated endlessly in various speeches and pamphlets, the basic proposition was "to abolish as rapidly as possible, the wage system, substituting co-operation therefore."[100] The idea of cooperation was so central to the Knights' vision that the *Journal* ran a specially edited section in each issue under the heading "Co-operation," which included reports from cooperative ventures around the world, extracts of cooperative tracts, potted histories of cooperation, advice for forming cooperatives, and the correspondence of members.[101] They also formed a fund to help promote cooperatives, and one of their major cooperative activists, John Samuel, wrote the most widely distributed "how-to" manual for starting a cooperative.[102]

The labor republicans saw the cooperative principle as a modern answer to republican problems for two interrelated reasons. First, as we have seen, labor republicans believed that the cooperative character of labor was already a *fact* about industrial society, but it had not yet been articulated as a principle. The principles of individual ownership and freedom of contract were in some sense in conflict with the realities of the economy that had grown up underneath them. In one pithy formulation, "men's expanding powers of cooperation bring them to the conscious ability to unite for new benefits; but this extension of individuality is forbidden in the name of individuality."[103] Cooperation was an alternative principle, suited both to the moral and social realities of an industrial republic. As one study of cooperation argued, "co-operation is equally adapted to large or small enterprises-to very moderate or most extensive operations," because it was a matter of who governed the work activity and who received the profits, not the scale of the undertaking.[104] This adaptability of cooperation reflected the underlying reality that both large and small undertakings shared the same essential feature of being coordinated, not isolated, labor activities.

Second, cooperation was not just a fact of industrial organization but also an alternative to the principle of "competition" defining the wage-labor system. It meant shared ownership and control of productive resources. As one proponent argued, there would be an evolution from a "degrading stage of mere wage slavery to one of profit-sharing, in which all are recognized as equals, or better still, to a universal system of co-operative production."[105] It must be noted that the distinction between profit-sharing, in which workers received some of the profits after debts and dividends were paid, and "true" cooperation,

[100] Jelley, *The Voice of Labor*, 203.
[101] The section was started by Henry Sharpe, first head of the Knights' Co-operative Fund. This section ran alongside feature articles on similar topics.
[102] Leikin, *The Practical Utopians*, 12–13. On Samuel's pamphlet, see John Samuel, "An Experiment Which May Be Tried in Any Local Assembly," *JUL*, July 1886, 2139.
[103] Lloyd, *Wealth against Commonwealth*, 178.
[104] Jelley, *The Voice of Labor*, 262.
[105] Ibid., 362, quoting David Ross.

which included worker ownership and management, was not always clear.[106] Cooperation had multiple meanings as an organizational principle,[107] but it nearly always meant something akin to every worker having access to productive resources through membership in an association of producers.

Even more important, unlike the conception of cooperation first put forward by the famous Rochdale pioneers, who were a major influence in American circles, labor republicans insisted on *producer*, not just consumer, cooperatives.[108] Consumer cooperatives aimed at using collective purchasing power to cut out middlemen, eliminate merchant profits, and sell at cost to keep basic goods cheap. Although labor republicans formed many consumer cooperatives, they were clear that the principle of cooperation had to be applied to production, otherwise it could hardly meet the challenge of wage-slavery. Shared ownership and control addressed structural dependence by giving a worker an alternative to selling his labor. It gave him control over more of what he produced, which meant freedom from the compulsion to work for another. As Sylvis put it, cooperation "renders the workman independent of necessities which often compel him to submit to hectoring, domineering, and insults of every kind."[109] Furthermore, as a form of control not just ownership, cooperative production eliminated workers' personal subjection to employers in the workplace. They were under their own, collective authority.

The identification of cooperative production with the recovery of control over work was one of the labor republicans' most important conceptual moves. Because industrial labor was cooperative as a matter of fact, there was no return to the farmer's individual control over his activity. Instead, the productive control of the free laborer could only mean equal, collective rule over their joint activity. That they were trying to make sense of how a worker could

---

[106] E.g., "Co-Operation: a Lecture Delivered before the Local Assemblies of Easton, PA., by Charles Summerman, of the State Labor Bureau of New Jersey," *JUL* VI, no. 17 (January 10, 1886); "To Wages Add Profits: Economic Doctrine Not Down in the Books," *JSP* 1, no. 8 (December 2, 1883).

[107] There were various meanings of cooperation in play at this time, not all of them theorized in republican terms. For a discussion of these meanings, see Rodgers, *The Work Ethic in Industrial America, 1850–1920*, 40–45; Leikin, *The Practical Utopians*, 4–6, 28. It is worth noting that this republican cooperative movement was not exclusively American and bears strong affinities to European socialist currents at the time. Fink, *Workingmen's Democracy*, 22–23. John Stuart Mill's discussion of cooperative enterprises in *Principles of Political Economy* articulates many of the same ideas, and there is evidence that some of the labor republicans were aware of his work. E.g. Ira Steward, *The Eight Hour Movement: A Reduction of Hours Is an Increase of Wages* (Boston: Boston Labor Reform Association, 1865), 9–10. On Mill's 'republicanism' see Urbinati, *Mill on Democracy: From the Athenian Polis to Representative Government*, 155–201.

[108] On the influence of the Rochdale Pioneers and their transformation in the American context, see Leikin, *The Practical Utopians*, 31–32.

[109] William H. Sylvis, "The Uses of Co-Operation," in *The Life, Speeches, Labors and Essays of William H. Sylvis*, ed. James C. Sylvis (Philadelphia: Claxton, Remsen & Haffelfinger, 1872), 392.

be *independent*, not just "not poor," further explains why they tended to identify cooperation with active worker management, not just profit-sharing. As one Knight put it, the advantage of "co-operative industry" over the "wage system" was that "each man can feel that he is a proprietor; when he can feel that he is working for himself and not for a master; when he can feel and know that his brain and muscle weighs equally in the scale."[110] Terence Powderly said nearly the same thing in 1880, during his first annual address to the General Assembly of the Knights of Labor, "the method by which we hope to regain our independence ... [is] by embarking in a system of COOPERATION which will eventually make every man his own master-every man his own employer."[111]

Ideally speaking, cooperation guaranteed independence in the workplace by inverting the relationship between worker and manager. "To abolish wage slavery and to be our own bosses"[112] generally did not mean rejection of technical expertise or the need for managers.[113] Instead, the principle was that managers would be accountable to workers, "running their own shops, choosing their own directors and overseers."[114] If the cooperative idea did not reject the need for managerial expertise it did reject the converse – that workers were naturally inferior or lacked the competence to make decisions about the daily workings of the business. It is important to note this aspect of the argument for cooperation. The critics of labor republicanism not only claimed workers had no legal or moral *right* to demand control over the workplace, they also rejected the idea that labor could exercise this control competently. For labor republicans, however, the connection between cooperative institutions and the idea of independence lay not just in the negative case against subjection to the boss, but also in the positive idea that workers had the capacity for self-government and should be free to develop and exercise these capacities in their daily lives. The positive and negative aspects of the argument were really two sides of the same coin – subjection was wrong because the worker had the positive capacity for independent judgment. "*What is it to be a* SLAVE?" asked a Knight in the Detroit *Labor Leaf,* "It is to be a person consciously capable of self-government, and to be, at the same time, subject to the will of another person."[115] Cooperation appealed to this conscious capability for self-government, imputing it to all workers, in contrast, say, to William Graham Sumner's famous claim that only "captains of industry" were competent to make economic decisions.[116]

This aspect of the cooperative message carried over into more immediate efforts to exercise control in the workplace that fell short of creating a

---

[110] Jelley, *The Voice of Labor*, 261.
[111] Powderly, *The Path I Trod: The Autobiography of Terence V. Powderly*, 269.
[112] "Chapters on Labor: Chapter VI," *JUL* VI, no. 2 (October 10, 1885), 1093–95.
[113] E.g., "Legalize Co-Operation," *KoL* 1, no. 42 (January 22, 1887); C. S. Griffin, "Our Letter Bag: Co-Operation," *KoL* 1, no. 39 (December 30, 1886).
[114] McKee, "Co-Operative Shoe Factory," 796.
[115] "What Is It to Be a Slave?," *Labor Leaf* I, no. 47 (September 30, 1885).
[116] Sumner, "The Absurd Effort to Make the World Over."

cooperative enterprise. For instance, in Wanskuck, Rhode Island an assembly of Knights protested against the hazardous intensification of work. Threatening various collective actions against management, the assembly convinced management to back down, and for a time the Knights assembly was "administering the shop-floor life as a whole, by establishing the pace, cooperation between workers, and evaluation of the final product."[117] In another example, a local assembly of garment workers at the Riverside Mills in Rhode Island saw management's decision to remove stools as the last straw in what they called a "whole history of petty tyrannies that they had been subjected to for many weeks past."[118] The Knights' threat of organized action forced the return of stools and other concessions. Here again, the assertion of collective control, from within the wage-labor relationship, allowed these Knights to limit their subjection to bosses. When the Knights in Thibodaux, Louisiana organized the strike of cane cutters against the plantocracy, one suspects that workers were drawn to this sense that they should not have to obey passively their overseers and might even one day run things themselves.[119]

Perhaps the most powerful evidence of the connection between cooperation and independence as a positive capacity of self-government is found in the extraordinary initiative of local Knights assemblies in setting up their own cooperatives, often without any initial guidance or help from their national organization. The Knights' local papers were full of announcements of new cooperatives formed – newspapers and textile mills, coopers and shoe-makers, glass blowers and miners, groceries and farms.[120] Moreover, the Knights spread the cooperative idea to groups that had been excluded from earlier phases of the cooperative movement, including unskilled workers, blacks, and women.[121] Female workers organized their own cooperatives and housewives even applied the cooperative concept to their own work, creating shared housework and purchasing schemes.[122] Here were workers taking seriously the idea that they did not just have to take orders. It is no surprise that cooperation made a quantum leap from prior decades, leading to roughly

---

[117] Buhle, "The Republic of Labor: the Knights in Rhode Island," 3–39.
[118] Quoted in ibid., 20.
[119] See description of this episode in the Introduction.
[120] Just about every issue of papers like *Labor Leaf*, *Knights of Labor*, and *John Swinton's Paper* contain such lists. For instance, the August 26, 1885 issue of *Labor Leaf* reports the earnings from the Industrial Cooperative Association of New England, and notes the activities of the Plymouth Rock cooperative shoe store, the Kingston Co-operative Foundry, and the Co-operative Store of Salem. Or, the November 13, 1886 issue of *Knights of Labor* reports on the following cooperatives: cigarmakers in Weaverville, Pennsylvania; glassmakers in Des Moines, Iowa; Philadelphia cigarmarkers and hatters; Wilmington glass-workers; Frankford textile workers; and women garment workers in Chicago.
[121] On this conservative dimension of earlier cooperative efforts, see Leikin, *The Practical Utopians*, 33–41.
[122] Levine, "Labor's True Woman: Domesticity and Equal Rights in the Knights of Labor," 326, 328–29.

500 producer cooperatives, and thousands of consumer co-ops, employing tens of thousands of workers.[123]

It should be noted that the Knights not only made the idea of cooperation more universal but also changed its scope. A national organization of labor made possible thinking of cooperative production not just as a local activity but also as coordinated economic activity on a national scale. They sometimes referred to cooperation as not just a few experiments but what they called "a universal system of co-operative production" or "integral co-operation:"

> not any kind, or any measure, of co-operation will outwork our emancipation from the wage-condition ... integral co-operation is the whole or complete organization of production and distribution for the benefit of the whole body of those concerned in the production.... A body of men in integral co-operation ... would practically have formed an industrial state, the members of which employing their own labor and consuming their own products would be self-sustaining, therefore independent of the money-market and of the wage-market.[124]

This view of cooperative production as an "industrial state" stood in contrast to the separate, utopian communities of the early Owenites and Fourierists for whom secession from wider society was a real possibility. The Knights also made thinkable a somewhat more centralizing vision than that of earlier cooperators, who, at most, conceived of city-wide markets. For labor republicans, the purpose of forming smaller cooperatives was so that they would grow, by brute success and by example, into a kind of republican state within a state that could continue to expand:

> If those members of the different branches of industry that believe the only solution to the labor question is co-operation, let them come to the front and organize our physical, moral and financial forces into a state within a state, that is, to produce what it becomes necessary to consume according to our natural wants; once accomplished, we would not have to depend on others for a bare living.[125]

Although formation of these local cooperative colonies could happen right away, and its members would immediately be free of the dependence of wage-labor, their wider aim was not separation from society but social transformation. Such colonies were viewed as exemplary instances of the possibilities for a nationally integrated cooperative system. As the *Journal* put it, they sought

> to influence such a large body of people as compose this nation, and we seek to bring its government into line with our ideas, we shall have a successful experiment to which we can refer, to emphasize our arguments.[126]

---

[123] Leikin, *The Practical Utopians*, 2.
[124] "Co-operation" *JUL* V, no.1 (May 25, 1884), p. 694. Also "Integral Co-operation," *JUL* IV, no.11 (1884), 664.
[125] Henry Fecker, "A Paper Read before L.a. 1450: Lawrenceburg, Ind., Jan 14, 1884," *JUL*, March 1884 657.
[126] Hasard, "Our Full Fruition," 46.

Cooperative colonies were not worlds unto themselves but inspiring examples of what it would mean to replace wage-labor with cooperation wholesale. Some labor republicans were aware that this integrated cooperative could only permanently succeed on a consciously organized, national basis. It needed the support of a background set of economic conditions, regulated by law, which made each cooperative's flourishing possible. Powderly summarized these demands, spelled out in greater detail in various platforms,[127] as "a just and humane system of land ownership, [public] control of machinery, railroads, and telegraphs, as well as an equitable currency system."[128] One issue of the *Journal* ran, with approval, a proposal to allow groups of workers to incorporate, issue government-backed debt, and form cooperatives that would be supported by government price and wage controls.[129] Nationalization of land and public utilities, a people's bank making credit available to producer cooperatives, and a system of labor legislation all entailed major transformations in property relationships and public regulation. Put another way, cooperation was only a way of eliminating the structural dependence of wage-laborers because it transformed the background structure of production and distribution. The change in this background structure was the condition of possibility for the creation and maintenance of an integrated economy of cooperatives.

At their most ambitious, some labor republicans even proposed creating a parallel cooperative economy that would expand over time. It would have its own public credit system and issue currency notes, based on labor time, usable in markets, created by the Knights, selling only cooperatively produced goods.[130] The author of "Chapters on Labor" even put forward an "Industrial Constitution" whose articles include the creation of a "federation" of producers whose purpose was to create a "unity of action between all the producers of each State and nation, and afterwards between the producers of the whole world." It would include a "federal fund," and a system for providing producers tools and land, as well as a propaganda arm for spreading information and coordinating activities.[131] Henry Sharpe went so far as to argue that "the Order has arrived at the time when its organization should be at least as complex as

---

[127] The Knights of Labor platform included appropriation of communications and transportation networks, cheap credit, constraints on banks, publicly managed money depositories, health and safety regulations, recognition of unions, redistribution of public lands to "actual settlers; not another acre for railroads or speculators," eight hours legislation, and a Bureau of Labor Statistics. Many of these were understood as preliminary measures on the way to a truly cooperative system. "Knights of Labor Platform – Preamble and Declaration of Principles."
[128] Powderly, *Thirty Years of Labor 1859–1889*, 514–15.
[129] "Important Action by the U.S. Senate (concluded)," *JUL* 3, no.4 (1882), 278.
[130] Leikin, *The Practical Utopians*, 43–46, 58–66; Horner, "Producers' Co-Operatives in the United States, 1865–1890," 191–93. See especially Henry Sharpe's proposals for the Cooperative Guild, published in the June 10 and 25 issues of the *Journal* as "Article I" and "Article II" as well as the articles such as Sharpe, "Co-Operation," 776–77.
[131] "Chapters on Labor: Chapter VII," *JUL* VI, no. 13 (November 10, 1885), 1119.

that of a State" able to administer a wide variety of programs.[132] Although this highly integrated version of the cooperative commonwealth remained notional, the much more successful system of boycotting as well as the ethos of buying only Knights-produced goods, was a partial realization of this effort to centrally coordinate economic activity in a way that supported the formation of cooperatives. Closely connected to this idea was the highly contentious issue of a national cooperative fund, run by the Knights of Labor, which would help cooperatives raise capital and compete against non-cooperative enterprises. Originally a voluntary fund, briefly made compulsory, the Knights saw it as a way of drawing on its hundreds of thousands of members to accumulate capital they could not acquire on credit markets or by selling shares. The fund itself was mismanaged from the start, but all accounts of cooperation during this period note that the dramatic growth of cooperatives was a consequence of the Knights' ability to support them financially and to coordinate buying efforts.[133]

The eventual failure, though partially attributable to the empirical decline of the Knights, was also linked to the ambiguities of cooperation itself. Many Knights thought that too much centralization or compulsory cooperation threatened the emancipatory aims of cooperation itself, and these views tended to win out in debates about the cooperative fund. Others thought local, decentralized action would be sufficient. This particular problem remained an unresolved puzzle in the cooperative vision of the labor republicans. But, in the broader scope of ideological controversy, it was mostly a family quarrel about means not ends. Nobody disputed that cooperative production was the way of eliminating subjection to employers and of making possible each person's "capabilities of self-government."

The argument in favor of cooperation marked an important conceptual shift away from the social assumptions of earlier republicanism. Where the individual producer had been the original instance of economic independence, it was now possible to separate the normative core of that individual's freedom from its earliest institutionalization. As one labor republican put it, "the remedy does not lie in the direction of a return to the old slow methods of production. But if the workman may not again aspire to a separate business carried on with his own capital in his own little shop, he may reasonably aim at something which would constitute its economic equivalent."[134] Not only did the cooperative ideal require distinguishing the free labor of the individual from the individuated assumptions of the small producer, it meant that free labor was established *in*

---

[132] Quoted in Leikin, *The Practical Utopians*, 61.
[133] On the fate of the fund, see Leikin, *The Practical Utopians*, 44–46. Leikin notes that the Knights' ability to centralize and coordinate information, capital, and practical assistance was crucial to the cooperatives that did develop. Ibid., 65–83. On the importance of Knights' centralized "network of support" to the effectiveness of local action, see also the discussion in Levine, *Labor's True Woman*, 98–101.
[134] "Labor's Disadvantage."

and *through* each laborer's relations with others, rather than *prior* to or *absent* these social relations. That is to say, independence or "non-domination" was no longer conceived as a way of acting without the need to coordinate one's own labor with others, but rather as equal control over that shared activity. Liberty was a quality of collectively regulated interdependent relations, rather than a legally guaranteed separation from others. In this sense, the cooperative ideal brought to the fore something that had always been true – independence, even of the yeoman farmer, had been predicated on a collective regulation of the production and distribution process. The cooperative principle extended this logic to make labor a kind of public activity. It introduced popular sovereignty into the workplace itself: "[T]here is to be a people in industry, as in government."[135] The space of politics itself was redrawn to include the daily relations coordinating the interactions of laborers. That is why, when labor republicans spoke about "a republicanization of labor, as well as a republicanization of government,"[136] they conceived of this republicanization in political terms, not just as an instrument for increasing wages.

The Value of Independence: Free Labor and Free Time

The change in the meaning of independence went hand-in-hand with a new way of thinking about its value. After all, the defense of cooperative production was not a straightforward glorification of work. To be sure, labor republicans held the idle rich in great contempt: "[I]f the wage system were abolished and the equities of co-operation placed in its stead, the vast army of non-producers would vanish, and humanity would be in a better condition."[137] But their target here was not leisure itself so much as those who lived off the dependent labor of others. In fact, labor republicans saw their conception of cooperative production as intrinsically linked to the quest for more leisure time. The cooperative commonwealth was not merely offered as an alternative community of free and virtuous producers, whose independence contrasted with an aristocratic ideal of slave-holding leisure. Instead, collective control over labor was a first step to gaining control over and expanding free time. The great value of independence was thus not just being able to develop one's capabilities *in* work, but also in gaining greater freedom *from* work. As the Knights put it, the aim of their organization was "to secure to the workers ... sufficient leisure in which to develop their intellectual, moral and social faculties ... to enable them to share in the gains and honors of advancing civilization."[138]

It is here that labor republicans believed they were fully resolving the longstanding paradox of slavery and freedom, a paradox that could be articulated

---

[135] Lloyd, *Wealth against Commonwealth*, 183.
[136] Steward, "Poverty," 434.
[137] Jelley, *The Voice of Labor*, 255.
[138] "Knights of Labor Platform," 30–31.

in terms of the relationship between production and consumption. One of the great evils of the existence of a class of dependent laborers was not merely the denial of the dignity of free production, but also the benefits of all around consumption. Sylvis presented this reunification of producer and consumer as a resolution of an ancient historical dilemma, originating with the separation of society into freeman and slave: "[M]an himself, shall waken from the trance of ages, and the producer and the consumer, the creator of enjoyments and he who revels in them, shall be one and indivisible once more."[139] But why, exactly, did free labor also mean less labor, and why was free labor not enough?

One reason they thought leisure was necessary for the development of individual capacities had to do with machine production. If various capacities of self-government could be developed in the workplace itself, industry also routinized work to the point where it could become deadening rather than self-developing.[140] Moreover, there was more to life than work. There was a whole series of relationships in which one might develop oneself: "[H]e who has become citizen, neighbor, friend, brother, son, husband, father, fellow-member, in one, is just by so many times individualized."[141] Unstructured time and opportunities for consumption were thus also essential elements to one's all around development. Work was the central thing but not the only thing. Its burdens could be lightened, and the enjoyment of leisure increased, if the full promise of machine production were realized.

Yet, if labor republicans were often dazzled by the growth of human productivity, they saw its potential used against them rather than for them.[142] As the author of the "Chapters on Labor" wrote, the Knights' project is, "to satisfy more and more every day the ever-increasing wants of mankind with the least possible effort, which we can accomplish only through the exercise of industry."[143] Statements like these signaled a disavowal of the somewhat more austere republicanism that saw the very demand for material comfort and cultivation as corrupting "luxe."[144] Yet they were also distinct from a later consumerism, which placed a value almost exclusively on the importance of having more material wealth. Labor republicans saw opportunities both for the expansion of material consumption and free time, which was why they put their hopes in a world in which "the laborer shall receive his fair share of the increasing wealth of the country created by his labor, and his proportionate

---

[139] Sylvis, "Address Delivered at Chicago, January 9, 1865," 172.
[140] "Some Economic and Social Effects of Machinery"; The Master Workman of L A 1573, "An Essay on the 'Evils Resulting From Long Hours and Exhaustive Toil'."
[141] Lloyd, *Wealth against Commonwealth*, 178.
[142] "A Sketch of Political Economy, Chapter XI," *JUL* V, no. 21 (March 10, 1885), 927; "Chapters on Labor: Chapter V (Continued)"; "Some Economic and Social Effects of Machinery"; "Industrial Ideas Chapter IV."
[143] "Chapters on Labor: Chapter I," *JUL* VI, no. 3 (1885), 998.
[144] On virtue and commerce, see Chapter 5.

share of the leisure which the inventions of the age permit."[145] Industrial production made some work less attractive, and increased both the appeal and possibility for enjoying free time.

Yet their lived reality remained long hours and low wages. The problem, according to labor republicans, was political not technological. Workers did not control property and thus did not control the impact of labor-saving technologies on their time, activity, and standards of living. Here is where cooperation entered as a solution. As Terence Powderly put it in an address to the General Assembly of the Knights of Labor,

> The machine must become the slave of the man, instead of keeping the man in attendance on and subordinate to the machine. A plan of co-operation through which the workingman may control the machine he operates must one day supercede the present system.[146]

Powderly's point was that workers could only benefit from machine production if they controlled the wealth it produced. The major benefit would be greater wealth with fewer hours of labor. As another Knight put it,

> At this rate, then, three and a half hours work would be sufficient to provide him with as much as he receives now for ten hours' work.... If all men ... were their own employers they would naturally benefit by the amount of wealth they produced, but our present wages system permits employers to absorb all the wealth produced, with the exception of a bare subsistence given to the laborer.[147]

The basic reason why cooperative production was linked to free time was that it would allow workers to "absorb" more of the wealth they produced.

Labor republicans worked out this general argument about cooperation and leisure in the language of political economy. Political economy was important because, as an increasingly authoritative discourse, it appeared to say that their project was impossible. For instance, eight-hours legislation was one of the dominant demands of the nineteenth-century labor movement as a whole, and of labor republicans in particular, because it was a first step to reclaiming control over their time.[148] One important argument in favor of this legislation, made famous by Ira Steward, who founded the Boston Eight Hour League, was the seeming paradoxical claim that "a reduction of hours is an increase in wages."[149] Prevailing political economy suggested this was impossible. There was a fixed wage fund, which limited the level of wages anyhow. But more to the point, reduced hours at a given wage meant lower total wages, pure and

---

[145] The Master Workman of L A 1573, "An Essay on the 'Evils Resulting From Long Hours and Exhaustive Toil,'" 160.
[146] Terence Powderly, "Opening Address to General Assembly," *KoL* 1, no. 27 (October 9, 1886).
[147] "Eight Hours a Day," *Labor Leaf* II, no. 2 (November 18, 1885), 2.
[148] Roediger, "Ira Steward and the Anti-Slavery Origins of American Eight-Hour Theory."
[149] A claim found in various of Steward's writings and speeches, especially Steward, *The Eight Hour Movement: A Reduction of Hours Is an Increase of Wages*. Ira Steward, *The Meaning of the Eight Hour Movement* (Boston: Ira Steward, 1868).

Labor Republicanism and the Cooperative Commonwealth

simple. Moreover, fewer hours worked meant less produced overall, and thus a decline in overall wealth; or, if wages *did* increase then profits declined, which would reduce incentives to produce wealth, again reducing aggregate wealth.[150] Steward had a number of responses to this argument, some of which led in the more limited direction of arguing that higher wages raised aggregate demand.[151] But the one that most interests us connected the debate about hours and wages to the political economy of cooperation itself.

For Steward, not to mention other leading Knights,[152] maximum hours legislation naturally led to cooperation. "Eight Hours reduction will give [laborers] the time necessary, and other questions will follow,"[153] said Steward. This process of reflection would allow workers to alter their demands. Starting at wanting higher wages they would come to demand the "republicanization of labor" itself.[154] From "the trial of the Eight Hour system ... there will be a call for the Six Hour system" and eventually "with Six Hours a day ... all industries will glide naturally and almost insensibly into Co-operation."[155] If, on the one hand, maximum hours legislation allowed workers to make more wage demands and eventually demand cooperative control, on the other hand, it was only cooperation that would allow this reduction of hours to be fully compatible with increased levels of consumption. Steward spelled out the reasons why:

We are sometimes asked, "whether we can accomplish as much in Eight hours as in Ten hours?" To this we reply: "Perhaps not, the first day, or even the first year, in some case; though in time, as inventions multiply, we are sure to produce very much more." But whether we can or cannot is not the question to ask us; it is whether we can *get* as much of what we *do* produce?[156]

In other words, because cooperation was based on workers controlling the full, or at least "fair," value of what they produced, it would take them fewer hours

---

[150] Steward identifies these as the main objections of his adversaries. Steward, *The Meaning of the Eight Hour Movement*.
[151] Steward, "Poverty," 428; Ira Steward, "A Reduction of Hours an Increase of Wages," in *A Documentary History of American Industrial Society*, ed. T. Fly (Norman: The Arthur H. Clark Company, 1910), 284–301; Montgomery, *Beyond Equality*, 249–60; Roediger, "Ira Steward and the Anti-Slavery Origins of American Eight-Hour Theory." On the development of underconsumptionist theories, and their adoption by the American Federation of Labor and other social reformers, see Currarino, *The Labor Question in America*, 60–85. Although some labor republicans eventually took the argument in this direction, it is a mistake to make it the whole of their view, as Glickman does. Lawrence Glickman, *A Living Wage: American Workers and the Making of Consumer Society*, (Ithaca: Cornell University Press, 1997), 93–128. See also, Alex Gourevitch, "Review: Rosanne Currarino's the Labor Question in America: Economic Democracy in the Gilded Age," *Historical Materialism* 21, no. 2 (2013), 179–90.
[152] Powderly, *Thirty Years of Labor 1859–1889*, 471–525; Jelley, *Voice of Labor*, 228–37; McNeill, *The Labor Movement*, 470–82.
[153] Steward, *The Eight Hour Movement: A Reduction of Hours Is an Increase of Wages*, 12.
[154] Steward, "Poverty," 434.
[155] Steward, *The Meaning of the Eight Hour Movement*, 15.
[156] Ibid., 9.

to earn substantially more than they earned during the longer hours of the current system. In *this* sense, fewer hours meant higher wages.

In fact, the shift to cooperation would ultimately make the standard of "higher wages" obsolete, as the worker would no longer be asking a separate employer to pay him more. As one Knight put it, the point of the cooperative organization of work was "to *change* the *form* of *demand* from *increase* of *wages* to *participation in profits*."[157] Or again, on William Sylvis' account, the change in demand was a change of principle: "[W]e will not only secure a fair standard of wages, but all the profits of our labor."[158] In their support, labor republicans regularly observed the enormous wealth of their society as proof that labor was already productive enough to meet everyone's needs at an ample level, *even if* hours were reduced.[159] If anything, they thought, it was surprising that anyone, especially students of political economy, thought it so difficult to both increase leisure time and consumption levels.

The mistake of mainstream political economy, according to labor republicans, was that it accepted some contingent social facts as necessary and then built its laws out of those facts. As the author of 'Sketches of Political Economy' wrote:

Although political economy, in its restricted sense, treats only of the laws which govern the production, distribution and consumption of wealth, we shall have frequent occasion to revert to the consideration of subjects previously mentioned.[160]

The "subjects previously mentioned" were the nature of human liberty and the role of property regimes in advancing or restraining that liberty.[161] In a sense, labor republicans thought it was true that reducing hours could not increase wages *if*, in the "restricted sense" of current political economy, one assumed that the labor contract was free and that political economy only pertained to voluntary transactions in markets. But here was the mistake – political economists had assumed what they could not prove: that the labor contract was free. It was not, and thus the laws of political economy described not the general laws of a system of free exchange but a system of domination.

According to labor republicans, the economic laws of a cooperative commonwealth, based on universal independence not wage-slavery, were different. They were based on the full realization of republican liberty and thus the full value of one's labor. Their political economy aimed to show that a cooperative economy was based on a different system of producing and exchanging value. This use of political economy was an advance over earlier republican

---

[157] Fales, "The Organization of Labor," 558.
[158] Sylvis, "Address Delivered at Buffalo, N.Y., January, 1864," 114.
[159] "A Sketch of Political Economy Chapter I"; "Industrial Ideas Chapter II"; "Chapters on Labor: Chapter V (Continued)"; McNeill, *The Labor Movement*, 475–6.
[160] "A Sketch of Political Economy Chapter I," *JUL*, May 25, 1884, 699.
[161] See especially Chapters 1 and 2 of the Sketch. See also "Industrial Ideas Chapter I"; "Chapters on Labor: Chapter I."

Labor Republicanism and the Cooperative Commonwealth

uses. As we saw previous chapter, the early Workies primarily imbued political economy, especially the labor theory of value, with the task of giving scientific expression to the worker's domination. We have already seen that labor republicans accepted this critical power of the labor theory of value. But they added to it the further role of giving a positive account of how a cooperative economy would function. They felt it necessary to demonstrate that a reduction in hours worked did not necessarily entail a reduction in prosperity – that is, a reduction in the ability to enjoy free time. Through this use of political economy, they sought to articulate the logic of a cooperative commonwealth, and to demonstrate how it made possible each laborer's independence by, at once, increasing his control over the work process while also increasing his opportunities not to work.

The primary way the labor theory of value served the argument for cooperation was by explaining why cooperation was instrumentally necessary for expanding the amount of free time available to workers. The defining feature of cooperation was that the worker controlled the value he created. That workers were so productive already meant it would take little time to produce those goods each worker and his family personally needed, leaving much more of the day free. That, for instance, is why for Steward the move from the wages to the cooperative system is not just about higher wages but ultimately a transformation of class relations:

> the simple increase of Wages is the first step on that long road which ends at last in a more equal distribution of the fruits of toil. For Wages will continue to increase until the Capitalist and Laborer are One.[162]

While under the wage-system the worker had to spend the whole day working for another to acquire those goods he needs, under the cooperative system the cooperator would "earn" goods of the same value in a much shorter amount of time. He would thus be a producer *and* consumer, creating wealth and having time and means to enjoy it. Here the labor theory of value, as an account of the time spent working, revealed why cooperative production was necessary to increase leisure time for all workers.

This argument was an essential step in establishing the *value* of independence. Independence, in the form of cooperative work, was an attractive political value in an industrial setting not just because it stood opposed to forms of economic domination, but also because it expanded the opportunities for self-cultivation. This is what the author of "Industrial Ideas" meant when he said

> man requires such surroundings as will enable him to develop and progress. These surroundings should be entirely independent of the good-will or caprice of his fellow men. If it be not so, man cannot be said to enjoy liberty.[163]

---

[162] Steward, *The Eight Hour Movement: A Reduction of Hours Is an Increase of Wages*, 6.
[163] "Industrial Ideas Chapter I," 2085.

If independence now meant the equally interdependent relations of cooperative producers, it found its value in the free development of each individual. That free development occurred not just in exercise of self-governing capacities at work, but also in the freedom to develop the whole range of capacities when at leisure.

Conclusion: The Paradox of Slavery and Freedom Revisited

Over the course of the nineteenth century, the labor republicans developed a novel vision of the cooperative commonwealth. It was novel for being industrial, not agrarian, and for imagining a society of producer cooperatives in which individuals governed themselves at work and cultivated themselves at leisure. This was a new way of conceiving of both the condition of republican liberty and its value as a political ideal. Historians of political thought have noted that the subtraction, addition, and modification of meaning is an inescapable part of putting ideas to use.[164] Absent these conceptual shifts, political ideas remain either irrelevant, vague, or at the very least, incommensurate with the task of persuading actors to act. This chapter has shown us that the labor republicans engaged in this characteristic form of "conceptual innovation."[165] They were, after all, not professional philosophers but political actors, hoping to persuade hundreds of thousands to support their cause in a dynamic and evolving historical situation. If we take a step back, we recall that it was not just the immediate context of the industrial revolution and the different class interpretations of republicanism that shaped labor republican thinking. They also inherited the much longer standing paradox of slavery and freedom and the related effort to universalize republican liberty.

From the standpoint of this paradox, we can gain a new, more global appreciation of the significance of labor republicanism. It was no mere American exception. Instead, it was an attempt to make sense of wage-labor from the standpoint of an established tradition of thinking about freedom and politics. If that tradition provided the basic evaluative ideas, it was the new historical developments – permanent wage-labor, industrial production, class conflict, new juridical and economic discourses – that forced a clarification and evolution of those concepts. Labor republicans did not merely borrow the moral force of the republican contempt for slavery. They also deepened and modified it by developing an analysis of the structural and personal forms of domination specific to permanent wage-labor. Moreover, by developing the positive argument for cooperative labor, they gave an answer to how republican liberty could be universalized in industrial conditions, not just as a nostalgic

---

[164] Quentin Skinner, *Visions of Politics Vol. 1: Regarding Method* (Cambridge: Cambridge University Press, 2002), 103–44.
[165] Ibid., 87, 145–57.

negation of those conditions. Finally, in the process of identifying economic independence with cooperative production, they gave a new account of the value of that independence – as a condition that made possible self-cultivating leisure, not just free labor.

Historians of political thought have shown that a standard feature of republican thought has been the idea that "it is only possible to be free in a free state."[166] We might summarize the labor republican contribution by saying that they added the thought that "it is only possible to be free in a free society." Indeed, to labor republicans, a certain kind of defense of the formally "free state" (i.e., constitutionalism, representative government, and legal equality) had become the means by which a few arrogated to themselves the benefits of liberty, converting the universalizing aspirations of earlier republicans into the basis of a new kind of aristocratic privilege. The original promise of political republicanism had been betrayed and, in certain hands, become a "false idea of liberty ... defended by the governing classes!"[167] The paradox of slavery and freedom had been reconstituted under this laissez-faire republicanism.

The labor republicans do not have to have been fully aware of the paradox of slavery and freedom for them to have been part of it. Although sometimes self-conscious that they were part of a grand historical drama,[168] they were just as often concerned entirely with the present. Under the pressures of the moment, labor republicans pushed the republican theory of liberty in unexpected directions. Although their thoughts possessed an internal coherence, they did not have the aims of a system builder beginning from first principles and following out each logical inference. Instead, faced with the fact of industrial wage-labor and the inherited but underdetermined ideal of free labor, labor republicans gradually worked out a series of intermediate steps, regarding the nature of economic domination in industrial capitalism, the role of political economy in analyzing these relations, and the relationship between cooperation, technology, work and leisure. It is only in retrospect that we can reconstruct the coherence as if it were a systematic whole.

At this point, we might be inclined to ask just how universal the labor republican project was. I do not mean how successful it was in practice, but whether it truly sought to eliminate dependent labor. A powerful test of this question lies in their views on women and labor. If women were to perform uncompensated labor for men, then that would leave in place a class of dependent workers, casting doubt on the universality of their vision. A complete study of the role of women in the Knights is beyond the scope of this book,

---

[166] Skinner, *Liberty before Liberalism*, 60.
[167] "Chapters on Labor: Chapter V (Continued)" 1082.
[168] There are numerous references to thoughts like "the whole process of civilization has been to emancipate human beings from the condition of slavery." "Wages Slavery and Chattel Slavery," 702.

but others have done much of the work, leaving us with enough information to draw the following conclusions.[169] It is undoubtedly true that, until the rise of the Knights of Labor, cooperation was a highly masculine ideal, and presupposed that women would serve a subordinate and separate role.[170] The economic independence of men was predicated on the domestic service of women. However, the Knights, although they never shed certain ideas about "true womanhood" and female domesticity, were far more progressive in claiming equal political and economic rights and meaningful public roles for women than any organization of the day, not to mention many subsequent labor organizations.[171] They were the first organization to call for "equal pay for equal work"; they defended female suffrage; they gave women leadership positions within the organization; and they created a bureau of women's work. Women organized their own Knight assemblies and participated in mixed ones; they formed numerous cooperatives and trade unions; and most of the leading feminists of the day, from Mother Jones to Susan B. Anthony, at some point held membership in the Knights.

The Knights even extended their critique of dependent labor to include housework and domestic service. They were the first to organize domestic servants, nearly all of whom were women. Labor papers recognized "'the housekeeping wives of laboring men' as a 'class of people'" whose working days were sometimes harder and longer than those of their paid husbands.[172] The Knights were also committed to educating women as citizens, and their reading rooms and papers promoted key feminist works of the day, such as August Bebel's *Women and Socialism*.[173] They tended to take women seriously as possessing the same "capacities for self-government" as men.

There is little doubt that the Knights labor culture was often masculine and fraternal,[174] that women faced sexism, and this sexism was sometimes destructive to the Knights efforts to make their appeals truly universal.[175] But even a brief glance at some of the Knights' major papers and most significant strikes shows that the logic of their argument was powerful enough not only to draw women to their own, independent action, but also to drive Knights to public

[169] The material for the following discussion is taken from Robert E. Weir, "A Dubious Equality: Leonora Barry and Women in the KOL," in *The Knights Unhorsed: Internal Conflict in a Gilded Age Social Movement* (Wayne State University Press, 2000), 141–60; Levine, *Labor's True Woman*; Levine, "Labor's True Woman: Domesticity and Equal Rights in the Knights of Labor"; Weir, *Beyond Labor's Veil*, 51–55, 180–90.
[170] Leikin, *The Practical Utopians*, 26, 41–46.
[171] Weir, "A Dubious Equality: Leonora Barry and Women in the KOL," 141–60; Levine, *Labor's True Woman*; Levine, "Labor's True Woman: Domesticity and Equal Rights in the Knights of Labor."
[172] Levine, "Labor's True Woman: Domesticity and Equal Rights in the Knights of Labor," 328.
[173] Ibid., 327.
[174] Weir, *Beyond Labor's Veil*, 51–55.
[175] Weir, "A Dubious Equality: Leonora Barry and Women in the KOL."

expressions of support for and pride in the public exercise of power by women. Articles like "What Women Are Doing" described new jobs and social roles for women; "Knights of Labor and Women's Rights" reminded readers of the Knights' support for "equal pay for equal work" and for "equal rights for woman, not only in the field of industry, but of legislation"; "The Present Need of Women" told readers that wage-labor oppressed women too; "Organization For Women" celebrated women's self-organization in strikes and cooperatives; "Women Not Wanted" scorned social conventions not allowing women to go outside unaccompanied by men.[176] One article even noted that women were editing their own bible, based on their own reading and interpretation of the text, which included greater gender equality and sympathy for labor reform.[177] It is also worth recalling support of self-organization and equal rights for women contrasted with the conservative views that employers of women trotted out to, among other things, suppress their participation in strikes and boycotts.[178]

In sum, to the degree Knights *did* share widespread views of women's natural difference, they did *not* tend to think women deserved simply to work for men, and did believe women deserved economic and political independence. The best evidence of the universality of their general message is the degree to which women took it as a sign to act on their own initiative and organize and educate themselves, even against sexist views of some male Knights. Historians who have studied this issue closely have therefore come to the conclusion that, "[t]he Knights' commitment to equal rights inherently challenged conventional notions of domesticity and woman's sphere. Yet the Knights simultaneously asserted industrial reform and social renewal in the name of domestic idealism."[179] These "seemingly contradictory goals" arose from the fact that their arguments about wage-labor and republican liberty were in some tension with an inherited view of "true womanhood."

In all, although not entirely successful in overcoming certain prejudices, labor republicanism was not just some defensive attempt to defend the craft privileges of white male workers. It was well in advance of much public opinion at the time. The attempt to universalize economic independence was, for a time, a serious project with real bite, bringing housewives and carpet-weavers, black plantation workers, and white shoe makers, together in a single organization with the shared purpose of replacing wage-labor with cooperative production.

---

[176] Mary P. Hankey, "What Women Are Doing," *JUL* VII, no. 40 (June 10, 1887), 2430; "Knights of Labor and Women's Rights," *JUL* VII, no. 17 (January 25, 1887), 2246; "The Present Need of Woman"; "Organization for Women," *JUL* VII, no. 19 (January 22, 1887), 2262; "Women Not Wanted," *JUL* VII, no. 14 (November 25, 1886), 2212.
[177] "A Bible for Women," *KoL* 1, no. 34 (November 27, 1886).
[178] Levine, "Labor's True Woman: Domesticity and Equal Rights in the Knights of Labor," 327.
[179] Ibid., 330–31.

Coda: From Freedom to Virtue

If labor republicans appealed to republican liberty to argue for profound social change, then we should recall that the concept did not always generate such a transformative vision. It is important to mark the difference. Recall from Chapter 1 that the plebs of ancient Rome claimed their freedom in the form of basic concessions. Their *libertas* was defensive, aimed at restricting the most arbitrary forms of power, not offensive, in the sense of radically altering social relations. Of course, to claim this minimal liberty they engaged in numerous offensive actions, most famously the "secessions" of the fifth and fourth centuries BC. It is no stretch to say that when plebeian soldiers "seceded" or fled Rome instead of fighting its wars, they were engaging in some of the earliest recorded general strikes. Livy claimed this withholding of military labor nearly brought down the Roman republic more than once.[180] But the resultant victories were mostly defensive: representation through the tribune, abolition of debt-bondage and basic procedural protections from the magistrates. As one historian of political thought puts it, "for Livy, the tribunes are initially a sort of shield, a largely protective weapon – not a sword, a primarily offensive weapon."[181]

The original bequest of Roman political theory therefore comes across as rather modest. The plebs were mostly "satisfied with their liberty consisting primarily in the persons and powers of the tribunes and were not terribly interested in moving onto the highest levels of the *cursus honorum* or attaining a more proactive role in shaping their own collective destiny."[182] A constitutional balance between given social orders guaranteed non-domination. This way of thinking about freedom presupposed a premodern social ontology in which society was formally constituted as separate orders. Recall from Chapter 1 that this is why plebs worried about "the arbitrary power of an order in Roman society, an order with immense material and coercive power that would be otherwise unchecked."[183] Republican liberty was compatible with radical inequality and strict hierarchy precisely because plebs just sought a space free from arbitrary rule by their superiors.[184]

As in many other areas of political theory, Machiavelli inaugurates the reconfiguration of these inherited ideas by moving in the direction of a more "offensive" republicanism. On the one hand, in his commentaries on Livy, Machiavelli adopts the classical social ontology. He says "since in every republic there is an upper and a lower class, it may be asked into whose hands it is best to place the guardianship of liberty."[185] One answer, says Machiavelli, is

---

[180] Livius, *The History of Rome, Vol. 2*, book 1.
[181] Kapust, "Skinner, Pettit and Livy: the Conflict of the Orders and the Ambiguity of Republican Liberty," 393.
[182] Ibid., 397.
[183] Ibid., 398. See also discussion in Chapter 1.
[184] This is the force of Kapust's critique of Skinner and Pettit. Ibid. 389–98.
[185] Niccolo Machiavelli, *The Discourses*, trans. Leslie J. Walker (New York: Penguin Classics, 1998), 115.

that "in the former there is a great desire to dominate and in the latter merely the desire not to be dominated."[186] Taken in isolation, this quotation, which neo-republicans have used,[187] reproduces the defensive picture of republican liberty. But we know that Machiavelli also showed more than just sympathy for the "populares" against the "ottimati," he sometimes supported quite violent, quasi-revolutionary claims by the poor against privilege.[188] The liberty of the people here started to mean the conquest of social and economic power, not formal protections.

Machiavelli's world, however, remains a society of orders. Freedom is either something asserted by lower orders against the upper class, or the product of the clash of orders, but it does not describe the same condition for all. It is only with the reorganization of society into formally free individuals that the independence of each citizen could be conceived as something uniform, equally and universally owed to all. Only then can we imagine someone like William Sylvis looking forward to the day in which "Capitalist and Laborer are One."[189] As we have seen, the constitution of society as a body of formal equals is also the historical precondition for the rise of new relations of structural and personal domination against which labor republicans presented their cooperative alternative. Labor republicans claimed their liberty in a fluid, rather than static, social order in which everyone was at least nominally recognized as equally free.

Importantly, labor republicans did not see themselves as making an abstract moral appeal to their betters but as making a demand for practical solidarity among all those members of the dependent, laboring class. The theory of the cooperative commonwealth was in this sense intrinsically connected to a specific sociopolitical practice: that those denied liberty seize it for themselves. Here was the full shift from a "defensive" to "offensive" conception of republican liberty. The transformation of society required forms of social and political cooperation. Such collective action was only possible if workers developed and exercised certain qualities in themselves. They needed not just a conception of liberty but a sense of virtue.

---

[186] Ibid., 116.
[187] Skinner, "The Republican Ideal of Political Liberty," 292–309.
[188] See especially Yves Winter's superb essay. Yves Winter, "Plebeian Politics: Machiavelli and the Ciompi Uprising," *Political Theory* 40, no. 6 (November 8, 2012), 736–66. Also McCormick, "Machiavelli against Republicanism: On the Cambridge School's 'Guicciardinian Moments,'" 615–43. For a different appraisal of the redistributive element in Machiavelli see Nelson, *The Greek Tradition in Republican Thought*, 49–86.
[189] Steward, *The Eight Hour Movement: A Reduction of Hours Is an Increase of Wages*, 6.

5

Solidarity and Selfishness

The Political Theory of the Dependent Classes

> The Knights have learned that they are powerless to accomplish anything individually, and so labor for their whole class. It is the correct idea – Solidarity. It will sweep all systems based on individual selfishness out of existence.
>
> Maud, Breaking the Chains[1]

In 1826, Langdon Byllesby wrote, "history does not furnish an instance wherein the depository of power voluntarily abrogated its prerogatives, or the oppressor relinquished his advantages in favour of the oppressed."[2] A year later, Byllesby's fellow Worky, William Heighton, explained the formation of the Working Men's Party of Philadelphia on the same grounds. Workers "are beginning to discover, that FROM THEMSELVES ALONE, ALL their help must come."[3] Throughout the nineteenth century, labor republicans would return to this political sentiment. In 1865, William Sylvis reminded his audience of iron-molders that "all popular governments must depend for their stability and success upon the virtue and intelligence of the masses … tyranny is founded upon ignorance, and liberty upon education."[4] If popular governments required an educated and virtuous public, it was the working majority's task to organize and educate itself. Sylvis continued, "without an effort on the part of the masses themselves, their condition must forever remain the same … an effort to be successful must be a united one."[5] Two decades later, the anonymous author of "Industrial Ideas" in the *Journal of United Labor* wrote, "let us not boast of liberty if we require politicians to advise us, governments to tax us, bosses in order to produce, merchants to exchange our products. If we are slaves, we must learn to

---

[1] Gantt, "Breaking the Chains: a Story of the Present Industrial Struggle," 99.
[2] Byllesby, *Observations on the Sources and Effects of Unequal Wealth*, 5.
[3] Heighton, *The Principles of Aristocratic Legislation*, 4.
[4] Sylvis, "Address Delivered at Chicago, January 9, 1865," 129–30.
[5] Ibid., 164.

live without masters. Let us be our own government, our own capitalist, our own employer, or liberty will forever be a delusion-never a reality."[6]

From their earliest incarnation onward, labor republicans married the argument that a free government required virtuous citizens to a belief that workers had to act on their own and the common interest. The political ideal of a "cooperative commonwealth" was inextricably tied to the practice of workers acting together to realize that ideal. There was a simple sociological reason for looking to the dependent worker as the agent that would carry forward the "republicanization of labor."[7] If it was true that the dominating class had an interest in the dependence of propertyless workers, then there was little reason to expect that class to, as Byllesby had put it, "voluntarily abrogate its prerogatives" and create a cooperative commonwealth. The particular interests of the propertied ran against the general interest in universal republican liberty. It was only "from themselves alone," as Heighton put it, that dependent workers could possibly hope for independence.

The self-confident, even triumphant, register in which labor republicans made their appeals concealed a deep unease. If the dominant class was suspect because its self-interest prevailed over public virtue, there was good reason to doubt that anyone would act virtuously. Why think the workers had any better chance of publicly spirited action? Experience only confirmed the worry. Looking back on the failures of post-Civil War labor organizing, one Knight of Labor wrote, "in all the efforts of the past to organize labor, the spirit of selfishness has predominated. A lack of unity has prevailed, a want of confidence in each other, a determination to be bell-sheep, or no sheep at all." This lack of unity was a political failure, a failure to produce the bonds of solidarity that would forge workers into citizens. The Knight continued, we must

> banish forever the spirit of selfishness from their minds, sweep it out of their assemblies, and to unite together ... to stand a solid compact body ... to feel that our brother's weal is our weal, and our brother's woe is our woe ... then will we be able to direct and control legislation in the interests of labor; to grade the wage system so that eight hours shall constitute a day's labor; to own our own factories, mills and work-shops, build railroads and ships, mine our own coal ... and break the back of these rings and monopolies that are now grinding us to the earth.[8]

Corruption of public spirit by "the spirit of selfishness" was a long-standing republican worry, here applied to labor's inability to act collectively. Selfishness plagued not just the dominators but the dominated, keeping society in a state of corruption and servitude. Yet labor republicans knew that they could not, in a classical vein, simply oppose virtue to self-interest. They recognized that political life had to be based on a "realistic" sense of individual motivation. In

---

[6] "Industrial Ideas Chapter II," 2098.
[7] Steward, "Poverty," 434.
[8] Nicholas O. Thompson, "'An Important Question,'" *JUL* II, no. 3 (July 15, 1881), 127.

response to this challenge, the Knights and their predecessors felt the need to develop a way of thinking about virtue as something neither absolutely counterposed to self-interest nor simply assimilated to it.

Out of this practical demand emerged a new way of thinking about virtue. Labor republicans started their reasoning from the decidedly non-ideal circumstances of their own industrial society, rather than from the standpoint of the ideal republic. Their analysis of these social conditions led them to a point of connection between interest and virtue: the particular interests of dependent workers in this society were potentially identical with the general interest in universal republican liberty. But labor republicans also knew that various obstacles stood in the way of workers acting on that shared interest, which was why, though it was a "realistic" basis for collective action, this action would not spontaneously arise. As a consequence, they came to see virtue as the habits of solidarity required to act collectively in the relevant ways. Moreover, they sought to find institutional forms and educational processes through which each individual could acquire these habits. In all, they identified the politics of virtue with the practices of self-organization and self-education through which workers acted collectively to transform society.

To understand what is new and important in this way of thinking, we must first remind ourselves of a few features of scholarly debate about civic virtue. Although what follows is only be a brief sketch of the main themes, it is sufficient for our purposes. We see that there are three main assumptions that structure current scholarship: (1) that civic virtue is primarily about preserving free institutions; (2) that inculcating virtue mainly involves coercive socialization by the state; and (3) that there is an inescapable dialectic of virtue and commerce. As we then see in the second part of this chapter, the labor republican approach to civic virtue challenges each of these assumptions and presents us with a different way of thinking about the role of civic virtue in modern society.

Civic Virtue in Theory and History

In political philosophy, the concept of civic virtue is possibly even more controversial than republican liberty. That is because the politics of virtue has generally been associated with coercive socialization into shared traditions and institutions. Such coercion is thought to be at odds with modern individualism and commercial activity. These worries about civic virtue break down into three interrelated elements: (1) the politics of virtue is essentially conservative; (2) it is, anyhow, necessarily coercive; and (3) civic virtue is inconsistent with modern commerce.

First and Second Worries: Coercive Socialization and the Preservation of Free Societies

Civic virtue is usually understood as the "qualities of character that equip citizens to share in self-rule," of which the most important is "the willingness to put the common good above our private interests."⁹ The primary function of civic virtue is that it preserves free institutions from defeat or decay. On this civic republican view, "some bonding between the individual and the community must exist beforehand, otherwise 'citizens' will only participate for instrumental reasons, reasons which have to do with the private rather than the public self."¹⁰ The community must have a preexisting identity to which the citizen is attached and that the state upholds. Purely instrumental attachment to the state, of the kind promoted by commercial, liberal societies, is an inadequate basis for its preservation.¹¹ Institutions will not function properly if citizens do not sustain them for their own sake, and thus the function of civic virtue is to sustain these institutions. As a consequence, republicans say, liberal states that attempt to remain neutral undermine their own stability.

That civic virtue is primarily about preservation of the state's institutions leads to the second thought about coercion. Since public spiritedness itself is always susceptible to corruption, republicans tend to believe that the state must coercively inculcate and maintain virtuous dispositions in its citizens. As Quentin Skinner puts it, "for the republican writers ... the deepest question of statecraft" has always been "how can naturally self-interested citizens be persuaded to act virtuously"?¹² Republican authors have placed "their faith in the coercive powers of the law," which can "force us out of our habitual patterns of self-interested behavior" and "into discharging the full range of civic duties."¹³ Freedom requires free institutions; but free institutions require virtuous citizens; civic virtue is the product of coercive state policy. In his sympathetic survey of modern republicanism, Adrian Oldfield summarizes this position in its most hard-nosed form:

The moral character which is appropriate for genuine citizenship does not generate itself; it has to be authoritatively inculcated. This means that minds have to be manipulated.¹⁴

Other interpreters of the republican tradition might use softer language, but they agree on the basic point. Republicans conventionally insist that there are values and attitudes "for the state to promote" not just "constraint[s] on how the state is to pursue other goals."¹⁵ The state cannot simply be neutral with respect to the

---

⁹ Sandel, *Democracy's Discontent*.
¹⁰ Dagger, *Civic Virtues*, 163. See also Pettit's argument for "the need for civility." Pettit, *Republicanism: A Theory of Freedom and Government*, 246–51.
¹¹ This argument has found particular favor among legal republicans. Sunstein, "Beyond the Republican Revival;" Michelman, "Law's Republic"; Ackerman, *We the People: Foundations*, 3–33.
¹² Skinner, "The Republican Ideal of Political Liberty," 304–05.
¹³ Ibid., 305.
¹⁴ Adrian Oldfield, *Citizenship and Community: Civic Republicanism and the Modern World* (New York: Routledge, 1990), 164.
¹⁵ Pettit, *Republicanism*, 97. See also Viroli, *Republicanism*, 241–270; Maynor, *Republicanism in the Modern World*, 68–89; Richard Dagger, *Civic Virtues*, 17–31; Sandel, *Democracy's Discontent*, 25–54.

goals and qualities of its citizens.[16] The inculcation of virtue is about coercive socialization into the practices and traditions of a particular community and about developing an active concern for the good of that community.

It is no surprise that some scholars associate this politics of virtue with repression, or at least with a deeply conservative mode of politics. The focus on "civility,"[17] "concord,"[18] "civic education,"[19] shared traditions and national cohesion,[20] all smack of a political theory whose aim is not a robust and self-critical political life, but the active preservation of existing institutions and celebration of past deeds.[21] For example, Benjamin Rush, an important figure in early American politics, once said, "I consider it is possible to convert men into republican machines." This "conversion" required recognizing that "every man in a republic is public property. His time and talents-his youth-his manhood-his old age-nay more, life, all belong to his country."[22] Pointing to Rush's comments, the political theorist Don Herzog concludes that, "the republican tradition has an element of hostility to individualism itself, if virtuous citizens are unpleasantly like robots."[23] Critics like Herzog back up these worries by pointing to the actual proposals inspired by this tradition, which all seem to involve the curtailment of individual rights and the coercive enforcement of duties: a national draft or public service, mandatory voter registration, uniform civic education, far-reaching economic regulations and reorganization of city life, even state support for religion.[24]

Worse yet, if republicanism turns its citizens into machines, it is bound to be even more unjust to those not recognized as capable of virtue in the first place. That is why, historically, republican communities have tended both toward the internal exclusion of subject populations and the external domination and colonization of "inferior' peoples."[25] The historian David Roediger once argued

---

[16] Dagger, *Civic Virtues*, 183–87; Oldfield, *Citizenship and Community*, 152–54; Sandel, *Democracy's Discontent*, 3–54.
[17] Pettit, *Republicanism*, 174–202.
[18] Oldfield, *Citizenship and Community*, 23, 163.
[19] Dagger, *Civic Virtues*, 120–25.
[20] Michelman, "Law's Republic"; Sandel, *Democracy's Discontent*, 317–52.
[21] Don Herzog, "Some Questions for Republicans," *Political Theory* 14, no. 3 (August 1986), 486; McCormick, "Machiavelli against Republicanism: On the Cambridge School's "Guicciardinian Moments,'" 619–36; Epstein, "Modern Republicanism, or, the Flight From Substance," 1635. It is worth noting that some conservative theorists *have* seized on these aspects of the theory of civic virtue to defend traditional institutions, like the family and religion. See, e.g., Mary Ann Glendon, ed., *Seedbeds of Virtue: Sources of Competence, Character, and Citizenship in American Society* (Lanham: Madison Books, 1995).
[22] Rush quoted in Herzog, "Some Questions for Republicans," 486.
[23] Ibid., 486–7. See also Epstein, "Modern Republicanism, or, the Flight From Substance," 1635–36.
[24] Maynor, *Republicanism in the Modern World*, 174–202; Dagger, *Civic Virtues*, 117–74. For the most far-reaching republican proposals, see Oldfield, *Citizenship and Community*, 156–74; Sandel, *Democracy's Discontent*, 329–51.
[25] On the American example of this dynamic, see Aziz Rana, *The Two Faces of American Freedom* (Cambridge, MA: Harvard University, 2010), 20–175. See also recent discussions

that it was just this kind of thinking that led nineteenth-century white workers to identify their right to free labor as a racial privilege: "[I]t was not difficult to move toward considering the proposition that Black oppression was the result of 'slavishness' rather than slavery. White revolutionary pride could thus open the way for republican racism."[26] The nominally universal ideal of free labor runs aground on the particularism of a theory of virtue that holds only some are fit for freedom.

Republicans will reply that their liberal critics have no alternative theory for how to maintain support for their regimes. Their liberal regimes will degenerate into just the despotisms they fear.[27] But there is no need to go any further here. The contours of debate are clear enough. Both as a view of history and as a matter of political theory, republicans and their critics tend to share the two assumptions that civic virtue has primarily a preservative function and that it is inculcated through coercive socialization by the state. Scholars differ as to whether these are good or bad things and what conclusions we can draw from history.

The Third Worry: The Dialectic of Virtue and Commerce

Labor republicans have played little role in scholarly debates about these first two issues, but they have garnered more attention when it comes to the third: the relationship of virtue to commerce. J. G. A. Pocock set the terms of the historiographic debate with his famous claim that the "dialectic of virtue and commerce was a quarrel with modernity."[28] For the ancients, virtue could only be cultivated under conditions of arms-bearing, landed proprietorship and quasi-permanent military mobilization. An economy based primarily on agriculture and inherited land ownership made possible a stable personality "who affirms his being and his virtue by the medium of political action."[29] Modern trade and finance introduced fluid forms of property, redirecting energy to money-making and to social relationships based on temporary agreements, not long-standing social ties. Opinion – rather than independent thought – grounded judgment, generating a "chaos of appetites, productive of dependence and loss of personal autonomy, flourishing in a world of rapid and irrational change."[30] In the modern period, the substitution of a politics of virtue for "a more modern and more realistic sense of political behavior" based on the free play of

---

about Tocqueville's defense of French imperialism in Algeria. Jennifer Pitts, "Republicanism, Liberalism, and Empire in Post-Revolutionary France," in *Empire and Political Thought*, ed. Sankar Muthu (Cambridge: Cambridge University Press, 2012), 261–91.

[26] Roediger, *The Wages of Whiteness*, 35. Roediger went much too far in making his point, but he does articulate the objection with the most gusto. For a more balanced treatment of race and empire in the republican tradition see Rana, *The Two Faces of American Freedom*, 20–175.

[27] Dagger, *Civic Virtues*, 108; Skinner, "The Republican Ideal of Political Liberty," 301–06; Oldfield, *Citizenship and Community*, 164.

[28] Pocock, *The Machiavellian Moment*, 546.

[29] Ibid., 550.

[30] Ibid., 486.

interests "marked an end of the classical conception of politics."[31] On this narrative, the only remaining scholarly question becomes when modern commerce overtook classical virtue.[32] Liberal scholars tell a similar story but in a less nostalgic tone. They have reconstructed "political arguments for capitalism before its triumph,"[33] a "politics, not of duty but of happiness, not of frugality but of opulence,"[34] and a defense of humanitarian tolerance against the "ferocity of the ancients."[35] But regardless of the value put on the narrative of decline, it is essentially one of epochal confrontation between virtue and interest, glory and peace.

Michael Sandel has argued that labor republicans fit this narrative and there is evidence to support his view. For instance, we can find Terence Powderly arguing that maximum hours legislation is necessary because,

> we further hold that intelligence and virtue in the sovereignty are necessary to a wise administration of justice, and that as our institutions are founded on the theory of sovereignty in the people, in order to their preservation and perpetuity, it is the imperative duty of Congress to make such wise and just regulations as shall afford all the means of acquiring the knowledge requisite to the intelligent exercise of the privileges and duties pertaining to sovereignty.[36]

Powderly and others[37] argued that without leisure time to study politics, workers could not possibly acquire this "intelligence and virtue," let alone virtuously exercise their capacities. Sandel interprets such statements as evidence that labor republicans developed a "political economy of citizenship."[38] On Sandel's view, labor republican support for eight-hours legislation and similar measures was about creating the economic opportunities for workers to become competent citizens who can commit themselves to political life rather than to their work.

---

[31] Wood, *The Creation of the American Republic, 1776–1787*, 606.

[32] Unlike Wood and Pocock, for whom the turning point is the end of the eighteenth century, Sandel believes the end of the nineteenth century marks the "decisive moment in America's transition from a republican public philosophy to the version of liberalism that informs the procedural republic." It is when a "political economy of growth and distributive justice" based on neutrality and self-interest and supercedes a "political economy of citizenship" based on the cultivation of virtue. Sandel, *Democracy's Discontent*, 200.

[33] Albert O. Hirschman, *The Passions and the Interests: Political Arguments for Capitalism before Its Triumph* (Princeton, NJ: Princeton University Press, 1996).

[34] David Wootton, "Introduction: the Republican Tradition: From Commonwealth to Common Sense," in *Republicanism, Liberty, and Commercial Society, 1649–1776*, ed. David Wootton (Stanford: Stanford University Press, 1994), 39.

[35] Paul Rahe, "Antiquity Surpassed: the Repudiation of Classical Republicanism," in *Republicanism, Liberty, and Commercial Society*, ed. David Wootton (Stanford: Stanford University Press, 1994), 236–41. Recall, too, Judith Shklar's contrast "between cruel military and moral repression and violence, and a self-restraining tolerance." Judith N. Shklar, *Ordinary Vices* (Cambridge, MA: Harvard University Press, 1995), 5.

[36] Powderly, *Thirty Years of Labor 1859–1889*, 88.

[37] Sylvis, "Address Delivered at Chicago, January 9, 1865," 129–30.

[38] Sandel, *Democracy's Discontent*, 123–25.

On this interpretation, the "last great act of the Renaissance"[39] was not the creation of the American Constitution, with its interest-based vision of political motivation, but rather the defeat of the Knights of Labor. They were the last to campaign on behalf of classical virtues against the tide of liberal-capitalist triumphalism.[40] In their wake, an entirely different set of virtues, centered on working and earning, replaced classical virtue. As Judith Shklar, much more sympathetic to this historic shift, once summarized it, a "vision of economic independence, of self-directed 'earning,' as the ethical basis of democratic citizenship took the place of an outmoded notion of public virtue ... we are citizens only if we earn."[41]

Although it can muster some evidence in its favor, this interpretation suffers from straightforward difficulties, beginning with the fact, observed in the previous chapter, that labor republicans did not object to the production and accumulation of wealth. They celebrated leisure and consumption not merely for their political uses but in themselves, as opportunities for self-cultivation. And while they believed an active and virtuous citizenry was necessary to keep officials in check, they gave no pride of place to public life nor did they see the world of work and consumption as mere base necessity but as a site for the experience of freedom itself. Moreover, they did not neutrally affirm political "participation" as a good in itself, the way civic republicans like Sandel have done. Labor republicans supported only particular kinds of political engagement – those of instrumental value to their reform project.

Perhaps, then, given their favorable view of consumption and leisure, labor republicans were the opposite of what figures such as Pocock and Sandel believe. Perhaps they were using an inherited language to affirm the values of bourgeois life? If labor republicanism was not so much driven by classical anxieties about luxury but rather by the quest for middle-class respectability, then it would fit with a different scholarly paradigm for interpreting the relationship between virtue and commerce. On this "liberal beginnings" view, virtue and commerce were not starkly opposed historically. Instead, republican language was the "chrysalis" in which liberal ideas and practices were born. As two scholars put it, "liberalism as we know it was born from the spirit of republicanism, from attempts to adapt republicanism to the political, economic, and social revolutions of the eighteenth century and the first decades of the nineteenth."[42] We saw one version of this argument in Chapter 2, in the birth of a laissez-faire republican defense of freedom of contract, but the interpretation can also be applied to the development of the concept of virtue. Scholars say that thinkers such as Adam Ferguson and Adam Smith used republican language, but for the purposes of giving new value to – as well

---

[39] Pocock, "Review: Virtue and Commerce in the Eighteenth Century," 120.
[40] Sandel, *Democracy's Discontent*, 197–200.
[41] Shklar, *American Citizenship*, 67.
[42] Katznelson and Kalyvas, *Liberal Beginnings*, 4.

as expressing anxiety about – market competition and its requisite virtues.⁴³ The market – rather than the polis – became the site of agonistic struggle and thus the display of virtues. Scholars have assembled numerous examples that support this "liberal beginnings" interpretive paradigm.⁴⁴ For instance, the historian of political thought Isaac Kramnick observes how in seventeenth- and eighteenth-century England, "the middle class wrapped itself in [a] new notion of virtue," in which "corrupt political man" was contrasted "with virtuous and productive economic man."⁴⁵ As Joyce Appleby showed, these ideas carried over into the capitalist transformation of early America.⁴⁶ But does this interpretation fit labor republicanism?

Undeniably, labor republicans spoke a language that bled into the middle-class moral reform projects of the late nineteenth century. Ira Steward argued that "habits of thought and observation have not been cultivated"⁴⁷ because the "operative or mechanic employed by a corporation fourteen hours a day"⁴⁸ has no opportunity to do so. When identifying the specific "habits of thought and observation" denied to the worker, he does not, like a classical republican, focus exclusively or even mainly on the virtues of public life:

> His labor commences at half-past four in the morning, and does not cease until half-past seven, P.M. How many newspapers or books can he read? What time has he to visit or receive visits? to take baths? to write letters? to cultivate flowers? to walk with his family?⁴⁹

Taking baths, cultivating flowers, and walking with one's family are not exactly heroic acts of selfless devotion to the common good. They are minimal requirements of social respectability, the habits and manners of one who hopes to escape what Adam Smith called the dreaded invisibility of poverty.⁵⁰ These are the virtues required to make a decent public appearance, not an excellent one. Steward sounds here like one of Kramnick's anxious middle-class aspirants, worried about corruption from below as much as from above, and

---

⁴³ Ibid., 18–87.
⁴⁴ See the account Kalyvas and Katznelson give of Madison and Paine's role in using republican language to make toleration an important virtue. Katznelson and Kalyvas, *Liberal Beginnings*, 109–14. The revaluation of wealth in the republican tradition has been convincingly traced back to the early modern Italian city-states, where it would be quite odd if a group of bankers and merchants had signed up to classical republicanism only to criticize their own commercial activities. Jurdjevic, "Virtue, Commerce, and the Enduring Florentine Republican Moment: Reintegrating Italy into the Atlantic Republican Debate."
⁴⁵ Isaac Kramnick, "Republican Revisionism Revisited," *The American Historical Review* 87, no. 3 (June 1982), 629–64, 663.
⁴⁶ Appleby, *Capitalism and a New Social Order*. See also Appleby's account of Jefferson and the use he makes of republican views of virtue to celebrate commercial farming. Appleby, "The 'Agrarian Myth' in the Early Republic," 253–76.
⁴⁷ Steward, *The Eight Hour Movement: a Reduction of Hours Is an Increase of Wages*, 9.
⁴⁸ Ibid., 7.
⁴⁹ Ibid., 4–5.
⁵⁰ Adam Smith, *The Theory of Moral Sentiments* (Indianapolis: Liberty Fund, 1976), 50.

Solidarity and Selfishness
147

celebrating the private virtues of prudent self-control and moderation. Steward moralistically derided the way workers indulged "frequently in the most debasing amusements," and thought that a great benefit of limiting hours of labor was that it "gives time and opportunity for the ragged – the unwashed – the ignorant and ill-mannered, to become ashamed of themselves and their standing in society."[51] Moreover, other labor republicans, most famously Powdely himself, seemed to be single-mindedly obsessed with temperance,[52] on the grounds that alcohol destroyed family harmony and personal character. What clearer sign that the Knights were deploying the language of virtue in the service of bourgeois morality?

Some historians have indeed interpreted labor republicanism in this light.[53] Lawrence Glickman argues that, by the end of the nineteenth century, a kind of republican, "producerist" argument for eight hours and the full fruits of one's labor became a liberal, "consumerist" demand for private leisure time and acquiring the necessary income to enjoy it.[54] Reformers mainly aimed at cultivating those virtues associated with the appropriate use of one's leisure time.[55] Steward and Sylvis's heirs – such as the later George McNeill, George Gunton, and even Samuel Gompers – gradually modified the republican critique of wage-labor to accommodate this rise of middle class values. They retreated from trying to control the workplace itself. Instead, they turned ideas about the economic basis of active citizenship into an argument for material comfort, and redefined virtue as those qualities required to consume, rather than act, well. This group made middle-class respectability, with its concomitant scorn for those unable to work themselves out of poverty, the main goal for the laboring classes.[56] The relevant virtues of the citizen became, on the one hand, hard work and discipline, and on the other hand, temperance, modesty, care for family life, fidelity to one's union, and commitment to the nation.[57]

---

[51] Steward, "A Reduction of Hours an Increase of Wages."
[52] Weir, *Beyond Labor's Veil*, 212–14. Over the course of the 1880s, Powdely tried to drive the Knights closer to groups such as the Women's Christian Temperance Union, whose leading figure, Frances Willard, frequently appeared in the *Journal* after 1886.
[53] Grob, *Workers and Utopia: A Study of Ideological Conflict in the American Labor Movement, 1865–1900*; Glickman, *A Living Wage*.
[54] Glickman, *A Living Wage*, 24–29. This is to a degree also Roediger's view of Steward. Roediger, "Ira Steward and the Anti-Slavery Origins of the Eight Hour Theory."
[55] Ibid.
[56] See also Currarino, *The Labor Question in America*. Currarino's view is that labor and social reformers such as Gunton, Gompers, and Jane Addams, along with a new wave of professional economists, *expanded* the conception of citizenship by defining it with respect of economic participation in social life. Middle class living standards were part of the rights of citizenship, not a shift from those concerns.
[57] Glickman argues that this "consumerist" turn in the argument for eight hours and higher wages gradually transformed the demand for "full fruits of one's labor" into a "living" or "fair" wage, and that the latter eventually became associated with an "American standard of living." Recent immigrants, such as Chinese and Southern and Eastern Europeans, who failed to demand higher wages and more leisure time were frequently dismissed, on this account, as lacking virtue and

Here we have a classic case of "liberal beginnings," in which a republican conception of virtue gradually mediates the development of what becomes a set of liberal virtues. The orientation toward private life and the satisfaction of subjectively determined needs overtakes an emphasis on participation and the common good.

But the labor republicans, though they did argue for many of these things, were neither the last act of the Renaissance nor the first act of consumer society. On the one hand, although they did employ the language of civic virtue, they did not do so to affirm the superiority of a life dedicated to politics. On the other hand, republican ideas about virtue were not merely the sign under which they attempted to turn workers into respectable members of bourgeois society. There were virtues that they wanted to develop and exercise that did not fit with the existing logic of the market.

Beyond Nostalgia and Assimilation: Realizing the Cooperative Commonwealth

The problem with existing interpretive strategies is their failure to connect virtue to the related concept of solidarity and its role in the cooperative commonwealth. If we are to understand what labor republicans thought about the concept of virtue, we first have to appreciate the problem they were trying to solve. We have already seen that labor republicans did not accept the range of opportunities that commercial society made available to them. They did not, as the "liberal beginnings" thesis has it, accept the terms of that society and seek ideological accommodation to it. They wanted to transform it, to replace its existing economic and social logic with a new one. Yet this was no nostalgic project of return to the virtues of the classical city-state; it was a forward-looking project of social and political transformation – about achieving the "freedom yet to come." But creating a cooperative commonwealth was extraordinarily difficult. For one, it required overcoming the forms of social domination, direct state coercion, and political culture arrayed against them. These were the non-ideal circumstances that shaped their thinking.

In response to this challenge, they developed a "political theory of the dependent classes." This theory reversed earlier republican thinking by arguing that the class most likely to act virtuously was not the already independent class of property owners but those dependent workers who had not yet realized

---

undeserving of membership in labor organizations: "[B]y promoting the idea that living standards are a function of race and gender, white male workers maintained that others were incapable of expanding their social needs and consuming respectably. By defining "American-ness" and civilization against the "other," the discourse made consumption as much a terrain of exclusion as production had ever been." Glickman, *A Living Wage*, 191. For different assessments of this consumerist turn see Gourevitch, "Review: Rosanne Currarino's the Labor Question in America: Economic Democracy in the Gilded Age"; Rana, *The Two Faces of American Freedom*, 176–236.

Solidarity and Selfishness

their freedom. The great challenge for this turn to the dependent classes was that labor republicans faced not just external repression but internal divisions among members of that class. Here, for instance, is Ira Steward fretting about the way the laboring classes undermined themselves:

> Think of it, you mechanics, who affect a social distinction between the uncultivated laborer and yourself; on election day the capitalist and the common laborer unite and vote you down, and the rest of the year you and the shrewder capitalist unite and keep down and away from you the "common and unclean" laborer.[58]

The one group who could use their collective power to create a cooperative commonwealth seemed unable to act together as a group. This problem pushed labor republicans to develop a way of thinking about virtue as a form of solidarity that workers inculcated in themselves, through their own self-organization and education, rather than via the coercive apparatus of the law. Although it involved a critique of "selfishness" and a thoroughgoing attempt to sculpt the passions and ideas of workers, labor republicans never understood the project of inculcating virtue as one in conflict with each worker's self-interest – especially the worker's fundamental interest in economic independence. Instead, virtue was conceived as the habits of solidarity, where solidarity was the willingness to act collectively on the understanding that the individual best advanced his or her own interests cooperatively, in social and political action together with others, rather than competitively, against others. As we shall now see, this way of thinking about virtue cut across the three scholarly assumptions we have mentioned so far. Labor republicans sought to transform not preserve institutions, to cultivate virtue in themselves rather than have virtue coercively inculcated, and saw no fundamental conflict between the economic interests of each worker and virtuous action.

Virtue and Solidarity

Let us begin with the "political theory of the dependent classes." If we start there, we can understand why labor republicans saw civic virtue not as the matter of individuals participating separately and virtuously in the public sphere, but as a form of solidaristic action by members of a specific class.

"The Causes that Ruen Republicks": The Political Theory of the Dependent Classes

The political theory of the dependent classes is an idea we can trace back to the earliest days of the American republic. William Manning must have spoken for many of the discontented debtors, farmers and "mechanicks" of the late eighteenth century when he argued that "the causes that ruen republicks … always arises from the ungoverned dispositions & Combinations of the few, &

---

[58] Steward, "A Reduction of Hours an Increase of Wages," 292.

the ignorance of the Many."⁵⁹ Since the wealthy "few" lived off the dependence of the laboring "many," said Manning, "they are interested in having mony scarse & the price of labour & produce as low as possible."⁶⁰ Such policy "always brings the many Into distress & compels them into a state of dependence on the few for favours & assistance in a thousand ways."⁶¹ This economic dependence, in other words, made "the many" subject to the arbitrary power of the idle "few:" "the advantages the few Receiv from the Scarcity of Money … [is that] it brings the Many into wants & nesecatyes[,] obliges them to Come to them for Justis Mercy & forbairance."⁶² On this view, the ruling few shared a fundamental interest in keeping the many economically dependent on them.

According to Manning, economic condition acted on the sentiments. Since the few enjoy the rare luxury of "ease & rest from Labour," they develop "a sense of superiority" and "look down with two much contempt on those that labour."⁶³ For Manning, the shared interest in unequal dependence produced general dispositions hostile to republicanism.⁶⁴ The few,

cant bare to be on a level with their fellow cretures, or submit to the determinations of Lejeslature whare (as they call it) the Swinish Multitude are fairly represented…& are ever hankering & striving after Monerca or Aristocracy whare the people have nothing to do in maters of government.⁶⁵

This social analysis gave Manning to believe that the idle few had neither an interest in political equality nor the virtue to overcome this self-interest. On the other hand,

the Labourer being contious that it is Labour that seports the hole, & that the more there is that live without Labour … so much the harder he must work, or the shorter he

---

⁵⁹ Manning, "The Key of Liberty," 212. Historians have found strong evidence that the kinds of ideas Manning developed were shared by many of his peers. Some, like those leading the land riots and regulations, may well have been more radical than Manning. See Cotlar, *Tom Paine's America*, 144–60; Merrill and Wilentz, "William Manning and the Invention of American Politics;" Alan Taylor, "Agrarian Independence: Northern Land Rioters After the Revolution"; Ruth Bogin, "Petitioning and the New Moral Economy of Post-Revolutionary America." See discussion in Chapter 3.
⁶⁰ Ibid., 219.
⁶¹ Ibid.
⁶² Manning, "Some Proposals for Makeing Restitution to the Original Creditors of Government," 329.
⁶³ Manning, "The Key of Liberty," 218.
⁶⁴ Of course, Manning is quick to add that "their is a large number in all orders who are true frinds to Liberty," but it is evident that Manning's heart is not in this qualification. In the next sentence he qualifies his qualification, saying "I also believe that a large majority of them are actuated by very different prinsaples." Ibid., 212. It is, nonetheless, important to note that Manning does not believe the professions ought simply to be abolished, but that they should be paid only what any person requires, rather than make off with the majority of labor's products. Ibid., 222–31.
⁶⁵ Ibid., 220.

Solidarity and Selfishness   151

must live, this makes the Labourer watch the other with a jelous eye & often has reason to complain of real impositions.⁶⁶

The laborer's immediate interest in not being exploited, or not working longer than he needed, made him attentive to those conditions that tended to produce dependence. All dependent workers thus had an interest in universalizing independence. The immediate interest in avoiding domination by the few gave the average laborer a further interest in achieving economic equality. However, the great limit on the laboring majority was their ignorance, which was why Manning proposed the creation of a "Sociaty of Labourers"⁶⁷ with its own press.⁶⁸ The latter would educate workers and publicize the actions of officers, while the former would be a way of organizing pressure on republican institutions.

Although he was unknown in his own time, Manning had already outlined the basics of a political theory of the dependent classes. In decades to come, this theory would reappear and grow in popularity.⁶⁹ Various labor republicans would argue that, while the ruling few had an interest in domination, the class of dependent workers had a common interest in economic independence.⁷⁰ Now that republican institutions were understood to require the economic independence of all, not just some, this class interest of workers was also a common interest of all committed republicans. The coincidence of their long-run class interests with the general interests of a republic made workers potentially agents of republican transformation. But certain features of the present, such as ignorance, stood in the way of them developing the relevant virtues of action.

By the 1820s, we see the sharpening of this general idea. For instance, Langdon Byllesby and Thomas Skidmore were especially scathing in their criticism of philanthropic appeals to the rich to redistribute property. Byllesby laments that earlier thinkers "addressed themselves" to members "of society whose wishes and desires were adverse to their plans, or those who had no feelings of personal interest in them."⁷¹ Byllesby then continued with the quotation that opened this chapter: "[H]istory does not furnish an instance wherein the depository of power voluntarily abrogated its prerogative, or the oppressor relinquished his advantages in favour of the oppressed."⁷² Thus when

---

⁶⁶ Ibid., 218.
⁶⁷ Ibid., 248.
⁶⁸ On the rapid growth during the 1790s of a democratic press, with the purpose of disseminating knowledge and politicizing those not used to expressing opinions, see Cotlar's fascinating discussion Cotlar, *Tom Paine's America*, 13–48.
⁶⁹ I have discussed the preceding material in greater detail in my Gourevitch, "William Manning and the Political Theory of the Dependent Classes."
⁷⁰ E.g., Orestes A Brownson, "Brownson's Defence: Defence of the Article on the Laboring Classes," *Boston Quarterly Review* (1840), 1–94; Sylvis, "Address Delivered at Chicago, January 9, 1865"; "Wages Slavery and Chattel Slavery," 702.
⁷¹ Byllesby, *Observations on the Sources and Effects of Unequal Wealth*, 4.
⁷² Ibid., 5.

Byllesby says "the design of the following pages" is "to excite a train of popular reflection, and course of social discussion"[73] he is not making a general "civic" appeal to the public sphere, but is instead addressing that fraction of citizens with an identifiable interest in republican institutions: "[T]he following matter is planned more particularly for the service of those whose labour is the origin of wealth which they do not enjoy."[74] Although a Society of Labourers and a labor press[75] were but a twinkle in Manning's eye, by Byllesby's time workingmen's parties and their labor presses had made their presence felt. Most notable among these first labor presses were *Mechanics' Free Press* (Philadelphia) and *Working Man's Advocate* (New York). When figures such as Heighton defended the formation of "a UNION OF OPERATIONS among Working People" on the grounds that "they are beginning to discover, that FROM THEMSELVES ALONE, ALL their help must come,"[76] they were reaffirming the connection between class interest and virtue.

By 1865, when William Sylvis intoned, "*it is not what is done for people, but what people do for themselves, that acts upon their character and condition*,"[77] these ideas had become a fixed feature of republican thinking. The italicized quotation was originally from a republican tract from 1840 that celebrated the assertion of "popular control over the actions of monarchs"[78] and identified that assertion as itself a process of self-education. Sylvis had now incorporated this "political" republican phrase into an argument for the political capacities of laborers:

Is there any reason why we should not occupy a social position equal to other men? Labor is the foundation of the entire political, social, and commercial structure. Labor is the author of all wealth; it is labor that breathes into the nostrils of inert matter its commercial existence. And yet we are told by the aristocracy – by these sticklers for the divine right to rule the world – that we are only fitted to be the "hewers of wood and drawers of water;" and, therefore, should be kept in constant subjection.[79]

Sylvis' contemporary, Ira Steward, sounded similar notes: "Wealthy people have no interest in contrasting their situation with the poor, for this reason[:] that it is the extreme poverty of the masses, which makes the ease and leisure

---

[73] Ibid., 6.
[74] Ibid., 4–5.
[75] Although, as Cotlar has shown, a democratic press emerged soon after the Revolution, a self-consciously labor press had to wait until the 1820s. Cotlar, *Tom Paine's America*, 13–48.
[76] Heighton, *The Principles of Aristocratic Legislation*, 4.
[77] Sylvis, "Address Delivered at Chicago, January 9, 1865," 169.
[78] Both quotation are taken from Henry Carey, *Principles of Political Economy: Part the Third; of the Causes Which Retard Increase in the Numbers of Mankind, Part the Fourth; of the Causes Which Retard Improvement in the Political Condition of Man* (Philadelphia; London: Lea & Blanchard; John Miller, 1840), 162–63. The line that Sylvis quotes is actually from a republican tract by Laing, which Carey quotes, and which Sylvis most likely read in Carey rather than the original.
[79] Ibid., 111–12.

of the Wealthy possible."[80] In 1885, the anonymous author of "Chapters on Labor" in the *Journal of United Labor*, said much the same: "[T]he workers can hope for nothing favorable at the hands of governments, nor of politicians, nor of statesmen. They must take their own affairs into their own hands and emancipate themselves."[81]

The political theory of the dependent classes was, undoubtedly, something of a rhetorical gesture by men seeking to spur their audience to action. It appealed both to the power and resentment of workers. But it also managed to fuse, in a new way, the social analysis of interests with the political theory of virtue. On the one hand, the theory accepted that self-interest was an inescapable motivation in political life. One could not simply base one's politics on the hope that people would radically suppress their private interests in the name of a virtuous commitment to the common good. Yet, on the other hand, labor republicans argued that the "realistic" analysis of interests gave reason to believe that there could be a connection between partial and general interests. Interest and virtue were not at odds, at least in principle. However, the challenge was that the long-term interest of each person in economic independence was unachievable unless each person recognized that his self-interest was unattainable through individual efforts alone. As Terence Powderly put it, "[t]he condition of one part of our class can not be improved permanently unless all are improved together."[82] But this fact was not always immediately apparent to each actor. The deep problem here was one of practical action, not just rational understanding; of subjective orientations, not just objective social position. A worker's position in the social structure did not in itself guarantee he would act "virtuously," it only gave reason to believe he would. Here was where specifically political virtues mattered, including having the desires, knowledge, and competence required to commit to and advance the shared goals of an organization. After all, if the social analysis was correct, why was it that workers had not yet done what it was already in their interest to do? It turned out virtuous subjective dispositions did not spontaneously arise from within the wage-labor system. They had to be cultivated.

"To See is to Desire ... to Desire is to Struggle": Need and Discontent
Like classical thinkers before them, labor republicans thought that the cultivation of virtue began with sculpting of habit and desire.[83] However, on the classical view, the cultivation of virtue was about eliminating corrupting selfishness and disruptive factionalism so as to ensure the stability of the republic. Labor republicans turned this idea on its head by arguing that the main purpose of sculpting desires was to *produce* "factional" discontent. That, for instance,

[80] Steward, *The Eight Hour Movement: A Reduction of Hours Is an Increase of Wages*, 12.
[81] "Chapters on Labor: Chapter VII" 1119.
[82] Powderly, *Thirty Years of Labor 1859–1889*, 121.
[83] Subheading quotation from Steward, *The Eight Hour Movement: A Reduction of Hours Is an Increase of Wages*, 13.

is what Ira Steward had in mind when he said, "Few ... insist upon more pay now, but they are in competition with the great body of laborers who do not, and who never will, until, in the language of John Stuart Mill, 'a change has been wrought in their ideas and requirements.'"[84] To generate this shift in "requirements," Steward thought it necessary "to make a man feel as keenly as possible, the meanness of his position or of his behavior."[85] Although this might sound like a middle-class reformer trying to shame poor workers into personal programs of moral uplift, it was more radical than that. Instead, as Steward continued, "[t]he masses must be made discontented with their situation, by furnishing them with the leisure necessary to go about and observe the dress, manners, surroundings, and influence of those whose Wealth furnishes them with leisure."[86] McNeill, Steward's protégé, put it more bluntly: the key is "to disturb this class of men from their sottish contentment by an agitation for more wages or less hours, is to lift them up in the level of their manhood to thoughts of better things, and to an organized demand for the same."[87]

For Steward and McNeill, the point was that the radical inequalities of their time had inscribed themselves on the workers' desires and conceptions of need. Long hours of work "robbed [laborers] of all ambition to *ask* for anything more than will satisfy their *bodily* necessities."[88] A Knight of Labor from Detroit complained:

One great evil of the long hours worked is that the man, woman or child at the end of a day's work is often physically incapable of doing anything requiring thought, and we cannot wonder if they seek silly amusements. They will read trashy novels, or go to a variety theatre or a dance, but nothing beyond amusement.[89]

It was unreasonable to ask the overworked to demand more, as their condition left them without time to enjoy it, and habituated many to their position. Workers with a bit of leisure would begin to compare their situation to others and give more open expression to the desire for better housing, clothes, food. This, in turn, would require higher wages and shorter hours to enjoy them. That is why they thought "reducing the hours of labor acts more directly on the habits and thoughts of the people than any other measure heretofore proposed."[90] As workers began to demand more, they would come in contact with society's resistance to satisfying these needs, which would generate discontent.

Labor republicans conceived these new desires rather widely, not just as physical but also cultural needs. In their most romantic moments, labor republicans even thought workers would become guardians of culture and virtue

---

[84] Ibid., 10.
[85] Steward, *The Eight Hour Movement: A Reduction of Hours Is an Increase of Wages*, 11.
[86] Ibid., 11–12.
[87] McNeill, *The Labor Movement*, 472–73.
[88] Steward, *The Eight Hour Movement: A Reduction of Hours Is an Increase of Wages*, 4.
[89] Gnomon, "'Gnomon' and His Critics," *JUL* IV, no. 9 (January 1884), 631.
[90] McNeill, *The Labor Movement*, 472.

against the vulgarian capitalists. For instance, in *Breaking the Chains*, the only novel written about the Knights by a Knight,[91] the author has two Knights, Maud and Harry, attend a production of King Lear. Their rapt enjoyment – "They had read and re-read the play, discussed and studied it, so that they understood every word said and knew what every movement meant... they trudged homeward, oblivious of fatigue, their souls sublimated" – is contrasted with the boredom and status-conscious superficiality of the boorish industrialist and corrupt politician, who spend the play ogling other members of high society – "Their souls being dead to art, the time must be whiled away with inane conversation."[92] The novel is somewhat clunky and didactic, but for that very reason it is most interesting as an insight into the Knights' attitudes about need and cultivation. Here we see their thinking about leisure at its most idealized – more leisure time would, or at least could, be used to develop and enjoy new and refined preferences.

With a taste for the freedom associated with greater leisure, workers would increasingly bridle at their ongoing subjection to employers at work. They would begin to see the advantages of a life in which one enjoyed the full independence of control over all of one's time. They would come to *need* their full republican liberty and demand a cooperative system in which "the Laborer and the Capitalist will be One!"[93] In turn, they would seek out new enjoyments that would reflect this cooperative spirit:

> Men will be stimulated but by higher motives; and stimulated, not so much from the desire of individual aggregations as for public aggregations, because and all others will be benefited therein. The demand for public parks in our great cities, although, perhaps, fostered in a measure by speculators and contractors, has its firm footing upon the common impulse for opportunities for public possessions for general enjoyment.[94]

Objects such as public parks were by their very nature "public aggregations." They could only be produced and consumed as a common good, a public thing, and thus represented a distinct kind of desire appropriate to a person committed to the republican values of cooperation. What began as a demand for higher wages and fewer hours would develop into the need for the benefits of independence itself.

In other words, labor republicans started in the ostensibly private realm of passion and desire because they hoped to denaturalize dependence. They wanted to expose the way in which relations of domination were internalized as conceptions of need. The awakening of desire would alert the individual worker to the limits of his society, thus generating a demand for social

---

[91] For a masterful discussion of the politics of various treatments of the Knights in prose and verse, see Weir, *Beyond Labor's Veil*, 145–230.
[92] Gantt, "Breaking the Chains: A Story of the Present Industrial Struggle," 78.
[93] Steward, *The Meaning of the Eight Hour Movement*, 4.
[94] McNeill, *The Labor Movement*, 476.

change. Again, unlike their classically oriented predecessors, labor republicans hoped to increase discord rather than concord; the virtuous worker was one discontent with his station and subjection. In Steward's pithy summation: "to see is to desire ... to desire is to struggle."[95]

"The People are Reading for Themselves": Self-Education and the Production of Knowledge

But how to direct this discontent at its proper object? Here labor republicans moved from the emancipation of desire to its education. The industrial system not only stunted needs but also produced ignorance and prejudice. Those condemned to long hours could not read or had little access to information, producing an "aristocracy of intellect" appropriate to "monarchical governments" not republican ones.[96] This put the current economy at odds with the cultivation of virtue. Recall Terence Powderly's view that, "intelligence and virtue in the sovereignty are necessary." For this reason, Powderly felt "it is the imperative duty of Congress to make such wise and just regulations as shall afford all the means of acquiring the knowledge requisite to the intelligent exercise of the privileges and duties pertaining to sovereignty."[97] The most important of these regulations was "to ordain that eight hours' labor ... should constitute a day's work."[98]

Importantly, the defense of the eight-hours law was but the starting point for a wider argument about knowledge and education. Having time to study political questions was a necessary, but insufficient, condition for the development of a citizen's competence because, *even with* leisure time, a proper education was hard to come by. Political leaders showed only an instrumental interest in the labor question and often held anti-republican views. When it came to the study of political economy, labor republicans distrusted existing sources:

> The bitter experience of the past has proven that this all important subject is not, nor can it ever, become the business exclusively of the Politician, Statesman or Legislator. But it is and forever must remain by its own peculiar terms, the business and the science of the people everywhere.[99]

The dominant texts of law and political economy only provided intellectual ballast for the current system of "wage-slavery." Moreover, the press generally treated labor organizations unfairly and was frequently seen to be a source of misinformation.[100] A Grand Secretary of the Knights, Robert Layton, warned

---

[95] Steward, *The Eight Hour Movement: A Reduction of Hours Is an Increase of Wages*, 13.
[96] William H. Sylvis, "Aristocracy of Intellect," in *The Life, Speeches, Labors and Essays of William H. Sylvis*, ed. James C. Sylvis (Philadelphia: Claxton, Remsen & Haffelfinger, 1872), 444.
[97] Powderly, *Thirty Years of Labor 1859–1889*, 88.
[98] Ibid.
[99] Robert D. Layton, "Salutatory," *JUL*, October 15, 1881, 156.
[100] E.g., "The True and the False," *JUL* 3, no. 7 (November 1882), 335–336; Weir, *Beyond Labor's Veil*, 152–55, 227–30, 260–67.

Solidarity and Selfishness

that he had "long been impressed with the fact that he who relies upon the newspapers for information will be the worst deceived man that ever lived," backing up his suspicions with evidence that the Pittsburg Daily Dispatch not only misquoted him but invented an entire interview.[101] According to Steward, this was no accident: "Capital, with swift enterprise, can pay for heralding to the ears of ignorance favorite catch-words, while its control of the daily press and party machinery leaves the intelligent workingman, of slender means, in a mortifying minority."[102] This was a common allegation:

> the capitalists, have made millions, with which they have monopolized the means of obtaining news, which they falsify by bogus telegrams, and use other direct means to influence public opinion. They have monopolized the channels of news as their coworkers in capitalism had already monopolized credit, exchange and production.[103]

In short, even if workers had time to acquire the "intelligence" or education expected of sovereign citizens, available educational materials were sorely lacking. Sylvis's "aristocracy of intellect" was reproduced less by formal exclusion from education than by the continual disinformation and misrepresentations promoted by existing sources of knowledge.

If labor republicans could summarize this general mis-education in a single phrase, it was that dominant forms of knowledge failed to give the worker a "true sense of his surroundings."[104] Rather than promote the virtues of solidarity, existing forms of knowledge promoted competition and division. They separated workers by skill and party, by region and creed. Steward believed that the inadequate knowledge of political economy and the political system available through mainstream educational sources meant, "Workingmen ... until educated up to an interest in matters of real importance ... will be found, every election day, in company with master Capitalists, voting down schemes for their own emancipation!"[105] Looking back on failed efforts in the 1860s and 1870s to organize workers into a single, national labor union or party, Powderly remarked:

> Partisan prejudice was at that time strongly bedded in the workingmen, and it required an education, which they had not then received, to enable them to philosophically view the introduction of measures which might one day force them to take action against the party to which they were at that time attached.[106]

If nobody was going to educate workers properly, workers would have to do it themselves.

Here the labor republicans generally, and the Knights of Labor in particular, made a major *practical*, not just theoretical, contribution to republican culture.

---

[101] "The True and the False," 335–36.
[102] Steward, "A Reduction of Hours an Increase of Wages," 292.
[103] "Chapters on Labor VI (Cont)," *JUL* VI, no. 12 (October 25, 1885), 1105–07, 1106.
[104] Ibid., 62.
[105] Steward, *The Eight Hour Movement: A Reduction of Hours Is an Increase of Wages*, 12.
[106] Powderly, *Thirty Years of Labor 1859–1889*, 76–77.

The traditional understanding of a "civic education" was that it was provided by and for the state, a thought at least as old as the early Jeffersonians. The labor republicans, in contrast, pursued a strategy of "self-education." The main role for the state, to the extent that it could be controlled, was certain regulatory limits, such as maximum-hours laws, and some public schooling. But it was up to worker-citizens to provide the actual educational content, through their own institutions. The most important and longest standing of these institutions was the independent labor press. We have seen that, as far back as the 1790s, figures such as William Manning, argued for a cheap magazine, published by a "Sociaty of Labourers," to ensure "the Majority" were "furnished with the meens of knowledge" and that the machinations of the Few were "detected & surprised."[107] The workingmen's parties of the 1820s and 1830s created the first actual labor presses, and labor journalism experienced qualitative growth again after the Civil War. For example, by the 1880s, not only did the Knights of Labor have its official *Journal of United Labor*, but numerous local assemblies published their own, usually cooperatively run, papers, such as Chicago's *Knights of Labor* and Detroit's *Labor Leaf*.[108] Fellow-traveling papers, such as *John Swinton's Paper*, also gave them favorable coverage.

These labor presses provided knowledge and political experience missing from mainstream sources. They were a mix of news, alternative literary culture, organizing advice, official correspondence, and perhaps most importantly, lessons on political economy and cooperation. For instance, the *Journal* not only had its regularly running series of articles and selections on "Co-operation," but also included extracts from famous cooperative thinkers, reports of producers and distributors cooperatives, and serialized lectures, such as the "Sketch of Political Economy," "Chapters on Labor," and "Industrial Ideas."[109] The latter were serious treatments of fundamental questions, drawing on major thinkers, such as Ferdinand Lassalle and John Stuart Mill, and on central concepts, like the labor theory of value. The Journal also coordinated the acquisition of economic data relevant to workers, operating as a kind of de facto bureau of labor statistics. As Theodore Cuno, a New York Knight and first official statistician of the Knights of Labor, put it:

We must inform ourselves upon the condition of the wage-working masses, in order to be enabled to create a healthy public opinion upon the subject of labor, and the justice of its receiving a full and just renumeration. Without reliable facts and figures we cannot proceed with our work of demonstrating, that every one who works for wages is

---

[107] Manning, "The Key of Liberty," 250.
[108] Weir calculates that the number of newspapers overall doubled between 1880 and 1890. Weir, *Beyond Labor's Veil*, 153.
[109] "Sketch of Political Economy" ran from May 25, 1884 to March 25, 1885 (although the last article says to be continued, I could find no record of another installment). "Chapters on Labor" ran from June 10, 1885 to May 25, 1886. "Industrial Ideas" ran from June 10 to September 25, 1886.

Solidarity and Selfishness　　159

robbed of about two-thirds of the value of his labor. Let ever Statistician go to work earnestly. They should endeavor to give me exact figures in regard to.[110]

These papers combined basic information and theoretical education in order to "create a healthy public opinion" among its readers.

Beyond providing information, the labor papers also served to stimulate and develop workers' political capacities. They did so by engaging them in ways that mainstream society did not. For instance, the papers served as fora for public debate and discussion, through letters and published contributions by readers. Each issue of the *Journal*, as well as of many local Knight papers, usually included queries and speeches from local assemblies and individual Knights. They published and answered requests for advice. The general education toward which these presses aimed, then, was not just in facts and theories, but in the development of those "capacities for self-government" that society did not stimulate but on which the cooperative commonwealth would depend. As one Knight put it, "the people are reading for themselves; they are reading labor papers."[111]

The labor press was one among a wide range of experiments in self-education. Sylvis, for instance, argued: "We must erect our own halls wherein we can establish our own libraries, reading- and lecture-rooms, under the control and management of our own men; and we must have time to use them."[112] These reading rooms, lecture circuits, study groups, debating societies, and lending libraries sprang up in numerous local and district assemblies.[113] Powderly noted with pride "the establishment of workingmen's lyceums and reading-rooms"[114] and thought they showed "laboring men" that they "had the same right to study social, economic, and political questions that their employers had."[115] There is no existing study of the content of these reading rooms, which varied by locale, but we know from advertisements in papers and other sources that they included works on political economy, cooperative tracts, labor journals, and literature. For instance, a *Journal of United Labor* advertisement for "how and where to get knowledge" includes information on subscribing to the publications of the Co-operative Newspaper Society in Manchester, England.[116] In *Breaking the Chains*, the author has Maud, the heroine Knight, say the

---

[110] "Statisticians Attention!," *JUL* 2, no. 5 (October 15, 1881), 158.
[111] S. M. Jelley, *The Voice of Labor*, (Chicago: A. B. Gehman & Co., 1887) 363.
[112] Sylvis, "Address Delivered at Buffalo, N.Y., January, 1864," 114.
[113] There is no book-length treatment of the reading rooms and lecture circuits. The best discussion of the educational culture of the Knights is Weir, *Beyond Labor's Veil*, 277–319. See also Fink, *Workingmen's Democracy*, 10–11; Oestreicher, *Solidarity and Fragmentation*, 90–91; Levine, "Labor's True Woman: Domesticity and Equal Rights in the Knights of Labor," 327–28. In my reading of papers like the *JUL*, *KoL*, and *Labor Leaf* just about every issue advertised public lectures and books for sale.
[114] Powderly, *Thirty Years of Labor 1859–1889*, 68.
[115] Ibid., 56.
[116] "How and Where to Get Knowledge," *JUL* 3, no. 8 (November 1882), 369.

following, which is likely a reasonable approximation of many reading room selections: "We have read Adam Smith, Malthus, Ricardo, Carlyle's 'Past and Present,' Henry George, and somewhat of Herbert Spencer, as well as translations of several of Lasalle's political pamphlets."[117] Other works included material on the "woman question," economic pamphlets, and labor histories written by Knights or their sympathizers.[118]

Speeches and lectures were another important practice. In November 1882, the Journal started announcing public lectures that different Knights could provide to any local assembly, and solicited lectures from members on any topic. The announcement for the Journal's new special section on public lectures included the statement "the one thing needed by the wage-workers of America is education upon labor subjects, and especially upon cooperation."[119] The first list included such topics as "co-operation: its advantages and benefits" and "The Mission of the Knights of Labor"[120] and the range of offerings quickly expanded in the following years. As the Knights grew, so did their lecture circuit, both in quantity and subject. For instance, Leonora Barry, who became the highest ranking woman in the Knights of Labor, gave hundreds of lectures on the rights of women, the labor question, and related topics.[121] Knights also promoted lectures by non-Knights, including speeches by a popular land reformer, Henry George, or the famous 1886 tour of two British socialists, Edward Aveling and Eleanor Marx (Karl Marx's daughter).[122]

Of these many experiments with self-education, we must note two things. First, they fit neatly with the general emphasis on independence. Although independence was, in the objective sense, just the lack of material dependence on another's will, it was also understood more robustly to be a condition in which an individual took advantage of that lack of dependence to develop and exercise his or her own abilities. This thought came through in an educational message

---

[117] Gantt, "Breaking the Chains: A Story of the Present Industrial Struggle," 83.

[118] On the former, see the list in Susan Levine, "Labor's True Woman: Domesticity and Equal Rights in the Knights of Labor," 327. Important works by Knights or fellow-travelers include Victor Drury's *Polity of the Labor Movement*, McNeill's *Labor Movement, The Problem of To-day*, Henry George's *Poverty and Progress*, and James Sullivan's *Working People's Rights*.

[119] "Our Lecture Bureau," *JUL* 3, no. 7 (November 1882), 333.

[120] Ibid., 333–35.

[121] On Barry, see Weir, "A Dubious Equality: Leonora Barry and Women in the KOL"; Levine, "Labor's True Woman: Domesticity and Equal Rights in the Knights of Labor." Levine's contrast between Barry and Elizabeth Rodgers, and Leikin's discussion of Fannie Allyn, are both instructional about the often contradictory messages that came out in these lectures and wider roles assigned to women. Levine, "Labor's True Woman: Domesticity and Equal Rights in the Knights of Labor"; Leikin, *The Practical Utopians*, 107–9.

[122] See advertisements in *KoL*, *JSP*, and *Labor Leaf* throughout late-1886. Notably, Aveling and Marx showed up in Chicago during the volatile Haymarket trial, and addressed the dubious legal proceedings in their speeches. Their appearance in Chicago was preceded by threats from employers and the mayor, though these threats turned out to be empty. See the November and December 1886 issues of *KoL*.

that spoke directly to workers, through their own presses, which involved them writing their own speeches and pamphlets, and setting up their own libraries and reading rooms. To think for oneself was part of becoming free from the will of another. And the practice of reading, thinking, and debating was itself part of the education. Second, these educational initiatives were a practical necessity, not just an expression of independence. The natural tendency of most cultural institutions, even under conditions of freedom of the press, was to "foster prejudices rather than cultivate intelligence."[123] Only their own cultural institutions could provide the alternative information and stimulus that could educate workers into a "true sense of their own surroundings"[124] and a full sense of their competence as political actors.

Competition or Solidarity: The Necessity of Self-Organization
Yet the culture of competition against which labor republicans strained was not just the intentional product of journalists or propagandists. It also arose from the institutional conditions of the labor market itself. Labor republicans recognized that, in response to this competitive culture, they had to create a counter-culture of solidarity in order to cultivate the virtues of cooperation. The system of "competition," as they sometimes called capitalism, pitted workers against each other, creating the impression that each person could realize his fundamental interests through his own efforts alone. In developing their argument against this market ethos, labor republicans did not reject the very idea of self-interest, but criticized the way in which the culture of competition misrepresented a worker's interests in the first place. A certain kind of selfishness was in conflict with self-interest. The conceptual move distinguishing selfishness from self-interest is important because it situates them at a particular moment in the development of republican thinking about commerce: it was not the very activity of producing and accumulating wealth that was corrupting, but the historically specific culture of the labor market. In fact, unlike romantic anti-capitalists or austere civic humanists, labor republicans were quite willing to celebrate the production of wealth and the habits of leisure, so long as all enjoyed the benefits.

Labor republicans recognized that there was a certain truth to the culture of competition. Competition among workers was reasonable insofar as workers had no institutionalized way of pursuing their interests together. As Terence Powderly put it, "all who interest themselves in producing for the world's good must be made to understand that their interests are identical."[125] Their interests were identical because their social position meant there was no way for *all* workers to obtain that independence without cooperating. No individual could pursue his own interests fully without pursuing the interests of others, "an

---

[123] Sylvis, "Address Delivered at Chicago, January 9, 1865," 113.
[124] Powderly, *Thirty Years of Labor 1859–1889*, 62.
[125] Ibid., 258–59.

effort to be [individually] successful must be a united one."¹²⁶ Of course, there were various ways in which any particular worker could escape his status as a wage-laborer, but only on condition that he leave others behind, and accept the insecurity of his new social position. If each worker shared a fundamental interest in free labor then it remained the case, as we have seen Powderly say, that "the condition of one part of our class can not be improved *permanently* unless all are improved together."¹²⁷ Labor republicans thus defended the principle of solidarity in the name of self-interest rather than in the name of self-sacrificing virtues. As Steward put it, "we must remember that by an inexorable law of *self-interest*, we are bound to lift up the lowest and most degraded laborer."¹²⁸

How, then, to interpret their critique of "the spirit of selfishness"?¹²⁹ This would appear to be a classic republican argument against self-interest in the name of virtue. However, as the following quotation demonstrates, they were careful to distinguish selfishness from self-interest: "[C]o-operation is based on moral science. It implies the virtues of stability, honor, and fraternity. It is also the child of intelligent self-interest."¹³⁰ *Selfishness* was the willingness to improve one's own condition even if it meant leaving others behind. *Self-interest* was the interest each had in pursuing a secure independence that could only be achieved together with others. Selfishness, in other words, was expressed in the attempt to pursue one's own freedom without regard to the freedom of others – an individual expression of the labor market's general culture. Although labor republicans invoked the "virtues of stability, honor, and fraternity," they did not do so to promote a duty to uphold a common good over and against private interest – the vestigial formula of the citizen-warrior ready to sacrifice himself for his patria. Instead, they were protesting against the market as a *cultural* institution, which taught an individual to conceive his fundamental interest in independence narrowly, and to see his own good as distinct from the good of all others. As Sylvis said,

> I am fully imbued with the great American idea of individual independence, and much as I admire it as a characteristic of our race, yet I cannot fail to see that, if adhered to in our dealings with capitalists, it must sooner or later bring us to one common ruin.¹³¹

For Sylvis, the spontaneous understanding of the "great American idea of independence" was the one created by the market, which is to say selfishness. Each might hope to become his own employer or a businessman hiring others, but that was an independence won at the expense of others.

---

¹²⁶ Sylvis, "Address Delivered at Chicago, January 9, 1865," 164.
¹²⁷ Powderly, *Thirty Years of Labor 1859–1889*, 121 emphasis added.
¹²⁸ Steward, *The Eight Hour Movement: A Reduction of Hours Is an Increase of Wages*, 18.
¹²⁹ Thompson, "'An Important Question,'" 127.
¹³⁰ "Co-Operation – the Condition of Its Success," *JUL* V, no. 1 (April 25, 1884), 666.
¹³¹ Sylvis, "Address Delivered at Buffalo, N.Y., January, 1864," 107.

Solidarity and Selfishness

The culture of selfishness made itself felt in a variety of situations. It led to short-term calculations, and contributed to craft, sectional, and party divisions among workers, undermining their ability to act collectively to overcome their shared dependence. It also appeared in unplanned local strikes and participation in strikebreaking. A frequent target of opprobrium was craft distinctions that left workers unwilling to organize unskilled workers or to support other strikes and collective actions. Many labor republicans thought craft narrowness was based on a fundamental misunderstanding of the logic of industrial society, which anyhow was turning the skilled into unskilled. As Powderly put it, "steam and electricity have forever broken the power of one trade or division of labor to stand and legislate for itself alone, and with the craft that selfishly legislates for itself alone I have no sympathy."[132] Although the Knights' historical relationship to craft-unions was fraught and ambivalent, shifting between acceptance of them and opposition to their separate existence, Knights were popular precisely because of their openness to unskilled labor and their wider message of labor solidarity.[133] Another example of unworthy selfishness was the tendency to vote for one of the mainstream political parties – behavior often flowing from an electoral promise to improve some workers' short-run conditions or protect some specific sector of labor. For Sylvis, the only way to counter this tendency to use the suffrage poorly was organization: "Combination, or union among workingmen, may be looked upon as the first step towards competence and independence."[134] Overall, then, "selfish" behavior, like empty electoral partisanship, craft narrowness, and strike-breaking stood in contrast with the virtuous but still self-interested action oriented to collective advancement.

If cooperative activity was consistent with individual self-interest, it is important to note that labor republicans did not *call* the orientation towards this action "self-interest" because it was not a purely calculating attitude. Instead, they called it solidarity. This solidarity had a rational basis, but it was fundamentally a spontaneous disposition, the habit of identifying one's own good with the universal, shared good of all workers: "[T]here are certain habits, certain attributes of character without cultivation, of which there can be no individual progress, and therefore no social progress. These habits and this character is to make the man an independent being."[135] Note again that these habits were not in conflict with a citizen's interest in independence but rather constitutive of the relations that make that independence possible. As Sylvis put it, the

---

[132] Terence Powderly, "Message to the Noble Order of the Knights of Labor of America, Philadelphia, May 3, 1886," in *Labor: Its Rights and Wrongs*, ed. Terence Powderly (Westport, CT: Hyperion Press, Inc., 1886), 73.
[133] Weir, *Beyond Labor's Veil*, 46–55; Fink, *Workingmen's Democracy*, 126–30, 156–72.
[134] Sylvis, "Address Delivered at Chicago, January 9, 1865," 164.
[135] Sharpe, "Co-Operation."

results flowing from our organization is the universal and wide-spread acquaintance that has sprung up among the members: a feeling of brotherhood everywhere exists; an interest in each other's welfare has broken down, to a vast extent, that old feeling of selfishness that used to exist among us; a feeling of manly independence has taken the place of that cringing and crawling spirit that used to make us the scorn of honest men.[136]

Solidarity cast off the mentality of dependence by making visible to each his power as a potential agent. And it did so by showing how the real exercise of that power was necessarily linked to others exercising that power jointly with him. But this solidarity could only develop if these separate workers gave institutional expression to the otherwise abstract identity of interests among them. Such institutions had to make cooperation, rather than competition, a practical ethos not just an idea.

Solidarity was therefore a virtue linked to a specific institutional practice: the self-organization of workers as workers for achieving social and political ends. From its earliest manifestation in the workingmen's parties of the 1820s and 1830s through to the heyday of the Knights of Labor in the 1880s and 1890s, the cultural logic of labor republicanism was organizational. Uriah Stephens, founder of the Knights of Labor, wrote in the *Journal of United Labor*:

The work to which this fraternity addresses itself ... enters a field occupied by no other organized effort ... that of knitting up into a compact and homogeneous amalgamation all the world's workers in one universal brotherhood, guided by the same rules, working by the same methods, practicing the same forms for accomplishing the same ends.[137]

In the name of this universal brotherhood, Stephens proclaimed "Creed, party, and nationality are but outward garments."[138] With the creation of organizations through which workers could press demands and exercise their political agency, labor republicans embraced and recast the republican idea of active citizenship. Participation was not a process of maintaining existing free institutions but of conflictual engagement with current regimes of state and property. That was the full meaning of solidarity.

This "feeling of brotherhood," to which labor republicans regularly referred, was inescapably organizational because it did not produce itself. It was something generated and maintained – "knitted together" – through the cultural activities of this counter-hegemonic institution. For instance, Robert Weir's extraordinary reconstruction of the culture of the Knights of Labor reminds us that the genesis of solidarity reached deep into the day-to-day life of sport and leisure. "The KOL neither privatized nor trivialized leisure," writes Weir, "Knights took their battles over the issue [of leisure] into the nation's parks, streets, buildings, and public spaces."[139] The Knights developed a rich internal

---

[136] Sylvis, "Address Delivered at Chicago, January 9, 1865," 167.
[137] Uriah S Stevens, "Ideal Organization I" I, no. 2 (June 15, 1880), 24.
[138] Ibid., 24.
[139] Weir, *Beyond Labor's Veil*, 282.

symbolic world of picnics, sports, emblems and song.[140] More controversially, they also developed various secret rituals of membership, which fell away, though not entirely, during the rapid growth of the mid-1880s.[141] These cultural practices were a response to how to cultivate the virtues of solidarity in a competitive, unjust society. Self-organization made tangible the bonds of cooperation that could, potentially, be generalized if the cooperative commonwealth were made real.

Of course the point of organization was not just the production of shared sentiments through cultural activities but the practical exercise of agency. The Knights led a chaotic course through the labor conflicts of the late nineteenth century, never acquiring the mastery of their fate for which they hoped. But they led boycotts, strikes, and organizing campaigns, advocated policies, and endorsed and ran candidates. The empirical history of these various experiments has been told elsewhere.[142] What matters here is that actions like the boycott were understood as at once a test and proof of the value of collective action. The experience of that collective power was itself an education in the way each individual's power was increased through cooperative organization: "As individual atoms, the members of our Order are helpless; as the cohering atoms of a mighty association, they become a power."[143] Such actions required an extensive campaign of education, development of sympathies, reorientation of daily economic practices, and willingness to sacrifice short-term interests to the long-term aims of the campaign. Boycotts and strikes tested and were exercises in solidarity because they often came at great cost to those who lost wages, were tempted to cross picket lines, or were asked to pay more for Knight-made goods. They *did* involve personal sacrifices of many participants and in that sense involved the exercise of certain virtues.

These campaigns also required breaking through "partisan prejudice" that divided workers and led them to vote against their interests. One Knight drew the parallel between ancient and classical political corruption: "The monopolists of Rome defended themselves and crushed opposition by hiring their own dupes to use the dagger. The monopolists of America have defended themselves and attempted to crush their opponents at the election by hiring their dupes to use the ballot."[144] The only way to break these partisan commitments was to create an alternative organization to carry loyalties and articulate demands.[145] During the peak of political activity in the 1880s, for instance, one Knight proclaimed

---

[140] Ibid., passim.
[141] See Weir's fascinating discussion, ibid., 19–66.
[142] Norman Ware, *The Labor Movement in the United States*; Fink, *Workingmen's Democracy*; Oestreicher, "Socialism and the Knights of Labor in Detroit, 1877–1886"; Leikin, *The Practical Utopians*; Weir, "A Fragile Alliance."
[143] Sharpe, "Co-Operation."
[144] "Ancient and Modern Monopolies," *KoL* 1, no. 32 (November 13, 1886).
[145] Powderly, *Thirty Years of Labor 1859–1889*, 76.

> Some of the specific aims and objects of the [Knights] are ... to educate the members to an intelligent use of the ballot, for their own benefit and protection, free from restraint of party or undue influence of employers or monopolies.[146]

This included voting for Knights, or candidates they endorsed, rather than along party lines – an effort that enjoyed very limited empirical success.[147] Nevertheless, here again, the point was that the cultivation of virtue was inseparable from the kinds of action it was supposed to promote. The virtue was expressed in and developed by organized activity.

If politics was the classical domain for the exercise of virtue, to labor republicans the ultimate test was found in the economy. The virtues of solidarity were a precondition for the creation and maintenance of cooperatives themselves:

> Political action cannot reorganize the industrial system. Nothing short of a reorganization of the industrial system can abolish poverty and give equal opportunity to all. Co-operation is the only means whereby the poor can obtain a just share of the profits and honors of advancing civilization.[148]

Labor republicans famously disagreed with each other about the precise role of politics,[149] and the Knights changed positions over the course of its existence. But one very consistent thought was that control of the state could not, on its own, produce an economy of independent producers if those producers themselves did not understand and act on the principles of cooperation. As one article in the *Journal of United Labor* put it

> The organization of working men into societies, the amalgamation of these in a central body; the coalescence of these in turn in a trades union, are all well *as far as they go*. The principle, however, must be carried further, and applied in political life to the ballot, representation and legislation. It must be carried further still, and applied to trade itself; the masses must institute and *own their own industries*.[150]

For the masses to "institute and *own their own industries*" they had to be willing to engage in and relate to these enterprises in a different way from a mere job. Otherwise, the same logic of competition would undermine the very political economy they were trying to institute.

Cooperatives required virtuous members because they were voluntary organizations. As one Knight put it,

> Co-operation ... the word has come to have the special significance of *voluntary* working together. All that working together which is not voluntarily entered into, such,

---

[146] Jelley, *The Voice of Labor*, 203.
[147] On the Knights' relationship to party politics, see Fink, *Workingmen's Democracy*; Kim Voss, *The Making of American Exceptionalism*; Weir, "A Fragile Alliance."
[148] Henry E. Sharpe, "Co-Operation," *JUL*, January 15, 1884, 706.
[149] Fink, *Workingmen's Democracy*; Weir, *Knights Unhorsed*.
[150] Fales, "The Organization of Labor."

for instance, as that of convicts or soldiers in the ranks, is not termed co-operation. Co-operation is the antithesis of slavery.[151]

Cooperatives were a form of free labor, in contrast to wage and chattel slavery, if its members entered them voluntarily. But if cooperatives were formed voluntarily then, for one, their formation depended on a willingness of disparate individuals to create joint enterprises, rather than assume the traditional form of capital-labor relations. Furthermore, their success depended upon the dispositions of their members to maintain a commitment to the long-run health of the enterprise, and to consider each member's interests equally, rather than consider his own short-term self-interest.

In other words, labor republicans here transposed a familiar republican argument about free *political* institutions onto *socioeconomic* ones. If free political institutions only remained free if citizens were virtuous, the same held for cooperative economic enterprises, especially because these enterprises had the same basic purpose as political institutions: the independence of each member. But cooperatives could not rely on the employer's coercion or the discipline of the labor market the way the current system did. In order to accumulate the capital to compete and to make business decisions that would support the flourishing of the cooperative venture, each needed to see it as something more than just a temporary stint off which to make as much money as possible, regardless of what happened to the other cooperators. Moreover, as they grew, they would have to withstand hostility from enemies. For instance, citing the example of the National Association of Master Plumbers, who in 1885 forced manufacturers of plumbing materials not to sell to plumber cooperatives, John Swinton said, "any co-operative scheme, in any line of industry, that becomes strong enough to threaten the supremacy of capitalism, will very surely find the whole power of capitalists pitted against it."[152] For cooperatives to resist degenerating into internally inegalitarian or exploitative enterprises, its members needed to remain voluntarily committed to its rules and principles.

For this reason, labor republicans thought cooperatives ultimately rested on the moral qualities of their members:

Every lover of his fellowmen, every one who believes in education, nay, every one who understands how he is linked to the great man and how much he has himself at stake, will enter into cooperative work, not for the mere immediate gain in cash, but for that higher, permanent, moral gain which must come, which always does come, from giving man an interest in something outside of himself, which comes from the awakening of the moral and intellectual faculties in association and from practice experience in the management of property.[153]

---

[151] "Co-Operation," *JUL* IV, no. 6 (October 15, 1883), 580.
[152] "A Coward's Blow at Co-Operation," *JSP* 2, no. 91 (July 5, 1885).
[153] Sharpe, "Co-Operation," 597.

Absent the "awakening of the moral and intellectual faculties" cooperative work would, at best, be an external burden, and at worst, be seen just as another source of instrumental benefit for the individual.

This way of thinking about virtue and cooperation was extraordinarily demanding. The difficulties of accumulating capital, of competing with better capitalized private businesses, and of facing legal repression and illegal sabotage[154] were major obstacles to the long-run flourishing of cooperative enterprise.[155] That labor republicans nonetheless tended to blame failures on themselves, despite these external obstacles, speaks to their cast of mind. As an editor of the *Journal*'s cooperation section put it,

> all the failures have resulted either because the purpose was unattainable or because there was not co-operation.... To be a true co-operator, member of a *voluntary* association, a man must be one of the noblest of the race; he must be truthful, honest and industrious, for he must be loyal to his promises, he must keep his contracts, and to do that without fear of punishment before him, he must be a being of higher morality than the average man.[156]

Phrases such as "noblest of the race" and "higher morality than the average man" pointed to the burden that labor republican thinking placed on workers. Such thinking was a natural consequence of thinking that, on the one hand, they were wage-slaves, while, on the other hand, and for that very reason, they were the only possible agents of economic transformation. Who else would exercise true "nobility," in any socially effective way, in oppressive circumstances? But the kinds of habits required to overcome all of the pressures, distractions, and limits of the present required something extraordinary of each individual. These habits were virtues in the sense that they were forms of excellence, or high moral performance, exercised in the face of the many impediments to and temptations away from successful collective action by the dependent classes.

The Fragility of Virtue: Solidarity and Exclusion

The danger of this kind of thinking is not hard to see. If the success of the cooperative commonwealth depended on the agency, and therefore the virtue, of the dependent classes themselves, then at some point it was hard not to blame these wage-slaves for their servility. Consider the following:

> If we neglect or refuse to do it, let things remain as they are, we shall justly be the prey of monopolists, the serfs of lords of land, slaves of lords of labor, and victims of lords of law ... [leaving] no addition to the legacy bequeathed us by our patriotic forefathers,

---

[154] E.g., "Legalize Co-Operation," *KoL* 1, no. 42 (January 22, 1887); "A Coward's Blow at Co-Operation."

[155] On these challenges, see Leikin, *The Practical Utopians*; Clare Dahlberg Horner, "Producers' Co-Operatives in the United States, 1865–1890," (University of Pittsburgh Press, 1978).

[156] "Co-Operation," 581.

who did what they could ... but left an unfinished superstructure for those who came after them to complete.¹⁵⁷

In this quite extraordinary passage, Knight's founder Uriah Stephens is not saying that it is justifiable to make some human beings into slaves. But when he says "we shall justly be ... slaves of lords of labor" he *is* saying something akin to workers get what they deserve. If only those who are dominated can overcome their servitude, and doing so requires the exercise of unusual and extraordinary attributes, then it sounds like servile natures get the only conditions they are fit for. Or, put another way, until the enslaved start behaving like they deserve their freedom, they deserve their slavery. Their failure to exercise virtues is ultimately a sign that they do not yet have the desires, or the knowledge, or the capacity to pursue their liberty.

Once one could blame the servile for their servility, it was not a very great leap to connect servile natures to racial and ethnic difference. Labor republicans drew these connections when it came to some Eastern and Southern Europeans and especially the Chinese. For instance, one long article on "Hungarian serfs" in the *Journal* denounces the "lowest degredation [sic] into which these people have fallen." It accuses Hungarians of being perfectly happy to eat sausages "covered with slime" and of other living habits unworthy of "Americans or other white men" – unworthy because the latter demanded their independence, not mere survival.¹⁵⁸ Despite recognizing that these contract immigrant laborers were dependent on their employers for just about everything, and thus had little bargaining power, the editors of the *Journal* nonetheless blamed the Hungarians for putting up little resistance and thus for displaying servility they found characteristic of that nationality as whole. Aside from the very exceptional case of New York Knights hoping to organize Chinese assemblies, the Knights were also quite famously anti-Chinese. They favored legislation barring Chinese labor from coming to the United States.¹⁵⁹ Although this sometimes reflected the fact that they did not want to compete with the "coolie" or bonded labor of these groups, it was more often justified with reference to "barbaric" racial characteristics of the Chinese. One Knight said, "the Chinese in our midst are the natural product of a pagan climate and a despotic soil.... The Chinese are controlled by a central authority ... their stolidity, brutality, subservience, and docility are the result of their training."¹⁶⁰ Powderly, though more attentive to the way Chinese workers were coerced laborers, also criticized "their habits, religion, customs, and practices" as incompatible with the republican spirit.¹⁶¹ One lurid article in

---

¹⁵⁷ Stevens, "Ideal Organization I," 24.
¹⁵⁸ "Go-Stay," *JUL* 4, no. 1 (May 1883), 461.
¹⁵⁹ On the New York Knights who proposed organizing Chinese workers see, Weir, "A Fragile Alliance"; Weir, "'Here's to the Men WHO Lose!': the Hidden Career of Victor Drury."
¹⁶⁰ W. W. Stone, "The Knights of Labor on the Chinese Situation" *Overland Monthly and Out West Magazine* VII, no. 39 (March, 1886), 225–26.
¹⁶¹ Quoted, ibid., 229.

the *Journal* on the "cheapness of living ... among the Chinese and Hungarian laborers" condemns the way American workers are "compelled to compete with men who grow fat on a diet of wind pudding and sleep ... in quarters that would be uncomfortable as a pig-sty."[162] These last quotations are the more poignant for being found just beneath another article that, among other things, celebrates the inclusion of "a colored man" who was "representing a colored assembly" at a district gathering of Detroit-area Knights.[163]

It is easy to read these passages about the Chinese and Hungarians as examples of the inherently exclusionary tendency of the republican tradition's emphasis on the connection between liberty and virtue. Recall that the historian David Roediger interpreted earlier proslavery republicanism in just this way: "[I]t was not difficult to move toward considering the proposition that Black oppression was the result of 'slavishness' rather than slavery. White revolutionary pride could thus open the way for republican racism."[164] Once one starts arguing that liberty requires virtue, and observes that certain groups, especially at the bottom end of the labor market, appear not to exercise these virtues as fully as others, one quickly tends to racialize and blame victims, rather than condemn the special disadvantages that they face. Republicanism, it would seem, is inherently exclusionary.

Yet this way of interpreting is not so much wrong as it is one-sided.[165] Not only does it fail to grasp what drew labor republicans to their conception of virtue and what was new about it, it thereby leads to a misapprehension of why these exclusionary tendencies emerge. As we have seen, labor republicans began with the thought that the workers themselves had to be the agents of transformation and would have to transform themselves to become those agents. Only if they acted on their own behalf would the cooperative commonwealth truly be realized. This way of thinking about virtue derived from the hard realities of a society that was, to their mind, hostile to their conception of freedom. Their view was demanding not because of some commitment to ethnic and cultural unity. Instead, they made demands on workers because of the cultural and political obstacles that they had to overcome and because their social analysis led them to think they had to free themselves. The search for solidarity, and the virtues that maintained that solidarity, was first and foremost a response to these challenges. The universalizing character of this appeal to solidarity is not something that should be dismissed as a false universality, necessarily concealing the attempt to claim republican liberty as some kind of ethnic or cultural privilege.

[162] "Getting the Art of Living Down Fine," *JUL* V, no. 4 (June 25, 1884), 724.
[163] Ibid.
[164] Roediger, *The Wages of Whiteness*, 35. See discussion in Chapter 1.
[165] See also Cunliffe, *Chattel Slavery and Wage Slavery*; Mandel, *Labor, Free and Slave*; Eric Foner, "Abolitionism and the Labor Movement." On the Chinese, see Currarino's discussion and perhaps most importantly Glickman's discussion of the "American standard of living" and its connection with a "consumerist" racism toward immigrant consumption habits. Currarino, *The Labor Question in America*, 36–59; Glickman, *A Living Wage*, 78–92.

Instead, the latter was an ever-present possibility and danger, but not a straightforward logical consequence, of a demanding conception of virtue. The betrayal of the universal appeal to solidarity was a danger because of the very challenges that brought into being the labor republican theory of virtue in the first place: the challenges of a transformative politics under conditions of social domination. Rather than quickly reject the concept of virtue as antiquated and narrow, we can instead see reflected in labor republicanism a dilemma that persists for any theory of politics that takes as its starting point the aim of struggling against concrete relations of inequality and unfreedom. Moreover, the one-sided reading of labor republicanism as inherently exclusionary leaves no room to appreciate the extraordinary *inclusiveness* of their politics, not to mention the way in which it awakened the capacities of so many.

Conclusion: The Politics of Virtue Reconsidered

If we understand labor republican thinking about virtue as a response to the practical problem of self and social transformation, then we can better appreciate what was at once new and dangerous, inspirational yet fragile, in their political vision. The conceptual innovation of labor republicanism was to make the dependent, not independent, classes the bearers of virtue. Their partial interest in free labor, rather than the property-owning classes' interest in stability, was seen to be identical with the general interest in a cooperative commonwealth. This, in turn, led to a belief that virtue had to be inculcated through the self-education and self-organization of the dependent classes themselves. Labor republicans argued for the awakening of desire, the self-education of workers, and the cultural transformation of citizens without having to argue that this process of inculcation required massive coercive intervention of the state into religious and educational life. Moreover, their conception of virtue did not stand at odds with the production and accumulation of wealth. Instead, they sought to reorganize the basis of that economic activity so that all could enjoy its fruits under conditions of equal independence.

In this way, although labor republicans upheld the classical republican view that freedom required virtue, and that virtue had to be inculcated, they significantly transformed its basic coordinates in ways that cuts across the assumptions of contemporary scholarship. In the hands of labor republicans, the politics of virtue became primarily a theory of social transformation rather than institutional preservation, of self-education rather than coercive socialization, and of the fusion of virtue and interest. Equally significant, their ideas found practical expression in new cultural practices and sociopolitical organizations. The labor press and the reading room, the lecture circuit and the cooperative pamphlet, the local assembly and the national committee – these were radical "seedbeds of virtue."[166] They served to educate workers in the

---

[166] I take the phrase from a more conservative version of the account of the "seedbeds of virtue." Glendon, ed., *Seedbeds of Virtue*.

broad sense of "forming character" not just "acquiring knowledge." It is worth emphasizing that, because this conception of character formation departs from the more coercive tendencies of the classical ideal, and is aimed at transforming rather than preserving social institutions, it is a model for the politics of virtue that does not fall afoul of many conventional liberal criticisms. There is at least less reason to worry that the politics of virtue *naturally* leads to oppressive homogeneity and violation of individual rights; indeed, the broad aim of the labor republican project was to claim rights where they had been denied.

It is true that labor republicans made exceptional demands on workers themselves. As one Knight put it, "the workers become the arbiters of their own fate" only if they "learn and obey the laws of association," which include each worker making a "covenant with himself and with his fellows to exert self-denial, patience, determination, endurance, and all the virtue which go to make up a vigorous and virtuous character."[167] As we have seen, their theory even had a paradoxical structure: insofar as the dependent classes were "arbiters of their own fate" they were also the ones potentially to blame for their servility. They were at once unfree yet responsible, lacking in independence yet the agents of change. It is not hard to imagine the sense of betrayal when those who dedicated themselves to the rigors of "self-denial, patience, determination, [and] endurance" saw their fellows reject or ignore these virtues. This kind of thinking about virtue could easily collapse into appalling racial and ethnic stereotypes. If anything, the fragility of the theory was wider than any local, cultural prejudice. It set up its proponents for enormous impatience and intolerance of others even when this disappointment was disconnected from racial or ethnic views. It left some labor republicans ready to love humanity in general, but to become frustrated with actual human beings in particular.

Yet we must observe that the social-psychological fragility of this theory of virtue is inseparable from what made it so energetic, inspiring, and universalizing. After all, it made no sense to place significant demands on workers if one did not believe that they were potentially agents in their own emancipation, let alone capable of governing themselves in the workplace. We cannot forget how many formerly marginal groups – women, blacks, unskilled and immigrant workers – were so activated by this appeal to their agency that they took matters into their own hands, joining the organization in droves, creating unions, writing and lecturing, going on strike, forming cooperatives. No American organization was to be that successful in bringing together such disparate groups for decades. In fact, the emphasis on their own capacities to transform their situation, and the belief they could only do so collectively, was so successful that it nearly overwhelmed the Knights as an organization.[168]

---

[167] Sharpe, "Co-Operation."

[168] The difficulty in absorbing the demands for assistance in forming cooperatives and maintaining strikes is evident from the pages of the *Journal*. See for instance the message from the Secretary General of the Co-operative Board asking locals to stop asking for money from the national board. J. P. McGaughey, "Halt!" *JUL* VI, no. 24 (April 25, 1886), 2055.

Generally speaking, it is hard to imagine how one could announce the agency of a class of people without generating the expectation that they act in certain ways. To criticize the labor republican vision for being too demanding, therefore, might also be to call into question the very possibility of a dependent group being able to transform conditions they consider radically unjust.

That is why, if there is a lesson to draw from the demands of labor republicanism, it is perhaps the way it sheds light on *any* politics that understands itself to be egalitarian and radically transformative. The aim of the labor republicans was to universalize republican liberty and win inclusion for the excluded by transforming the social order. This aim generated not just a set of ideals but a new way of thinking about the political culture of a social movement that wanted to realize these republican ideals. The Knights made numerous political mistakes. They could have handled their popularity better, and they could have followed through on their own principles with greater consistency. But those political facts do not invalidate the novelty and importance of their contribution to political thinking. They did for civic virtue what they did for republican liberty. They kept alive a political language by reinventing it, thereby giving it a new universality.

Conclusion

"The Freedom Yet to Come"

It is easy to be seduced by historical distance. We might think that the labor republicans are a fascinating and inspiring group, but that their concerns are hardly ours. After all, at least in industrial countries, bosses no longer pay in scrip and pasteboard tickets, courts do not place entire towns under quasi-martial law, labor leaders do not get assassinated nor tent-cities of strikers mowed down by machine guns.[1] States do not send tanks to occupy labor-controlled cities[2]; in fact, the law recognizes labor's right to organize and to strike. What's more, the abject poverty of tenement dwellers and sugar cane cutters is (almost) entirely a thing of the past. Labor laws, welfare benefits, modern technology, and cheaper goods all mean that even those who live in poverty have access to much more of life's necessities, not to mention many luxuries, than workers of the late nineteenth century. Surely we have a right to some sense of moral superiority, to feeling that we do not live as they did.

Work and Domination Today

Of course, even if there is this great historical gap separating us from them, and even if we are entitled to some sense of social progress, we can still find ways to learn from labor republicans. Quentin Skinner argues powerfully that the task of historical reconstruction is "archeological." We recover lost ways of thinking so as to denaturalize the present:

[T]he intellectual historian can help us to appreciate how far the values embodied in our present way of life, and our present ways of thinking about those values, reflect a series

---

[1] Ross, "American Labor Violence: Its Causes, Character, and Outcome"; Hacker, "The United States Army as a National Police Force: The Federal Policing of Labor Disputes, 1877–1898"; Forbath, *Law and the Shaping of the American Labor Movement*.
[2] "From the Line of MOST Resistance," *American Federationist* 22 (1922), 263.

of choices made at different times between different possible worlds. This awareness can help to liberate us from the grip of any one hegemonal account of those values.[3]

It is easy to identify the "hegemonal account of those values" that labor republicanism denaturalizes. In current discourse, liberty is most frequently invoked to argue against worker attempts to exercise collective control over their labor, whether through regulation, unionization or organization of cooperatives. Economic freedom is understood to mean less regulation and lower taxes, the freedom of workers to make the contracts they like, and the related freedom of bosses to run the workplace as they see fit. It is certainly something of a surprise to discover that, for a time, vast numbers of people were energized by an account of freedom that ran in nearly the opposite direction. That surprise can translate into self-awareness and critical self-reflection. At the very least, it gives us pause before assuming that the only language for criticizing contemporary economic arrangements must come from other values *besides* freedom. Freedom can have a critical, not just apologetic, character.

But the connection with the nineteenth century is not that thin. There is a deeper sense in which, though there has been material progress, we should doubt the morally complacent attitude that assumes we have fully overcome the past. In fact, we can recognize important ways in which the problems the labor republicans addressed are still with us. Controversies over power and control in the workplace remain a part of our economic and political experience. The emancipating or constraining nature of labor contracts, and their relationship to wider economic inequalities, remains a central issue of the day. Although the particular manifestation of these conflicts differs in some ways from those of the nineteenth century, the driving moral concerns are the same.

For instance, in our time, employees have lost jobs for expressing or holding political views to which their bosses objected,[4] and employers have used their authority in the workplace to force employees to attend rallies, to listen to and distribute political messages, to influence their votes, and to donate to certain campaigns.[5] These are living examples of the labor republican worry that economic dependence on employers can translate into unequal political influence, thereby threatening our formal political freedom. Labor republicans thought that the only way to protect political equality was by ensuring a relatively equal distribution of wealth and the elimination of workplace domination. Only then could workers be sure their political views would not threaten them with severe economic punishment. As Henry Demarest Lloyd, author of *Wealth against Commonwealth*, wrote, there is no substitute for

---

[3] Skinner, *Liberty before Liberalism*, 116–17.
[4] Timothy Noah, "Bumper Sticker Insubordination," *Slate Magazine*, September 14, 2004; Brenda Howard, "I Left My Job Over a Computer-Desktop Hoodie," *The Washington Post*, August 16, 2013.
[5] E.g., Josh Eidelson, "Koch to Workers: Vote Mitt or Else!" *Salon.com*, October 18, 2012; Alec MacGillis, "Coal Miner's Donor," *The New Republic*, October 4, 2012.

"industrial liberty ... without which political liberty shrinks back into nothingness."[6] In our society, political liberty has not "shrunk into nothingness," but these political controversies remind us of the continuing salience of one of the labor republican worries. We might also note that the project of securing "industrial liberty" is a more thoroughgoing way of guaranteeing each citizen's political liberty than the chipping around the edges strategy of latter day campaign finance reformers.

Even more relevant are the extensive conflicts over issues that are not conventionally defined as "political." Bosses are challenged over hiring and firing, their control over the workplace, or for monitoring after hours activities. Recently, employers have fired workers for comments they made on Facebook,[7] their sexual orientation,[8] for being too sexually appealing,[9] or for not being appealing enough,[10] for trying to organize or support unionization,[11] for being "disloyal," or for some other kind of perceived disobedience.[12] Accusations about the "'arbitrary" use of power extend into day-to-day workplace relationships. Workers continue to complain about being forced to work in extreme heat or in physically hazardous conditions,[13] being refused bathroom and lunch breaks but being forced to stay even when their shift is up,[14] being denied the right to read or turn on air conditioning during breaks,[15] being forced to take

---

[6] Lloyd, *Wealth against Commonwealth*, 180.
[7] Ramona Emerson, "13 Controversial Facebook Firings: Palace Guards, Doctors, Teachers and More," *The Huffington Post*, October 17, 2011.
[8] J. D. Velasco, "Fired Gay Water Polo Coach and Supporters Protest at Charter Oak Board Meeting," *San Gabriel Valley Tribune*, October 7, 2011.
[9] Eric M. Strauss, "Iowa Woman Fired for Being Attractive: Looks Back and Moves On," *ABC News*, August 2, 2013.
[10] Amanda Hess, "How Sexy Should a Worker Be? The Plight of the Babe in the American Workplace," *Slate Magazine*, July 29, 2013.
[11] Alan Barber, "Pro-Union Workers Fired in Over One-fourth of Union Election Campaigns," *The Center for Economic and Policy Research*, March 4, 2009.
[12] On the strange case of the American Civil Liberties Union, which has fought these "arbitrary firings" by other companies, while wanting to make disloyalty a dischargeable offense for its own employees, see Ned Resnikoff, "ACLU Locked in Contract Dispute with Employee Union," *MSNBC*, July 25, 2013; and American Civil Liberties Union, "Legislative Briefing Kit: Wrongful Discharge," December 31, 1998.
[13] Tiffany Hsu, "Amazon Warehouse Employees Overheated Ahead of Holiday Season," *The Los Angeles Times*, September 19, 2011; Ian Urbina, "As OSHA Emphasizes Safety, Long-Term Health Risks Fester," *The New York Times*, March 30, 2013.
[14] Tanzina Vega, "In Ads, the Workers Rise Up ... and Go to Lunch," *The New York Times*, July 7, 2012; Todd Wasserman, "Amazon Dragged Into Applebee's Latest Jokey Campaign," *Mashable*, July 25, 2012; Bob Egelko, "Employers Must Pay if They Deny Lunch Breaks," *The San Francisco Chronicle*, February 18, 2011; Dave Jamieson, "Amazon Warehouse Workers Sue Over Security Checkpoint Waits," *The Huffington Post*, May 8, 2013.
[15] Meredith Bennett-Smith, "Indiana AT&T Technicians File Class Action Lawsuit Citing Grim Break Conditions," *The Huffington Post*, August 14, 2012; Lyneka Little, "AT&T Workers Claim Lunch Break Violations," *ABC News*, August 15, 2012.

random drug tests or perform other humiliating or irrelevant actions.[16] Notably, in nearly all these cases, the law protects the employer's authority to make these decisions without consulting workers. As a labor republican would be quick to note, employers do not *have* to exercise their power in cruel or malevolent ways. They might benevolently permit unlimited bathroom breaks, install temperature control systems, and comply with all safety recommendations. But whether they do this or not is beside the point from the standpoint of republican liberty. The problem is that employers have the *power* to do what they like on this and numerous other matters regardless of the will of the employees. That arbitrary power alone is what compromises the worker's liberty.

We might approach each of the instances listed here on a case-by-case basis and try to make individual judgments about which decisions were arbitrary or unjust. That is roughly how labor law operates. But the labor republican perspective allows us to see these as particular instances of a unified problem: Who is subject to whose will. Here is where we find continuity with the past. In fact, we might note, with some distress, that some of the exact same basic grievances still plague the workplace. The "abolition of the luncheon privilege" that George McNeill cited as a grievance so many decades ago[17] remains a contentious issue today. Employers spying on or demanding information about after hours activities, these days with respect to Facebook posts and sexual partners, stirred carpet-weavers to action in the 1880s.[18] But we do not need to show that the specific grievance is the same to demonstrate the relevant continuity with the past. Instead, the key commonality lies in the fact that economic struggles are not just about hours and wages but also power and control. The labor republican perspective is illuminating precisely because it identifies this common theme and allows us to trace disparate concerns back to a basic structural problem of unequal power relations. Freedom to form political views, use the bathroom, engage in leisure activities, determine what counts as a safe environment, and shape other aspects of one's work environment are some of the many issues that explain why economic domination is such a concern.

Moreover, as labor republicans would remind us, it is still the case that the labor contract, no matter how carefully regulated, cannot help but give employers the lion's share of this residual, discretionary authority. At heart, the contract is an agreement to sell the worker's capacity to labor to the employer and thus a transfer of rights of control over that property to the employer. If the employer is to make use of the employee's capacity for labor, then at some level the worker must make the employer's will his own. No matter how much one attempts to improve the worker's bargaining power, no matter how high the wages or good the hours, there is no way for the labor contract itself to cover

---

[16] For a list and discussion of related complaints, see Chris Bertram et al., "Let It Bleed: Libertarianism and the Workplace," *Crooked Timber*, July 1 2012.
[17] *Report of the Industrial Commission Vol 7*, 116.
[18] Susan Levine, *Labor's True Woman*, 56–59, 66–68, 73–81.

all of the eventual decisions that have to be made in the workplace itself. No matter how equal the two parties are when making the contract, that equality disappears once the contract is made.[19] Because of the incomplete character of contracts and the peculiarity of the labor commodity as something inseparable from the seller's will, a labor contract will always contain elements of subjection. The workplace is still a place where there are benevolent and malicious employers, but in both cases workers are subject to their boss's will.

Of course, this element of the labor republican critique would be less significant if the labor contract played a smaller role in our society. But that is not so. Although after the Great Recession of 2008 there was a dip in labor force participation, this was a temporary decline in the long-term historical trend whereby overall participation in the labor force has continually increased.[20] Here again, labor republican arguments are illuminating. Their argument that a form of structural domination complemented and reinforced domination in the workplace is in some sense even more applicable to us today. The majority, by some calculations the vast majority, of people have no other option but to sell their labor to an employer.[21] Current law protects a radical inequality of ownership such that, while some minimal economic benefits are available to those without work, few have a reasonable alternative to selling their labor. A worker cannot, as the Knights put it long ago, "produce without giving himself a boss or master."[22] Sometimes their employers are benevolent, or at least relatively hands off. And sometimes they monitor the activities of their employees in minute detail, including the number of times they get up from their desk, the duration of unscheduled breaks, and the number of seconds during which they are not performing a work-related activity.[23] Either way, structural domination

[19] I have discussed these issues at greater length in Gourevitch, "Labor Republicanism and the Transformation of Work."

[20] For instance, see the U.S. data, which shows that labor-force participation rates and employment to population ratios remain higher than any time prior to about 1978, even after the drop-offs from the recession of 2008. The Bureau of Labor Statistics supplies this information at the following Web sites: Labor force participation http://data.bls.gov/timeseries/LNS11300000 and employment to population ratio http://data.bls.gov/timeseries/LNS12300000. Eurostat data on the European countries show the same basic trends with some small variations. Data available at: http://epp.eurostat.ec.europa.eu/portal/page/portal/employment_unemployment_lfs/data/main_tables.

[21] For example, in the United States, calculations range from 60% to 80% of the working population of the United States. Doug Henwood, *After the New Economy* (New York: The New Press, 2003), 125; G. William Domhoff, "Wealth, Income, and Power," *Who Rules America*, http://www2.ucsc.edu/whorulesamerica/power/wealth.html; Edward N. Wolff, "The Asset Price Meltdown and the Wealth of the Middle Class," published online August 26, 2012, accessible at http://appam.confex.com/data/extendedabstract/appam/2012/Paper_2134_extendedabstract_151_0.pdf.

[22] "Industrial Ideas Chapter II," 2098.

[23] Rachel Emma Silverman, "Tracking Sensors Invade the Workplace," *The Wall Street Journal*, March 7, 2013; Chris Crowell, "Housekeeping Communication Gets More Efficient, High-Tech," *Hotelmanagement.net*, October 6, 2008.

translates into personal domination, and the latter reproduces the former insofar as very few workers can ever acquire enough capital to start their own business. And there is no way, within the existing methods of distributing control over productive resources, for all to escape the need to sell their capacity to labor. The labor republican critique of wage-labor is salient because it is able to show the way in which the structural and personal elements of economic domination relate to each other.

Moreover, it is not just the critique, but also elements of the labor republican alternative that have contemporary appeal. These days, courts and administrative bodies are the primary avenue for dealing with conflicts over power and authority in the workplace. In the United States, for instance, bodies like the Occupational Safety and Health Administration and the National Labor Relations Board, alongside criminal and civil courts, bear the responsibility for making administrative judgments and rulings on specific cases where disputes arise. It is worth recalling that labor republicans, though they supported many of the analogous reforms and indeed were a major force behind measures like the eight-hours law and the creation of state labor bureaus, did not see state regulation as the primary avenue for transforming economic relationships. In fact, in many respects, they saw many regulatory and administrative measures as a second best or temporary measure on the way to cooperative ownership and control of the workplace. In some cases, the creation of state labor bureaus were a kind of compromise or attempt to substitute for the creation of self-regulating, cooperatively controlled enterprises.[24]

One reason why labor republicans thought relatively self-regulating cooperatives were a superior solution to regulation by courts and administrative bodies was practical. The latter are very slow moving, often taking years to make a ruling, at which point many of those affected by the original grievance have experienced irreparable inconveniences and harms. Moreover, these institutions can only deal with a limited range of cases, and are easily influenced by the background inequalities of economic power that naturally arise when there is major inequality in control over wealth and productive property. No matter how good the labor law, there are a variety of reasons to believe it is a crude instrument, unable to deal with the immediacy, variety and complexity of many of the conflicts between labor and management in a workplace.[25]

---

[24] The Knights of St. Crispin, a shoemakers' organization that formed a number of cooperatives in the 1870s and 1880s, said: "We do not ask for a 'Bureau of Labor' to look into our condition; we propose to take care of ourselves." Quoted in Clare Dahlberg Horner, *Producers' Co-Operatives in the United States, 1865–1890*, 56fn6. On the Knights of St. Crispin as precursors to the Knights of Labor, see ibid., 53–70; Leikin, *The Practical Utopians*, 17–18.

[25] On the difficulty enforcing labor law, see Urbina, "As OSHA Emphasizes Safety, Long-Term Health Risks Fester." On the violation of labor law and the inability to enforce many workplace safety regulations, see, e.g., Harold Meyerson, "If Labor Dies, What's Next?" *The American Prospect*, September 13, 2012.

But there was a deeper reason for preferring the cooperative solution: it removes one of the fundamental sources of conflict and struggle from the workplace itself. If workers were their own employers, exercising relatively equal control over management and the work environment, then a number of problems would be solved. For one, the conflict of interest between employers, who wanted to employ workers for as long as possible at the lowest possible wages and under the least costly conditions, and their employees, who wanted the opposite, would mostly disappear. Making workers their own employers would dissolve the starkest conflict of interests. Certainly not all differences of opinion would go away. But cooperation would not merely make each worker's power roughly equal, it would also eliminate at least some of the differences over the reasonable exercise of that power. It is hard to imagine, for instance, a group of workers agreeing to create unnecessarily unpleasant or even dangerous conditions for themselves.[26]

That is but one example of the way in which a substantial amount of regulation would no longer be needed. Moreover, with workers exercising power directly, or through managers they controlled, it would be possible to make more particularized decisions about issues – such as hours, conditions, assessments of safety, introduction of new technologies, and so on – than state or national standards make possible. And these decisions could be more immediate, not to mention less costly, than hashing them out during interminable court or administrative battles. Furthermore, cooperative control also allows the elimination of the many small-scale, petty abuses that never rise to the level of being worthy of a court or arbitration battle, but which nonetheless persist in the current workplace.[27] In all, what might be surprising to us is that the argument for cooperatively run businesses was and is also an argument for *greater* self-regulation and thus against coercion of workers not just by bosses but by the state.

While viewing cooperatives as relatively self-regulating entities might jar against the normal polarities of arguing for "greater economic freedom" *or* "more regulation," it is an important part of their attraction. The idea of cooperative ownership and control is to reduce certain kinds of domination and thereby allow for greater freedom of individuals in the cooperative itself. That greater freedom is a natural consequence of believing one has created a workplace in which workers are their own employers, or at least exercise a greater degree of control than they do under a labor contract. It further assumes that

---

[26] I have left out, among other things, the important issue of global economic competition that could, in principle, force a group of producers down to a very low level of occupational safety if that were the only way to remain economically viable. Although an important issue, which would call for solutions at a level higher than the firm, one virtue of cooperative production would be the ability to distinguish when such conditions actually exist from when employers are simply using competition as an excuse not to pay for safe workplaces.

[27] I have discussed this in my Gourevitch, "Labor Republicanism and the Transformation of Work." see also Hsieh, "Rawlsian Justice and Workplace Republicanism."

workers are competent to exercise that control. Something of this confidence in the capacity of workers to collectively run their workplace has been lost to contemporary politics. One impulse guiding the demand for more labor regulation assumes that workers are victims, or at least, in an inescapable position of dependence – something like the old "wards of the state."[28] Workers are assumed to be nothing more than a dependent class that needs the external assistance of the law to achieve fairer and more equal dealings with employers. The point of cooperative production is not to use the law to balance the worker's inescapable dependence, nor to shift the economic relationship from the social inequalities of the labor market to the political equality of democratic law-making. Instead, its aim is to remove as much as possible that dependence at its origin, on the grounds that workers can, in fact, make competent decisions themselves.

Of course, this is not an argument against the very possibility of there being democratic law-making, in which regulations are the expression of equally free citizens establishing limits on the legitimate exercise of private power. But it *is* to say that labor republicans prompt us to think through institutional forms that secure each person's independence and that respect their capacity for the independent exercise of their will on the day to day level. Indeed, one suspects that local economic conditions that secure each person's independence are a precondition for a fully democratic form of law-making at the state level anyhow. Moreover, it is worth recalling here that workers saw cooperation not just as a change in laws of ownership and control but in culture. They argued that the kinds of informal norms of respect, authority, and mutuality that would arise in a cooperative workplace were more consistent with recognition of each person's independence than the hierarchical culture of existing workplaces. Although this was as much a hope as an argument, it had a reasonable basis. Informal norms tend to reinforce the relationships of power in which they develop.

One final appeal of labor republicanism is the value it places on leisure. The attempt to limit the hours of labor are a marginal part of contemporary politics, but it was an important and provocative feature of the labor republican social vision. For instance, most contemporary debate about technology seems to be about how it will make us better workers. Labor republicans remind us of an older idea, in which machines replaced workers rather than just made them better at their jobs. To the extent that technological innovation has *not* created a society in which all enjoy large swathes of true leisure time, so much as involuntary unemployment, not to mention overwork, this is not a technical

---

[28] For an example of this development in labor law, especially through the adoption by the state of a different rationale for regulating labor relations than the one presented by the labor movement itself, see James Gray Pope, "The Thirteenth Amendment versus the Commerce Clause: Labor and the Shaping of American Constitutional Law, 1921–1957," *Columbia Law Review*," *Columbia Law Review* 102, no. 1 (2002), 1–122.

so much as a political problem. The problem lies with who owns and controls labor-saving technologies and thus who reaps the benefits of their productive power.

The forgoing arguments in favor of labor republicanism are based on a very general description of the cooperative commonwealth, both in its own time and as it could function now. Must workers own as well as control, or can there be external ownership so long as it does not too greatly limit worker control? What about the domination of a minority of workers by the majority and other forms of informal domination? What about efficiency considerations and the incentives for innovation? How are credit and other forms of capital supposed to be made available to all workers? How would coordination among firms take place, and if through the market, should we see dependency on the market as a salutary discipline or form of domination? Finally, what about welfare rights for those who do not or cannot work, or whose firms fail?

Complete answers to these questions are well beyond the scope of this book. I offer a few brief points, but first I want to note what I am and am not saying about the labor republican legacy. I am not saying these nineteenth-century figures provide for us a clear recipe for economic reform, whose details and general principles require no further thinking. However, I do think they speak to the present more directly than just by denaturalizing our assumptions about the meaning of freedom and virtue. In ways we do not always admit to ourselves, their problems are not *radically* different from our own. We sometimes imagine ourselves so morally superior to the past that we see it merely as a repository of mistakes that we have long since overcome. There is plenty of evidence, however, that domination in the workplace and in the wider economy remains a deep and problematic issue. There is something profoundly compelling about a vision that responds to this problem not by trying to surround the contract with endlessly complex regulations and supervisory bodies, but by trying to transform the core relationship so that all can exercise a roughly equal measure of control over their daily activity. Of course, the challenge of this approach is that it demands of everyone a certain degree of democratic faith in the capacities of all workers. But that is a leap of faith worth taking.

Labor Republicanism and Its Predecessors

In arguing for the contemporary relevance of labor republicanism, I do not want to direct attention away from the historical arguments of this book. My primary aim was to recover the political ideas of the labor republicans and show that they contributed to a long-standing intellectual tradition. First, I wanted to show that neo-republican scholars have undersold the complexities of the relationship between slavery and freedom. It is not enough to note that, at its origins, freedom was the opposite of slavery. Classically, freedom also *presupposed* slavery. Moreover, the paradox of slavery and freedom was a central problem for nineteenth-century republicans because it had

Conclusion

a contemporary, not just ancient, referent: the modern revival of republican liberty *together with* chattel slavery. Attempts to solve this paradox spurred the development of the free labor ideal. When republicans began to argue that republican liberty should be a universal condition they finally began to "transcend their origins."[29]

Second, I wanted to show that this process of conceptual change forced modern republicans not only to confront the problem of slavery, but also to give an account of how republican liberty could be universalized in an industrial capitalist economy. Laissez-faire republicans responded by defending wage-labor as a universal condition of free labor. This forced labor republicans to deepen the republican analytics of servitude. They developed an account of both the structural and personal dimensions of domination. And they developed arguments to show how this domination was reproduced through the labor contracts that workers made with employers. In the face of these new forms of domination, and the collective character of industrial production, labor republicans made the further innovation of identifying independence with the self-governing conditions of workers' cooperatives, rather than with small-scale proprietorship or wage-labor. The somewhat unexpected result of these arguments was to modify not just the meaning, but also the value of republican liberty. Independence, they now argued, was valuable both because it afforded a condition of self-developing free labor and made possible greater leisure time.

We also saw that a reconceptualization of civic virtue came out of this new, cooperative thinking. Labor republicans transformed civic virtue into a politics of solidarity, in which those who suffered from servitude were also expected to be the agents of emancipation. In other words, the paradox of slavery and freedom was not just an intellectual puzzle regarding the universality of republican liberty; it was a practical puzzle regarding the process of universalization. Who had the practical interest in the cooperative commonwealth? Who, therefore, could realistically be expected to act virtuously? The answer was the dependent classes themselves, but only if they could transform themselves into agents capable of collective action.

Scholars have generally failed to take note of these contributions to republican thought because they have tended to ignore the nineteenth century, or they have written it off as the period of liberal ascendance. Perhaps, too, they have been guided by too narrow a sense of the problems their scholarship must address. After all, scholars such as Quentin Skinner and Philip Pettit have put a great deal of energy into arguing that the republican theory of liberty is "negative," and have taken pains to show that its modern progenitors, at least as far back as Machiavelli, have understood it that way.[30] They have put much less energy into proving the concept's universality and all that entails. I suspect that

---

[29] Pettit, *Republicanism*, 133.
[30] Skinner, "The Republican Ideal of Political Liberty"; Skinner, "Machiavelli's Discorsi and the Pre-Humanist Origins of Republican Ideas."

is because they have been engaged in a kind of argument with contemporary liberalism, especially as the terms were established by Isaiah Berlin in his famous essay on negative and positive liberty. In that essay, Berlin argued that the core fact of modern politics to which any theory of liberty must respond is "pluralism." What pluralism means is a matter of some controversy, which need not detain us here.[31] The point is, no matter how interpreted, the discovery of pluralism drives moderns to no longer think that one scale of values or a single conception of the good life is the same for all. Therefore, liberals might say, each must be left free to pursue his or her ends as he or she sees fit. More strongly, the fact of pluralism influences the *meaning* of freedom. Freedom is necessarily "negative," defined by the absence of interference or domination, not "positive" or defined by the achievement of specific ends or human capacities.[32] If there are plural ends and capacities, so the argument goes, then freedom just cannot meaningfully be identified with the exercise of an ability or the achievement of some particular end. Any positive concept must lead to extensive coercion of all those who disagree – "forcing" them to be free. The inescapable conclusion seems to be that this kind of coercion in the name of freedom makes an absurdity of the concept itself. Contemporary republicans have generally accepted these terms of the debate and either argued that their conception is negative or, somewhat less frequently, argued that a certain positive conception of liberty better attends to the facts of modern pluralism.[33]

This debate is important, but it has unduly narrowed the focus of historical scholarship. We saw throughout this book that another great fact of modern politics is not so much pluralism but the struggle for equality, with its

---

[31] It is worth noting that "pluralism" can be, as it was for Berlin, a meta-ethical thesis about the nature of values. On this view, there are incommensurable but objective values. In satisfying some we necessarily sacrifice others, and there is no objective principle that can allow us to settle them. For others, such as John Rawls and Charles Larmore and, in a quite different vein, Benjamin Constant, pluralism is an historical and sociological fact about modern life: There is more than one reasonable account of the good life out there, and we have no good way of arguing for the priority of any one of them. Yet for others, such as John Stuart Mill, pluralism is a thesis about human nature, or the necessarily diverse characters and thus diverse conditions under which individual human beings will flourish. Isaiah Berlin, "John Stuart Mill and the Ends of Life," in *Four Essays on Liberty* (New York: Oxford University Press, 1969), 173–206; Isaiah Berlin, "Two Concepts of Liberty," in *Four Essays on Liberty*, (Oxford; New York: Oxford University Press, 1979), 118–72; John Stuart Mill, "On Liberty," in *John Stuart Mill: On Liberty and Other Essays*, ed. John Gray (New York: Oxford University Press, 1998), 1–128; Constant, "The Liberty of the Ancients as Compared with That of the Moderns"; John Rawls, *Political Liberalism* (New York: Columbia University Press, 1996); Charles Larmore, "Political Liberalism," *Political Theory* 18, no. 3 (1990), 339–60.

[32] These connections are famously drawn in Berlin's essay. Skinner began self-consciously identifying the "neo-Roman" theory of liberty as negative, in contrast to other "positive" theories, at least as early as 1990. Berlin, "Two Concepts of Liberty"; Skinner, "The Republican Ideal of Political Liberty."

[33] Besides the aforementioned essays, see Skinner, "A Third Concept of Liberty"; Pettit, *Republicanism*, 17–50; Sandel, *Democracy's Discontent*, 26; Viroli, *Republicanism*, 38–42.

intellectual demand that political ideals be *universal* or applicable to all. The struggle for equality drew attention to whether republican liberty could overcome its inner "particularistic" connection to slavery. My suspicion is that scholars have allowed the terms of contemporary debate to affect the scope of their historical inquiries, rendering it difficult to make full sense of problems like the paradox of slavery and freedom. Yet when we turn our attention to the nineteenth century, the struggle for equality plays an undeniably central role in the transformation of republican thought. The key intellectual puzzle revolves around how to universalize republican liberty, not whether it is negative or positive. This only became an intellectual puzzle when a new class of actors seized on and challenged the dominant interpretations of the republican tradition itself. Scholars have, perhaps, been too preoccupied with their own questions to allow these historical voices to speak on their own terms.

Marx and the Cooperative Commonwealth

At the beginning of this book I said that the initial impulse behind this project was a Marxist criticism of the republican revival. By now we might wonder if the book has turned into its opposite – one long exercise in Marxist ventriloquism. Is all the talk of wage-slavery, the labor contract, propertyless classes, self-emancipation of workers, and cooperative production just a Marxism that dares not speak its name? The historical record only confirms the suspicion. Not only were some of the leading Knights of Labor, such as Terence Powderly, card-carrying Socialists,[34] but some were even members of Karl Marx's International Workingman's Association, and a number of them had read some of Marx's writings.[35] Or, if they weren't officially "Marxists," they looked like fellow-travelers, a hair's breadth away from the thing itself.[36] Yet we have to be careful not to read contemporary assumptions backwards into our intellectual and political history. For one, the most interesting thing about the labor republicans is precisely that most were not self-conscious Marxists. They understood their core ideas to be a natural extension of an inherited republican tradition, to which they added elements of political economy and cooperative theory. Marx did not have a monopoly on the critique of wage-labor, nor on

---

[34] Oestreicher, *Solidarity and Fragmentation*, 92.
[35] Joseph Buchanan, a leading Knight from Denver, was even a delegate to an IWA general assembly. Weir, *Knights Unhorsed*, 75–76. Theodore Cuno, the Knights' statistician, was a European émigré who had been close to Marx in the heyday of the IWA. Ira Steward and George McNeill had read some of Marx's work. Montgomery argues Steward naturally developed a view regarding the working day that is essentially the same as the one Marx develops in volume 1 of *Capital*. Montgomery, *Beyond Equality*, 249–60.
[36] Victor Drury, one of the most influential Knights in the New York scene, was an exiled Blanquist anarchist, and Joseph Labadie, leader of the Detroit Knights, was a former Socialist Party member-cum-anarchist. Weir, "Here's to the Men WHO Lose!: the Hidden Career of Victor Drury"; Oestreicher, *Solidarity and Fragmentation*, 79–85; Fink, *Workingmen's Democracy*, 18–37.

collective solutions to that problem. Labor republicans remind us that many of those ideas attributed to Marx are not so peculiar to his cast of mind. In fact, there is even a case to be made, though I cannot make it here, that something of the reverse is true. Marx was one of those nineteenth-century thinkers who inherited and radicalized the republican tradition.[37]

That said, there is still reason to articulate some Marxist concerns, especially to the degree that we think labor republicanism is relevant today. One worry is about the use of the labor theory of value. As we have seen, labor republicans often argued that cooperation would allow the producer to enjoy the "full fruits of his labor."[38] This claim had an analytic as well as moral dimension. Analytically, it was meant to explain the effects of economic dependence, or to describe the specific way in which a worker was forced to work yet lose control over most of what he produced. Morally, the labor theory of value was meant to express what an economic arrangement would be like in which workers were not subject to employers and were not forced, by economic need, to sell themselves.

But there was a deep ambiguity in the labor republican use of the labor theory of value, found in the vacillation between demanding the "full value" versus the "fair value." The *full* value refers to the entire value of what the worker produces, however that is calculated, whereas the *fair* value refers to some unspecified level of consumption relative to the amount of work performed. As Marx noted in his famous polemic against the Lasalleans, there are at least two problems with *either* of these ways of arguing for linking production to consumption. The first is analytical: A whole background set of social conditions – from infrastructure and the state to language and education – must first exist for any particular worker to be able to make his or her productive contribution. But if workers received the full value of what they produced then there would be no value left over to pay for all those background conditions, leaving workers unable to go on working. After all, a system of taxation and public spending would reduce the amount of value still in the worker's control to less than its "full" amount. But if workers only claim the "fair" value, the concept seems to lose its scientific character as an objective ratio, making it difficult to calculate and leaving the critic without a clear way of understanding each

---

[37] A suggestion that Quentin Skinner has made on a few instances: "I am very struck by the extent to which Marx deploys, in his own way, a neo-Roman political vocabulary. He talks about wage slaves, and he talks about the dictatorship of the proletariat. He insists that, if you are free only to sell your labour, then you are not free at all. He stigmatises capitalism as a form of servitude. These are all recognizably neo-Roman moral commitments." "Liberty before Liberalism and All That: Quentin Skinner Interviewed by Richard Marshall," *3am Magazine*, Monday, February 18, 2013, http://www.3ammagazine.com/3am/liberty-before-liberalism-all-that. I am grateful to William Clare Roberts for conversations on this topic and for sharing his writing on this subject with me. See also Lewis S. Feuer, "The North American Origins of Marx's Socialism," *The Western Political Quarterly* 16, no. 1 (March 1963), 53–67.

[38] "Industrial Ideas Chapter I," 2087.

individual's work as part of a social process. Both "full" and "fair," as concepts, represent the value a worker creates as a clearly measurable individual quantity, rather than grasping each person's work contribution as part of a social process. If each person's contribution presupposes a number of other people engaged in other activities, and an entire social infrastructure, it is unclear why we should view that person as exclusively, causally responsible for the value that his work adds.

Even if we could make this calculation, the second, moral problem would still remain. The claim to the full or fair value of one's labor links consumption directly and entirely to production. It is a way of saying that our ability to pay for goods, and thus satisfy our needs, should be strictly proportionate to the amount of work we do. But even if we accept that the amount of work someone performs, however measured, should somewhat determine his or her ability to consume, it is hard to accept the justice of a society that links consumption *exclusively* to the ability to work. Marx's formula, "from each according to his abilities to each according to his needs," controversial as it is in its pure form, captures at least one important truth: There are some needs that people should be able to satisfy without being able or even willing to work. Society owes it to each individual to meet his or her basic needs. We can imagine a number of welfare systems that can, or do, perform this function: An unconditional basic income, universal health care, and public pensions and education, as well as mass transit systems and public health programs. Yet it is unclear how the system of taxation required to finance these programs could be considered just if one believes that the ability to consume should be linked entirely to a person's willingness or ability to work. Such welfare schemes sound like they involve the unjust expropriation of the "fair" or "full" value of someone's labor. They are perhaps better seen as public goods and entitlements that each receives as a member of a complex, highly productive division of labor.

It is possible to accept this criticism without undermining the basic labor republican impulse. Recall, for instance, that the labor republican interest in the labor theory of value was to account for the kinds of social domination specific to the labor market, and to develop a theory of what a cooperative system would be like. Their mistake was, in some sense, to collapse ownership and control. The problem of control over the workplace is at least partially separable from ownership claims on the value that is produced. In fact, welfare systems that are based on unconditional provision of necessary goods, like a basic income and health care, can serve the republican project of eliminating forms of economic domination. If a citizen is able to fall back on a state-provided income, and is free to access health services regardless of whether he or she has a job, then that person is less easily made subject to an employer's will – something that would be important even when cooperatives are run by democratic majorities, not individual employers. A few contemporary theorists have even argued for an unconditional basic income on just these republican terms.[39] More broadly, the moral claim regarding which human needs should be satisfied can be separated from an argument about controlling the "full" or "fair" value of one's labor without challenging the basic labor republican project. Combining a welfare scheme for guaranteeing basic needs with cooperative control over work would be a way of advancing the labor republican project of enjoying both more freedom at work and freedom from work. It would do so, moreover, in a way that preserves the ideal of individuals as active agents of production, not just passive consumers – which is an advantage it would, or at least could, have over those reform programs *only* concerned with redistribution of income and public goods.

A further Marxist challenge for the labor republican project is political rather than moral. The issue here is voluntarism. One of Marx's most famous criticisms of earlier socialism was that it relied on the philanthropy of the wealthy or on a theory of gradual, historical change defined by the general enlightenment of society rather than class conflict. These "utopian" socialists refused to recognize the necessity of using the state's coercive powers to challenge the ruling class and centrally manage historical transformation.[40] As we saw, labor republicans certainly rejected appeals to philanthropy and they were confident in the agency of workers to overcome their dependence. However, although equivocal and internally divided on this matter, labor republicans were still voluntarists of a certain sort. They tended to think that central coordination of activities, especially through the coercive apparatus of the state or some large-scale organization like the Knights of Labor, was inconsistent with the cooperative project. Cooperatives lost their character as voluntary associations if, for instance, they raised their capital through mandatory contributions by members, or by taxation of the population at large.[41] Despite their far-reaching criticism of existing property relationships, they were often, though not always, surprisingly unwilling to challenge the property-rights of existing owners – with land distribution being a notable exception.[42] This might have been out of suspicion that the state could never really be democratically controlled, and thus could not be trusted; or it may have stemmed from an excessive optimism about the ability of workers to accumulate their own capital without state-led redistribution. But this ambivalence toward the state was also because of a certain voluntarist view of how cooperative organizations should be formed and

---

[39] Casassas, "Basic Income and the Republican Ideal: Rethinking Material Independence in Contemporary Societies"; Pettit, "A Republican Right to Basic Income?"; Pettit, *Republicanism*, 158–65. I have argued these proposals are inadequate from a republican standpoint in Gourevitch, "Labor Republicanism and the Transformation of Work."
[40] Karl Marx, "Critique of the Gotha Programme," in *The Marx-Engels Reader Second Edition*, ed. Robert Tucker (New York: W. W. Norton, 1978), 537–39.
[41] This was a divisive debate within the Knights of Labor, but the majority of Knights sided with voluntarism. See Leikin, *The Practical Utopians*, 43–46, 58–66.
[42] See for example A. J. Story, "The Land Question," *JUL* IV, no. 5 (September 15, 1883), 555–57; Weir, "A Fragile Alliance."

maintained.⁴³ This voluntarism informed a view of social change and economic reproduction that it is hard to credit as realistic. Especially today, it is hard to imagine how relatively poor workers could acquire enough capital to form cooperatives that could compete in major markets – not just in the interstices of the economy – let alone how these cooperatives could weather the long-run ups and downs of the market economy. As the best studies of cooperation during the late nineteenth century show, they were most successful when they had the support of the Knights, especially when, at its peak, the Knights were operating something like a state within a state.⁴⁴

To raise the funds, create the legal conditions, and maintain the credit environment necessary to sustain a network of cooperatives requires access to a considerable amount of property as well as control over the state. The state will still have to tax, pass laws, and enforce regulations, even if many of the reasons for labor regulation will have disappeared. Centralization and some amount of coercion are unavoidable. As a matter of political sociology, it was unreasonable for labor republicans to imagine that purely voluntary efforts, as they became successful, would be able seriously to challenge the class of private property-owners. Many knew it, though they were not always willing to follow through on the implications.⁴⁵ Moreover, as a matter of technical economics, some coordination – of capital flows, welfare claims, production decisions, regulation – was and is inescapable.

There is no need to settle the controversy over the relative superiority of market prices or state planning to register the general point that labor republicans failed to address some important ambiguities in their own argument. The cooperative commonwealth was a challenge to the economic prerogatives of an entire class, and it would require ongoing central coordination to create, let alone maintain, it. For these reasons, control over and use of the state seems to be an unavoidable part of the republican project, even if we accept that there are ways in which cooperative production might lead to a reduction in state regulation. This is all the more true if we accept the prior point, regarding the necessity of certain welfare programs, like a basic income and public health insurance. That too would have to be administered by the state.

The Politics of Republicanism

These are tentative criticisms, offered in the spirit of taking labor republicanism seriously as a contribution to our own ideas, not just as a defeated historical alternative. But of course, the history of how others thought is no substitute

---

[43] Fink, *Workingmen's Democracy*, 18–37.
[44] Leikin, *The Practical Utopians*, 57–88; Levine, *Labor's True Woman*, 99–102.
[45] E.g., "Legalize Co-Operation"; "Boycotting May Be Illegal"; Sharpe, "Co-Operation"; "Co-Operation: A Lecture Delivered before the Local Assemblies of Easton, PA., by Charles Summerman, of the State Labor Bureau of New Jersey."

for our own thinking. Moreover, there is no way to take labor republicans seriously without addressing their *political* challenge. By which I mean their view that the cooperative ideal was and is inextricable from the agent that makes it real. As we saw in Chapter 5, they argued that the central or hegemonic agent would have to be the dependent class of workers itself. Otherwise, there was some sense in which one could not say cooperative production secured the independence of each person. If an idea had to be coercively imposed on most people, then there is a way in which it was not an expression of their independent will and judgment. It was just an idea, imposed like any other.

Thus, although labor republican social analysis gave reason to believe that some amount of state coercion, in order to redistribute ownership and control, would be inevitable, we can easily understand why they were chary about taking that step, or at least over-emphasizing it. It is easy for the justification of coercion to take on a life of its own, not to mention narrow our sense of what counts as politics. In our own time, political philosophy sometimes collapses into the practice of coming up with rules for the legitimate use of state coercion, as if politics had no life beyond the state. We do well to understand why the labor republican conception of politics extended beyond the coercive state, to the practices of self-education and organization. If we, like they, start from actual conditions of inequality and domination, then we should also reflect on the processes by which dependent groups organize and educate themselves, and on the principles that underpin that kind of activity. Independence is not just an economic status that people possess, it is a political and social experience that people win for themselves. More often than not, they win that independence as a collective, even if they enjoy it as individuals.

Bibliography

Periodicals

John Swinton's Paper (JSP)
Journal of United Labor (JUL)
Knights of Labor (KoL)
Labor Leaf
The Liberator
Mechanics' Free Press
The Working Man's Advocate (WMA)
Young America (YA)

Primary Sources

Aristotle. *Politics*, trans. C. D. C Reeve. Indianapolis: Hackett, 1998.
    Rhetoric, trans. W. Rhys Roberts. New York: Courier Dover Publications, 2004.
Franklin, Benjamin. "A Modest Enquiry into the Nature and Necessity of a Paper Currency," in *The Works of Benjamin Franklin, Vol. I Autobiography, Letters and Misc. Writings 1725–1734*, ed. John Bigelow. New York: G. P. Putnam's Sons, 1904.
Brown, David. "Seditious Writings," in *The Faith of Our Fathers: An Anthology Expressing the Aspirations of the American Common Man 1790–1860*, eds. Irving Mark and Eugene L. Schwab. New York: Alfred A. Knopf, 1952.
Brownson, Orestes A. "Brownson's Defence: Defence of the Article on the Laboring Classes." *Boston Quarterly Review* (1840): 1–94.
Byllesby, Langdon. *Observations on the Sources and Effects of Unequal Wealth*. New York: Lewis J. Nichols, 1826.
Calhoun, John C. "Speech on the Reception of Abolition Petitions," in *Slavery Defended: The Views of the Old South*, ed. Eric L. McKitrick. New York: Columbia University Press, 1963.
Carey, Henry. *Principles of Political Economy: Part the Third; of the Causes Which Retard Increase in the Numbers of Mankind, Part the Fourth; of the Causes Which*

  Retard Improvement in the Political Condition of Man. Philadelphia; London: Lea & Blanchard; John Miller, 1840.
Carter, Nathaniel H., William L. Stone, and Marcus T. C. Gould. *Reports of the Proceedings and Debates of the New York Constitutional Convention 1821*. Albany: E. and E. Hosford, 1821.
Cicero. *On Duties*, trans. E. M. Atkins. Cambridge: Cambridge University Press, 1991.
  "On the Commonwealth," in *On the Commonwealth and On the Laws*, trans. James E. G. Zetzel. Cambridge: Cambridge University Press, 2003.
  On the Ends of Good and Evil, trans. H. Rackham. London: Loeb Classical Library, 1914.
  "On the Laws," in *On the Commonwealth and On the Laws*, ed. James E. G. Zetzel. Cambridge: Cambridge University Press, 2003.
  The Nature of the Gods, trans. H. Rackham. Cambridge: Harvard University Press, Loeb Classical Library, 1956.
Colquhoun, Patrick. *A Treatise on the Wealth, Power, and Resources of the British Empire*. London: Joseph Mawman, 1814.
Commons, John R. et al., eds. "Constitution of the Philadelphia Labour for Labour Association," in *A Documentary History of American Industrial Society Volume V: the Labor Movement*. Cleveland: The Arthur H. Clark Company, 1910.
Constant, Benjamin. "The Liberty of the Ancients as Compared with That of the Moderns," in *Constant: Political Writings*, ed. Biancamaria Fontana. Cambridge: Cambridge University Press, 1988.
Cooley, Thomas McIntyre. *A Treatise on the Law of Torts; or, the Wrongs Which Arise Independently of Contract*. London: Callaghan & Company, 1888.
De Voltaire, M. "Slaves," in *A Philosophical Dictionary Vol. 2*. London: W. Dugdale, 1843.
Debow, J. D. B. "The Interest in Slavery of the Southern Non-Slaveholder," in *Slavery Defended: The Views of the Old South*, ed. Eric L. McKitrick. Englewood Cliffs: Prentice-Hall, 1963.
Dew, Thomas. "Review of the Debate in the Virginia Legislature," in *Slavery Defended: The Views of the Old South*, ed. Eric L. McKitrick. Englewood Cliffs: Prentice-Hall, 1963.
Fisk, Theophilus. *Capital Against Labor: An Address Delivered at Julien Hall, Before the Mechanics of Boston, on Wednesday Evening, May 20*. Boston: Theophilus Fisk, 1835.
Fitzhugh, George. *Cannibals All!, or, Slaves without Masters*. Cambridge: Harvard University Press, 1988.
  "Sociology for the South," in *Slavery Defended: The Views of the Old South*, ed. Eric L. McKitrick. Englewood Cliffs: Prentice-Hall, 1963.
Gantt, T. Fulton. "Breaking the Chains: A Story of the Present Industrial Struggle," in *The Knights in Fiction: Two Labor Novels of the 1880s*, ed. Mary C. Grimes. Champaign: University of Illinois Press, 1986.
Godkin, E. L. "The Labor Crisis." *The North American Review* CV (1867): 177–213.
Hammond, James Henry. *Mudsill Speech*. The Congressional Globe, 1858.
Harrington, James. *The Commonwealth of Oceana and a System of Politics*. Cambridge: Cambridge University Press, 1992.
Heighton, William. *An Address Delivered before the Mechanics and Working Classes Generally, of the City and County of Philadelphia. At the Universalist Church, in*

Callowhill Street, on Wednesday Evening, November 21, 1827, by the "Unlettered Mechanic." Philadelphia: The Office of the Mechanics Gazette, 1828.

An Address to the Members of Trade Societies, and to the Working Classes Generally: Being an Exposition of the Relative Situation, Condition, and Future Prospects of Working People in the United States of America. Together with a Suggestion and Outlines of a Plan, by Which They May Gradually and Indefinitely Improve Their Condition. London: Sold at the Rooms of the Co-operative Society, Reprinted from Philadelphia Edition, 1827.

The Principles of Aristocratic Legislation Developed in an Address Delivered to the Working People of the District of Southwark, and Townships of Moyamensing and Passyunk. Philadelphia: J. Coates Jr., 1828.

Jefferson, Thomas. "Autobiography," in *Writings*, ed. Merrill D. Peterson. New York: The Library of America, 1984.

"Letter to Edward Coles," in *Thomas Jefferson: Political Writings*, eds. Joyce Appleby and Terence Ball. Cambridge: Cambridge University Press, 1999.

Notes on the State of Virginia. New York: Harpers & Row, 1964.

"To Benjamin Austin, January 9, 1816," in *Thomas Jefferson: Writings*, ed. Merrill D. Peterson. New York: The Library of America, 1984.

"To Dr. Edward Bancroft, Jan. 26, 1789," in *Thomas Jefferson: Political Writings*, eds. Joyce Appleby and Terence Ball. Cambridge: Cambridge University Press, 1999.

"To Dr. Thomas Humphreys," in *Thomas Jefferson: Political Writings*, eds. Joyce Appleby and Terence Ball. Cambridge: Cambridge University Press, 1999.

"To John Holmes, April 22, 1820," in *Thomas Jefferson: Political Writings*, eds. Joyce Appleby and Terence Ball. Cambridge: Cambridge University Press, 1999.

"To St. George Tucker, August 28, 1797," in *Thomas Jefferson: Political Writings*, eds. Joyce Appleby and Terence Ball. Cambridge: Cambridge University Press, 1999.

Jelley, Symmes M. *The Voice of Labor*. Chicago: A. B. Gehman & Co., 1887.

Kant, Immanuel. "On the Common Saying: 'This May Be True in Theory, but It Does Not Apply in Practice,'" in *Kant Political Writings*, ed. H. S. Reiss. Cambridge: Cambridge University Press, 1991.

Lincoln, Abraham. "Address to the Wisconsin State Agricultural Society," in *The Portable Abraham Lincoln* ed. Andrew Delbanco. New York: Penguin Books, 1992.

Livius, Titus. *The History of Rome, Vol. 2*, trans. B. O. Foster. London: Loeb Classical Library, 1922.

Lloyd, Henry Demarest. *Wealth against Commonwealth*. Englewood Cliffs, NJ: Prentice Hall, Inc., 1963.

Luther, Seth. *An Address to the Working Men of New England, on the State of Education, and the Condition of the Producing Classes in Europe and America* ed. George Evans. New York: The Office of the Working Man's Advocate, 1833.

Machiavelli, Niccolo. *The Discourses* trans. Leslie J. Walker. New York: Penguin Classics, 1998.

Madison, James. "Federalist No. 10," in *The Essential Federalist and Anti-Federalist Papers*, ed. David Wootton. Indianapolis: Hackett, 2009.

"James Madion, Note to His Speech on the Right of Suffrage," in *The Founders' Constitution*, eds. Philip B. Kurland and Ralph Lerner. Chicago: University of Chicago Press, 1821.

Manning, William. "Some Proposals for Making Restitution to the Original Creditors of Government." *William & Mary Quarterly* 46.2 (1989): 320–31.

"The Key of Liberty." *The William and Mary Quarterly* 13.2 (1956): 209–54.
Mark, Irving and Eugene L. Schwaab, eds. "The Memorial of the Non-Freeholders of Richmond, Virginian [1829]," in *The Faith of Our Fathers: An Anthology Expressing the Apsirations of the American Common Man 1790–1860*. New York: Alfred A. Knopf, 1952.
Marx, Karl. "Critique of the Gotha Programme," in *The Marx-Engels Reader Second Edition*, ed. Robert Tucker. New York: W. W. Norton, 1978.
McNeill, George E. *The Labor Movement: The Problem of To-Day*. New York: The M. W. Hazen Co., 1892.
Mechanick, A Brother. "To the MECHANICKS of PHILADELPHIA." *The INDEPENDENT GAZETTEER; or the CHRONICLE of FREEDOM* 11 Oct. 1783: 2.
Owen, Robert. *Two Discourses on a New System of Society as Delivered in the Hall of Representatives at Washington*. London: Whiting & Branston, 1825.
Paine, Thomas. "Agrarian Justice," in *Thomas Paine: Common Sense and Other Writings*, ed. Joyce Appleby. New York: Barnes & Noble, 2005.
   Rights of Man. New York: Citadel Press, 1991.
Phillips, Wendell. *The Labor Question*. Boston: Lee and Shepard, 1884.
Pickering, John. *The Working Man's Political Economy*. Cincinnati, OH: Thomas Varney, 1847.
Powderly, Terence. *Labor: Its Rights and Wrongs*. Westport, CT: Hyperion Press, 1886.
   Thirty Years of Labor 1859–1889. Columbus, OH: Excelsior Publishing House, 1889.
   The Path I Trod: The Autobiography of Terence v. Powderly. New York: Columbia University Press, 1940.
Powderly, Terence, ed. "Knights of Labor Platform – Preamble and Declaration of Principles," in *Labor: Its Rights and Wrongs*. Washington DC: The Labor Publishing Company, 1886.
Report of the Committee of the Senate upon the Relations between Labor and Capital, and Testimony Taken by the Committee: Volume I. Report of the Committee of the Senate upon the Relations between Labor and Capital, and Testimony Taken by the Committee: Volume I. Washington, DC: Government Printing Office, 1885.
Report of the Special Commission on the Hours of Labor and the Condition and Prospects of the Industrial Classes. Report of the Special Commission on the Hours of Labor and the Condition and Prospects of the Industrial Classes. Boston: Wright & Potter, State Printers, 1866.
Sallust. *Conspiracy of Catiline*, trans. Rev. John Selby Watson. New York and London: Harper & Brothers, 1899.
Sidney, Algernon. *Discourses Concerning Government Vol II*. Edinburgh: G. Hamilton and J. Balfour, 1750.
Simpson, Stephen. *The Working Man's Manual: A New Theory of Political Economy, on the Principle of Production the Source of Wealth*. Philadelphia: Thomas L. Bonsal, 1831.
Skidmore, Thomas. *The Rights of Man to Property!* New York: Alexander Ming, 1829.
Smith, Adam. *The Theory of Moral Sentiments*. Indianapolis: Liberty Fund, 1976.

Steward, Ira. "A Reduction of Hours an Increase of Wages," in *A Documentary History of American Industrial Society*, ed. T. Fly. Norman: The Arthur H. Clark Company, 1910.

"Poverty," in *Fourth Annual Report of the Bureau of Statistics of Labor*, ed. Massachusetts Bureau of Statistics of Labor. Vol. 173. Boston: Wright & Potter, State Printers, 1873.

The Eight Hour Movement: A Reduction of Hours Is an Increase of Wages. Boston: Boston Labor Reform Association, 1865.

The Meaning of the Eight Hour Movement. Boston: Ira Steward, 1868.

Stone, W. W. "The Knights of Labor on the Chinese Situation." *Overland Monthly and Out West Magazine* VII, no. 39 (March, 1886): 225–30.

Sullivan, James. *James Sullivan to Jeremy Belknap*, eds. Philip B. Kurland and Ralph Lerner. Vol. 1. Chicago: University of Chicago Press, 1986.

Sumner, William Graham. "The Absurd Effort to Make the World Over." *Forum* Mar. 1894: 92–102.

What Social Classes Owe to Each Other. New York: Harper & Brothers Publishers, 1883.

Sylvis, James C. "Biography of William H. Sylvis," in *The Life, Speeches, Labors and Essays of William H. Sylvis*, ed. James C. Sylvis. Philadelphia: Claxton, Remsen & Haffelfinger, 1872.

Sylvis, William H. "Address Delivered at Buffalo, N.Y., January, 1864," in *The Life, Speeches, Labors and Essays of William H. Sylvis*, ed. James C. Sylvis. Philadelphia: Claxton, Remsen & Haffelfinger, 1872.

"Address Delivered at Chicago, January 9, 1865," in *The Life, Speeches, Labors and Essays of William H. Sylvis*, ed. James C. Sylvis. Philadelphia: Claxton, Remsen & Haffelfinger, 1872.

"Aristocracy of Intellect," in *The Life, Speeches, Labors and Essays of William H. Sylvis*, ed. James C. Sylvis. Philadelphia: Claxton, Remsen & Haffelfinger, 1872.

"Co-Operation," in *The Life, Speeches, Labors and Essays of William H. Sylvis*, ed. James C. Sylvis. Philadelphia: Claxton, Remsen &Haffelfinger, 1872.

"The Uses of Co-Operation," in *The Life, Speeches, Labors and Essays of William H. Sylvis*, ed. James C. Sylvis. Philadelphia: Claxton, Remsen & Haffelfinger, 1872.

Tiedeman, Christopher Gustavus. *A Treatise on the Limitations of the Police Power in the United States*. St. Louis, MO: The F. H. Thomas Law Book Co., 1886.

Tocqueville, Alexis de. *Democracy in America*, trans. George Lawrence. New York: HarperCollins, 2006.

Tucker, St. George. *A Dissertation on Slavery, in Blackstone's Commentaries*, eds. Philip B. Kurland and Ralph Lerner. Vol. 1. Chicago: University of Chicago Press, 1986.

Warren, Josiah. "Letter from Josiah Warren," in *A Documentary History of American Industrial Society Volume v: the Labor Movement*, eds. John R. Commons et al. Cleveland, OH: The Arthur H. Clark Company, 1910.

Whitwell, Stedman. "Description of an Architectural Model From a Design by Stedman Whitwell, Esq. for a Community upon a Principle of United Interests, as Advocated by Robert Owen, Esq.," in *Cooperative Communities: Plans and Descriptions*, ed. Kenneth E. Carpenter. New York: Arno Press, 1972.

Secondary Sources

Ackerman, Bruce. *We the People: Foundations*. Cambridge, MA: The Belknap Press of Harvard University Press, 1991.

Adair, Douglass G. *The Intellectual Origins of Jeffersonian Democracy: Republicanism, the Class Struggle, and the Virtuous Farmer*. Lanham: Lexington Books, 1964.

Adamic, Louis. *Dynamite; the Story of Class Violence in America*. New York: Chelsea House Publishers, 1971.

American Civil Liberties Union, "Legislative Briefing Kit: Wrongful Discharge," (December 31, 1998).

Appleby, Joyce. *Capitalism and a New Social Order: The Republican Vision of the 1790s*. New York: New York University Press, 1984.

"Republicanism in Old and New Contexts." *The William and Mary Quarterly* 43.1 (1986): 20–34.

"The 'Agrarian Myth' in the Early Republic," in *Liberalism and Republicanism in the Historical Imagination*. Cambridge, MA: Harvard University Press, 1992.

Arky, Louis H. "The Mechanics' Union of Trade Associations and the Formation of the Philadelphia Workingmen's Movement." *The Pennsylvania Magazine of History and Biography* 76.2 (1952): 142–76.

Barber, Alan. "Pro-Union Workers Fired in Over One-fourth of Union Election Campaigns." *The Center for Economic and Policy Research* (March 4, 2009).

Benedict, Les Michael. "Laissez-Faire and Liberty: A Re-Evaluation of the Meaning and Origins of Laissez-Faire Constitutionalism." *Law and History Review* 3.2 (1985): 293–331.

Bennett-Smith, Meredith. "Indiana AT&T Technicians File Class Action Lawsuit Citing Grim Break Conditions." *The Huffington Post*, (August 14, 2012).

Berlin, Isaiah. "Two Concepts of Liberty." *Four Essays on Liberty*. Oxford and New York: Oxford University Press, 1979.

Bertram, Chris et al. "Let It Bleed: Libertarianism and the Workplace," *Crooked Timber*, (July 1, 2012).

Bestor Jr, Arthur E. "The Evolution of the Socialist Vocabulary." *Journal of the History of Ideas* (1948): 259–302.

Bogin, Ruth. "Petitioning and the New Moral Economy of Post-Revolutionary America." *The William and Mary Quarterly* 45.3 (1988): 392–425.

Brest, Paul et al. *Processes of Constitutional Decisionmaking: Cases and Materials*. 4 ed. Boston: Little Brown, 2003.

Brown, Robert Maxwell. "Back Country Rebellions and the Homestead Ethic in America, 1749–1799," in *Tradition, Conflict, and Modernization: Perspectives on the American Revolution*, eds. Richard Maxwell Brown and Don Fehrenbacher. New York: Academic Press, 1977.

Brunt, Paul A. "The Roman Mob." *Past & Present* 35 (1966): 3–27.

Buhle, Paul. "The Republic of Labor: the Knights in Rhode Island," in *From the Knights of Labor to the New World Order: Essay on Labor and Culture*. New York: Garland Publishing, Inc., 1997.

Burke, Martin J. *The Conundrum of Class: Public Discourse on the Social Order in America*. Chicago: University of Chicago Press, 1995.

Bushman, Richard L. "Massachusetts Farmers and the Revolution," in *Society, Freedom, and Conscience: The American Revolution in Virginia, Massachusetts, and New York*, ed. Richard M. Jellison. New York: W. W. Norton & Company, 1976.

Carter, Ian. "How Are Power and Unfreedom Related?," in *Republicanism and Political Theory*, eds. Cecil Laborde and John Maynor. Oxford: Blackwell Publishing, 2008.

Casassas, David. "Basic Income and the Republican Ideal: Rethinking Material Independence in Contemporary Societies." *Basic Income Studies* 2.2 (2008): 1–7.

Claeys, Gregory. "Introduction," in *The Politics of English Jacobinism: Writings of John Thelwall*, ed. Gregory Claeys. University Park: Pennsylvania State University Press, 1995.

"The Origins of the Rights of Labor: Republicanism, Commerce, and the Construction of Modern Social Theory in Britain, 1796–1805." *The Journal of Modern History* 66.2 (1994): 249–90.

Cotlar, Seth. *Tom Paine's America: The Rise and Fall of Transatlantic Radicalism in the Early Republic*. Charlottesville: University of Virginia Press, 2011.

Crowell, Chris. "Housekeeping Communication Gets More Efficient, High-Tech," *Hotelmanagement.net*, (October 6, 2008).

Cunliffe, Marcus. *Chattel Slavery and Wage Slavery: The Anglo-American Context, 1830–1860*. Athens: University of Georgia Press, 1979.

Currarino, Rosanne. *The Labor Question in America: Economic Democracy in the Gilded Age*. Urbana: University of Illinois Press, 2011.

Dagger, Richard. *Civic Virtues: Rights, Citizenship, and Republican Liberalism*. Oxford: Oxford University Press, 1997.

"Neo-Republicanism and the Civic Economy." *Politics, Philosophy & Economics* 5.2 (2006): 151–73.

De Ste Croix, G. E. M. "Review: Slavery." *The Classical Review* 7.1 (1957): 54–59.

Domhoff, G. William. "Wealth, Income, and Power" *Who Rules America*, accessible at http://www2.ucsc.edu/whorulesamerica/power/wealth.html.

Douglas, Dorothy W. "Ira Steward on Consumption and Unemployment." *The Journal of Political Economy* 40.4 (1932): 532–43.

Dubofsky, Melvyn. *Industrialism and the American Worker*. Arlington Heights, IL: Harlan Davidson, Inc., 1985.

Egelko, Bob. "Employers Must Pay if They Deny Lunch Breaks." *The San Francisco Chronicle*, (February 18 2011).

Emerson, Ramona. "13 Controversial Facebook Firings: Palace Guards, Doctors, Teachers and More." *The Huffington Post*, (October 17, 2011).

Epstein, Richard A. "Modern Republicanism, Or, The Flight From Substance." *Yale Law Journal* 97.8 (1988): 1633–50.

Ernst, Joseph A. "Shays's Rebellion in Long Perspective: The Merchants and the 'Money Question,'" in *In Debt to Shays: The Bicentennial of an Agrarian Rebellion*, Ed. Robert A. Gross. Boston: The Colonial Society of Massachusetts, 1993.

Fink, Leon. "From Autonomy to Abundance: Changing Beliefs about the Free Labor System in Nineteenth-Century America," in *Terms of Labor: Slavery, Serfdom, and Free Labor*, ed. Stanley L. Engerman. Stanford, CA: Stanford University Press, 1999.

"The New Labor History and the Powers of Historical Pessimism: Consensus, Hegemony and the Case of the Knights of Labor." *The Journal of American History* 75.1 (1988): 115–36.

Workingmen's Democracy: The Knights of Labor and American Politics. Urbana and Chicago: University of Illinois Press, 1985.

Finley, Moses. "Between Slavery and Freedom." *Comparative Studies in Society and History* 6.3 (1964): 233–249.
The Ancient Economy. Updated. Berkeley: University of California Press, 1999.
"Was Greek Civilization Based on Slave Labour?," in *Slavery in Classical Antiquity: Views and Controversies*, ed. M. I. Finley. Cambridge: W. Heffer & Sons Ltd., 1960.
Foner, Eric. "Abolitionism and the Labor Movement." *Politics and Ideology in the Age of the Civil War*. Oxford: Oxford University Press, 1980.
Free Soil, Free Labor, Free Men: The Ideology of the Republican Party before the Civil War. London, New York: Oxford University Press, 1971.
Nothing but Freedom: Emancipation and Its Legacy. Baton Rouge: Louisana State University Press, 2007.
The Story of American Freedom. New York: W. W. Norton, 1998.
"Workers and Slavery," in *Working for Democracy: American Workers from the Revolution to the Present*, eds. Paul Buhle and Alan Dawley. Urbana: University of Illinois Press, 1985.
Foner, Philip S. *History of the Labor Movement in the United States, Volume 1: From Colonial Times to the Founding of the American Federation of Labor*. New York: International Publishers, 1982.
Fones-Wolf, Ken. *The Boston Eight-Hour Men and the Emergence of American Trade Union Principles, 1863–1891*. Bethesda: University of Maryland Press, 1979.
Forbath, William. "Ambiguities of Free Labor: Labor and the Law in the Gilded Age." *Wisconsin Law Review* (1985): 767.
"Caste, Class, and Equal Citizenship." *Michigan Law Review* 98.1 (1999): 1–91.
Law and the Shaping of the American Labor Movement. Cambridge, MA: Harvard University Press, 1991.
Foxwell, H. S. "Introduction," in *The Right to the Whole Produce of Labor*, ed. H. S. Foxwell. New York: Macmillan and Co., Limited, 1899. v–cx.
"From the Line of MOST Resistance." *American Federationist* 22 (1922): 263.
Garnsey, Peter. *Ideas of Slavery from Aristotle to Augustine*. Cambridge: Cambridge University Press, 1996.
"Non-Slave Labour in the Roman World." *Cambridge Philological Society Supplementary Volume* no. 6 (1980): 34–47.
"Peasants in Ancient Roman Society," in *Cities, Peasants and Food in Classical Antiquity*, ed. Walter Scheidel. Cambridge: Cambridge University Press, 1998.
Social Status and Legal Privilege in the Roman Empire. Oxford: Oxford University Press, 1970.
Ghosh, Eric. "From Republican to Liberal Liberty." *History of Political Thought* XXIX.1 (2008): 132–67.
Gilbert, Amos. *The Life of Thomas Skidmore*, ed. Mark Lause. Chicago: Charles H. Kerr Publishing Company, 1984.
Gillman, Howard. *The Constitution Besieged: The Rise and Demise of Lochner Era Police Powers Jurisprudence*. Durham, NC: Duke University Press, 1993.
Glendon, Mary Ann, ed. *Seedbeds of Virtue: Sources of Competence, Character, and Citizenship in American Society*. Lanham, MD: Madison Books, 1995.
Glickman, Lawrence B. *A Living Wage: American Workers and the Making of Consumer Society*. Ithaca, NY: Cornell University Press, 1997.
Goodin, Robert E. "Folie Républicaine." *Annual Review of Political Science* 6.1 (2003): 55–76.

Gourevitch, Alex. "Labor and Republican Liberty." *Constellations* 18.3 (2011): 431–54.
  "Labor Republicanism and the Transformation of Work." *Political Theory* 41.4 (2013): 591–617.
  "Review: Rosanne Currarino's the Labor Question in America: Economic Democracy in the Gilded Age." *Historical Materialism* 21.2 (2013): 179–90.
  "William Manning and the Political Theory of the Dependent Classes." *Modern Intellectual History* 9.2 (2012): 331–60.
Greenberg, Joshua R. "'Powerful – Very Powerful Is the Parental Feeling': Fatherhood, Domestic Politics, and the New York City Working Men's Party." *Early American Studies: An Interdisciplinary Journal* 2.1 (2004): 192–227.
Grob, Gerald N. *Workers and Utopia: A Study of Ideological Conflict in the American Labor Movement, 1865–1900*. Evanston, IL: Northwestern University Press, 1961.
Gutman, Herbert. *Work, Culture and Society in Industrializing America*. New York: Vintage, 1976.
Hacker, Barton C. "The United States Army as a National Police Force: The Federal Policing of Labor Disputes, 1877–1898." *Military Affairs* 33.1 (1969): 1–11.
Hankins, James. "Exclusivist Republicanism and the Non-Monarchical Republic." *Political Theory* 38.4 (2010): 452–82.
Hansen, Mogens Herman. *The Athenian Democracy in the Age of Demosthenes*. Oxford: Blackwell, 1991.
Harris, David Anthony. *Socialist Origins in the United States*. Amsterdam: Van Gorcum & Co., 1966.
Hartz, Louis. *The Liberal Tradition in America*. New York: Harcourt, Brace & World, Inc., 1955.
Henwood, Doug. *After the New Economy*. New York: The New Press, 2003.
Hess, Amanda. "How Sexy Should A Worker Be? The Plight of the Babe in the American Workplace." *Slate Magazine*, (July 29, 2013).
Herzog, Don. "Some Questions for Republicans." *Political Theory* 14.3 (1986): 473–93.
Hirschman, Albert O. *The Passions and the Interests: Political Arguments for Capitalism before Its Triumph*. Princeton, NJ: Princeton University Press, 1996.
Hofstadter, Richard. *The American Political Tradition and the Men Who Made It*. New York: Knopf, 1973.
Hopkins, Keith. *Conquerors and Slaves*. Cambridge: Cambridge University Press, 1981.
Horner, Clare Dahlberg. *Producers' Co-Operatives in the United States, 1865–1890*. Ph.D Dissertation. University of Pittsburgh, 1978.
Horwitz, Morton J. "Republicanism and Liberalism in American Constitutional Thought." *William & Mary Law Review* 29 (1987): 57–74.
  Transformation of American Law, 1870–1960: The Crisis of Legal Orthodoxy. Oxford University Press, 1994.
Houston, Alan Craig. *Algernon Sidney and the Republican Heritage in England and America*. Princeton, NJ: Princeton University Press, 1991.
Hsieh, Nien-hê. "Rawlsian Justice and Workplace Republicanism." *Social Theory and Practice* 31.1 (2005): 115–42.
Hsu, Tiffany. "Amazon Warehouse Employees Overheated ahead of Holiday Season" *The Los Angeles Times*, (September 19 2011).
The Institutes of Justinian, trans. J. B. Moyle. Charleston, SC: BiblioBazaar, 2008.

Jameson, Michael H. "Agriculture and Slavery in Classical Athens." *The Classical Journal* 73.2 (1977): 122–45.

Jamieson, Dave. "Amazon Warehouse Workers Sue over Security Checkpoint Waits." *The Huffington Post*, (May 8, 2013).

Jones, A. H. M. "Slavery in the Ancient World," in *Slavery in Classical Antiquity: Controversies and Debates*, ed. Moses Finley. Cambridge: W. Heffer & Sons Ltd., 1960.

Jurdjevic, Mark. "Virtue, Commerce, and the Enduring Florentine Republican Moment: Reintegrating Italy Into the Atlantic Republican Debate." *Journal of the History of Ideas* 62.4 (2001): 721–43.

Kalyvas, Andreas, and Ira Katznelson. *Liberal Beginnings*. Cambridge: Cambridge University Press, 2008.

Kapust, Daniel. "Skinner, Pettit and Livy: The Conflict of the Orders and the Ambiguity of Republican Liberty." *History of Political Thought* XXV.3 (2010): 377–401.

Keyssar, Alexander. *The Right to Vote: The Contested History of Democracy in the United States*. New York: Basic Books, 2000.

King, J. E. "Utopian or Scientific? A Reconsideration of the Ricardian Socialists." *History of Political Economy* 15.3 (1983): 345–73.

Kramer, Larry. *The People Themselves: Popular Constitutionalism and Judicial Review*. New York: Oxford University Press, 2004.

Kramer, Matthew H. "Liberty and Domination," in *Republicanism and Political Theory*, eds. Cecile Laborde and John Maynor. Oxford: Blackwell, 2008.

Kramnick, Isaac. "Republican Revisionism Revisited." *The American Historical Review* 87.3 (1982): 629–64.

Krause, Sharon. "Beyond Non-Domination: Agency, Inequality, and the Meaning of Freedom." *Philosophy and Social Criticism* 39.2 (2013): 187–208.

Larmore, Charles. "Liberal and Republican Conceptions of Freedom," in *Republicanism: History, Theory and Practice*, ed. Daniel Weinstock. London: Routledge, 2004.

Laurie, Bruce. *Working People of Philadelphia, 1800–1850*. Philadelphia: Temple University Press, 1980.

Lause, Mark A. *Young America: Land, Labour, and the Republican Community*. Champaign: University of Illinois Press, 2005.

Lee, Daniel. "Popular Liberty, Princely Government, and the Roman Law in Hugo Grotius's De Jure Belli Ac Pacis." *Journal of the History of Ideas* 72.3 (2011): 371–92.

Leikin, Steven. *The Practical Utopians: American Workers and the Cooperative Movement in the Gilded Age*. Detroit: Wayne State University Press, 2004.

Levine, Susan. *Labor's True Woman: Carpet Weavers, Industrialization, and Labor Reform in the Gilded Age*. Philadelphia: Temple University Press, 1984.

  "Labor's True Woman: Domesticity and Equal Rights in the Knights of Labor." *The Journal of American History* 70.2 (1983): 323–39.

  "Liberty before Liberalism and All That: Quentin Skinner Interviewed by Richard Marshall" *3am Magazine*, (February 18, 2013), accessible at http://www.3ammagazine.com/3am/liberty-before-liberalism-all-that.

Lintott, Andrew. "Citizenship," in *A Companion to Ancient History*, ed. Andrew Erskine. West Sussex: Blackwell, 2009.

  Judicial Reform and Land Reform in the Roman Republic. Cambridge: Cambridge University Press, 1992.

  The Constitution of the Roman Republic. Oxford: Clarendon Press, 1999.

Little, Lyneka. "AT&T Workers Claim Lunch Break Violations." *ABC News*, (August 15, 2012).

Lowenthal, Esther. "The Ricardian Socialists." *Studies in History, Economics and Public Law* XLVI.I (1911): 5–105.

Lurie, Ronald, and Jonathan Labbe. *The Slaughterhouse Cases: Regulation, Reconstruction, and the Fourteenth Amendment*. Lawrence: University Press of Kansas, 2003.

Macpherson, C. B. "Harrington as Realist: a Rejoinder." *Past & Present* 24 (1963): 82–85.

Maddox, Graham. "The Limits of Neo-Roman Liberty." *History of Political Thought* XXIII.3 (2002): 418–31.

Maihofer, Werner. "The Ethos of the Republic and the Reality of Politics," in *Machiavelli and Republicanism*, eds. Quentin Skinner and Maurizio Viroli Gisela Bock. Cambridge: Cambridge University Press, 1990.

Mandel, Bernard. *Labor, Free and Slave: Workingmen and the Anti-Slavery Movement in the United States*. Champaign: University of Illinois Press, 1955.

Markell, Patchen. "The Insufficiency of Non-Domination." *Political Theory* 36.1 (2008): 9–36.

Maynor, John and Cecil Laborde. "The Republican Contribution to Political Theory," in *Republicanism and Political Theory*, eds. Cecil Laborde and John Maynor. Oxford: Blackwell Publishing, 2008.

Maynor, John W. *Republicanism in the Modern World*. Oxford: Polity, 2003.

McCormick, John P. "Machiavelli against Republicanism: on the Cambridge School's 'Guicciardinian Moments.'" *Political Theory* 31.5 (2003): 615–43.

Menger, Anton. *The Right to the Whole Produce of Labour*, ed. H. S. Foxwell, trans. M. E. Tanner. London: Macmillan and Co., 1899.

Meyerson, Harold. "If Labor Dies, What's Next?" *The American Prospect*, (September 13 2012).

Michelman, Frank I. "Law's Republic." *Yale Law Journal* 97.8 (1988): 1493–537.

Millar, Fergus. *The Roman Republic in Political Thought*. Hanover: University Press of New England, 2002.

Miner, Claudia. "The 1886 Convention of the Knights of Labor." *Phylon (1960-)* 44.2 (1983): 147–59.

Montgomery, David. *Beyond Equality: Labor and the Radical Republicans 1862–1872*. New York: Alfred A. Knopf, 1967.

Citizen-Worker: The Experience of Workers in the United States with Democracy and the Free Market During the Nineteenth Century. Cambridge: Cambridge University Press, 1995.

"Labor and the Republic in Industrial America: 1860–1920." *Le Mouvement social* 111.Georges Haupt parmi nous (1980): 201–15.

"The Working Classes of the Pre-Industrial American City, 1780–1830." *Labor History* IX (1968): 3–22.

"William H. Sylvis and the Search for Working-Class Citizenship," in *Labor Leaders in America*, ed. Warren Van Tine and Melvyn Dubofsky. Urbana and Chicago: University of Illinois Press, 1987.

Morgan, Edmund. *American Slavery, American Freedom*. New York: W. W. Norton & Co., 1975.

"Slavery and Freedom: The American Paradox." *The Journal of American History* 59.1 (1972): 5–29.

Mossé, Claude. *The Ancient World at Work*, trans. Janet Lloyd. New York: W. W. Norton & Company, 1969.
Nelson, Eric. "Liberty: One Concept Too Many?." *Political Theory* 33.1 (2005): 58–78.
  The Greek Tradition in Republican Thought. Cambridge: Cambridge University Press, 2004.
New, John F. H. "Harrington, a Realist?." *Past & Present* 24 (1963): 75–81.
  "The Meaning of Harrington's Agrarian." *Past & Present* 25 (1963): 94–95.
Nicolet, Claude. *The World of the Citizen in Republican Rome*, trans. P. S. Falla. Berkeley: University of California Press, 1980.
Novak, William. "The Legal Origins of the Modern American State," in *Looking Back at Law's Century*, eds. Robert Kagan and Austin Sarat Bryant Garth. Ithaca, NY: Cornell University press, 2001.
Ober, Josiah. *Mass and Elite in Democratic Athens: Rhetoric, Ideology, and the Power of the People*. Princeton, NJ: Princeton University Press, 1990.
Oestreicher, Richard. "A Note on Knights of Labor Membership Statistics." *Labor History* 25.1 (1984): 102–08.
  "Socialism and the Knights of Labor in Detroit, 1877–1886." *Labor History* 22.1 (1981): 5–30.
  Solidarity and Fragmentation: Working People and Class Consciousness in Detroit, 1875–1900. Urbana: University of Illinois Press, 1986.
  "Terence v. Powderly, the Knights of Labor, and Artisanal Republicanism," in *Labor Leaders in America*, ed. Warren Van Tine and Melvyn Dubofsky. Urbana and Chicago: University of Illinois Press, 1987.
Oldfield, Adrian. *Citizenship and Community: Civic Republicanism and the Modern World*. London; New York: Routledge, 1990.
Patten, Alan. "The Republican Critique of Liberalism." *British Journal of Political Science* 26.1 (1996): 25–44.
Patterson, Orlando. *Freedom Vol. 1: Freedom in the Making of Western Culture*. New York: Basic Books, 1991.
Pessen, Edward. *Most Uncommon Jacksonians: The Radical Leaders of the Early Labor Movement*. Albany: State University of New York Press, 1967.
  "The Ideology of Stephen Simpson, Upperclass Champion of the Early Philadelphia Workingmen's Movement." *Pennsylvania History* 22.4 (1955): 328–40.
  "The Workingmen's Movement of the Jacksonian Era." *The Mississippi Valley Historical Review* 43.3 (1956): 428–43.
  "Thomas Skidmore, Agrarian Reformer in the Early American Labor Movement." *New York History* 35.3 (1954): 280–96.
Pettit, Philip. "A Republican Right to Basic Income?." *Basic Income Studies* 2.2 (2007): 1–8.
  "Freedom in the Market." *Politics, Philosophy & Economics* 5.2 (2006): 131–49.
  "Republican Freedom: Three Axioms, Four Theorems," in *Republicanism and Political Theory*, eds. Cecil Laborde and John Maynor. Oxford: Blackwell Publishing, 2008.
  Republicanism: A Theory of Freedom and Government. Oxford: Oxford University Press, 1999.
Pitts, Jennifer. "Republicanism, Liberalism, and Empire in Post-Revolutionary France," in *Empire and Political Thought*, ed. Sankar Muthu. Cambridge: Cambridge University Press, 2012.

Pocock, J. G. A. "Review: Virtue and Commerce in the Eighteenth Century." *Journal of Interdisciplinary History* 3.1 (1972): 119–34.
  The Machiavellian Moment: Florentine Political Thought and the Atlantic Republican Tradition. Princeton, NJ: Princeton University Press, 2003.
Pope, James Gray. "Labor's Constitution of Freedom." *Yale Law Journal* 106.4 (1997): 941–1031.
  "The Thirteenth Amendment versus the Commerce Clause: Labor and the Shaping of American Constitutional Law, 1921–1957." *Columbia Law Review* 102.1 (2002): 1–122.
Rahe, Paul. "Antiquity Surpassed: the Repudiation of Classical Republicanism," in *Republicanism, Liberty, and Commercial Society*, ed. David Wootton. Stanford, CA: Stanford University Press, 1994.
Rana, Aziz. *The Two Faces of American Freedom*. Cambridge, MA: Harvard University, 2010.
Rawson, Elizabeth. "The Ciceronian Aristocracy and Its Properties," in *Studies in Roman Property*, ed. M. I. Finley. Cambridge: Syndics of the Cambridge University Press, 1976.
Resnikoff, Ned. "ACLU locked in contract dispute with employee union" *MSNBC*, (July 25, 2013).
Robbins, Caroline. *The Eighteenth Century Commonwealthman*. Indianapolis, IN: Liberty Fund, 2004.
Rodgers, Daniel T. *The Work Ethic in Industrial America, 1850–1920*. Chicago: University of Chicago Press, 1979.
Roediger, David R. "Ira Steward and the Anti-Slavery Origins of American Eight-Hour Theory." *Labor History* 27.3 (1986): 410–26.
  The Wages of Whiteness: Race and the Making of the American Working Class. New York: Verso, 1999.
Rorabaugh, William J. "'I Thought I Shall Liberate Myself From the Thraldom of Others': Apprentices, Masters, and the Revolution," in *Beyond the American Revolution: Explorations in the History of American Radicalism*, ed. Alfred F. Young. Dekalb: Northern Illinois University Press, 1993.
Ross, Philip, and Philip Taft. "American Labor Violence: Its Causes, Character, and Outcome," in *The History of Violence in America: A Report to the National Commission on the Causes and Prevention of Violence*, eds. Hugh Davis Graham and Ted Robert Gurr. 1969.
Rupprecht, Arthur Albert. *A Study of Slavery in the Late Roman Republic from the Works of Cicero*. Philadelphia: University of Pennsylvania, 1960.
Sandel, Michael J. *Democracy's Discontent: America in Search of a Public Philosophy*. Cambridge, MA: Harvard University Press, 1996.
Sawyer, Laura Phillips. "Contested Meanings of Freedom: Workingmen's Wages, the Company Store System, and the Godcharles v. Wigeman Decision." *The Journal of the Gilded Age and Progressive Era* 12.3 (2013): 285–319.
Schofield, Malcolm. "Cicero's Definition of Res Publica," in *Cicero the Philosopher: Twelve Papers*, ed. J. G. F. Powell. Oxford: Clarendon Press, 1995.
Schultz, Ronald. *The Republic of Labor: Philadelphia Artisans and the Politics of Class, 1720–1830*. New York: Oxford University Press, 1993.
  "The Small-Producer Tradition and the Moral Origins of Artisan Radicalism in Philadelphia 1720–1810." *Past & Present* 127 (1990): 84–116.

Scott, Rebecca J. *Degrees of Freedom: Louisiana and Cuba after Slavery*. Cambridge, MA: Harvard University Press, 2009.
Sellers, Charles. *The Market Revolution: Jacksonian America, 1815–1846*. Oxford: Oxford University Press, 1994.
Shalhope, Robert E. "Thomas Jefferson's Republicanism and Antebellum Southern Thought." *The Journal of Southern History* 42.4 (2007): 529–56.
Shklar, Judith. *American Citizenship: The Quest for Inclusion*. Cambridge, MA: Harvard University Press, 1991.
  Ordinary Vices. Cambridge, MA: Harvard University Press, 1995.
Silverman, Rachel Emma. "Tracking Sensors Invade the Workplace." *The Wall Street Journal*, (March 7, 2013).
Skinner, Quentin. "A Third Concept of Liberty." *Proceedings of the British Academy* 117.237 (2002): 237–68.
  "Freedom as the Absence of Arbitrary Power," in *Republicanism and Political Theory*, eds. Cecil Laborde and John Maynor. Oxford: Blackwell, 2008.
  Liberty before Liberalism. Cambridge; New York: Cambridge University Press, 1998.
  "Machiavelli's Discorsi and the Pre-Humanist Origins of Republican Ideas," in *Machiavelli and Republicanism*, eds. Gisela Bock, Maurizio Viroli, and Quentin Skinner. Vol. 120. Cambridge: Cambridge University Press, 1993.
  "The Republican Ideal of Political Liberty," in *Machiavelli and Republicanism*, eds. Quentin Skinner and Maurizio Viroli and Gisela Bock. Cambridge: Cambridge University Press, 1990.
  Visions of Politics Vol. 1: Regarding Method. Cambridge: Cambridge University Press, 2002.
Skocpol, Theda. *Protecting Soldiers and Mothers: The Political Origins of Social Policy in the United States*. Cambridge, MA: Harvard University Press, 1992.
Skydsgaard, J. E. "The Disintegration of the Roman Labour Market and the Clientela Theory," in *Studia Romana in Honorem Petri Krarup Septuagenarii*, ed. Karen Ascani. Odense, 1976.
Stanley, Amy Dru. *From Bondage to Contract: Wage Labor, Marriage, and the Market in the Age of Slave Emancipation*. Cambridge: Cambridge University Press, 1998.
Starr, Chester G. "An Overdose of Slavery." *The Journal of Economic History* 18.1 (1958): 17–32.
Steinfeld, Robert J. "Changing Legal Conceptions of Free Labor." in *Terms of Labor: Slavery, Serfdom and Free Labor*, ed. Stanley L. Engerman. Stanford, CA: Stanford University Press, 1999.
Stone, Geoffrey R. *Perilous Times: Free Speech in Wartime from the Sedition Act of 1798 to the War on Terrorism*. New York: W. W. Norton & Co., 2004.
Strauss, Eric M. "Iowa Woman Fired for Being Attractive: Looks Back and Moves On." *ABC News*, (August 2, 2013).
Sunstein, Cass. "Beyond the Republican Revival." *Yale Law Journal* 97.8 (1988): 1539–90.
Taylor, Alan. "Agrarian Independence: Northern Land Rioters after the Revolution," in *Beyond the American Revolution: Explorations in the History of American Radicalism*, ed. Alfred F. Young. DeKalb: Northern Illinois University Press, 1993.
Tise, Larry E. *Proslavery: A History of the Defense of Slavery in America, 1701–1840*. Athens: University of Georgia Press, 1987.

Tomlins, Christopher L. *The State and the Unions: Labor Relations, Law, and the Organized Labor Movement in America, 1880–1960*. Cambridge: Cambridge University Press, 1985.
Trachtenberg, Alan. *The Incorporation of America: Culture and Society in the Gilded Age*. New York: Hill and Wang, 1982.
Treggiari, Susan. "The Freedmen of Cicero." *Greece & Rome* 16.2 (1969): 195–204.
Urbina, Ian. "As OSHA Emphasizes Safety, Long-Term Health Risks Fester." *The New York Times*, (March 30, 2013).
Urbinati, Nadia. *Mill on Democracy: From the Athenian Polis to Representative Government*. Chicago: University of Chicago Press, 2002.
Vega, Tanzina. "In Ads, the Workers Rise Up ... and Go to Lunch." *The New York Times*, (July 7 2012).
Velasco, J. D. "Fired Gay Water Polo Coach and Supporters Protest at Charter Oak Board Meeting." *San Gabriel Valley Tribune*, (October 7, 2011).
Viroli, Maurizio. *Republicanism*. New York: Hill and Wang, 2002.
Voss, Kim. *The Making of American Exceptionalism: The Knights of Labor and Class Formation in the Nineteenth Century*. Ithaca, NY: Cornell University Press, 1993.
Ware, Norman. *The Labor Movement in the United States, 1860–1895: A Study in Democracy*. New York: Vintage Books, 1929.
Wasserman, Todd. "Amazon Dragged Into Applebee's Latest Jokey Campaign." *Mashable*, (July 25, 2012).
Weir, Robert E. "'Here's to the Men WHO Lose!': The Hidden Career of Victor Drury." *Labor History* 36.4 (1995): 530–56.
  "A Dubious Equality: Leonora Barry and Women in the KOL," in *The Knights Unhorsed: Internal Conflict in a Gilded Age Social Movement*. Detroit: Wayne State University Press, 2000.
  Beyond Labor's Veil. University Park, PA: Penn State Press, 1996.
  Knights Unhorsed. Detroit: Wayne State University Press, 2000.
Westermann, William L. "Slavery and the Elements of Freedom," in *Slavery in Classical Antiquity: Views and Controversies*, ed. M. I. Finley. Cambridge: W. Heffer & Sons Ltd., 1960.
Wilentz, Michael, and Sean Merrill. "William Manning and the Invention of American Politics," in *The Key of Liberty: The Life and Writings of William Manning, "a Laborer," 1747–1814*, eds. Michael Merril and Sean Wilentz. Cambridge, MA: Harvard University Press, 1993.
Wilentz, Sean. "Against Exceptionalism: Class Consciousness and the American Labor Movement, 1790–1920." *International Labor and Working Class History* 26 (1984): 1–24.
  Chants Democratic: New York City & the Rise of the American Working Class, 1788–1850. New York: Oxford University Press, 1984.
Winter, Yves. "Plebeian Politics: Machiavelli and the Ciompi Uprising." *Political Theory* 40.6 (2012): 736–66.
Wirszubski, Chaim. *Libertas as a Political Idea at Rome during the Late Republic and Early Principate*. Cambridge: Cambridge University Press, 1968.
Wolff, Edward N. "The Asset Price Meltdown and the Wealth of the Middle Class." published online (August 26, 2012), accessible at http://appam.confex.com/data/extendedabstract/appam/2012/Paper_2134_extendedabstract_151_0.pdf

Wood, Ellen Meiksins. *Peasant-Citizen and Slave: The Foundations of Athenian Democracy*. London: Verso, 1988.
  "Why It Matters." *London Review of Books* 30.18 (2008): 3–6.
Wood, Gordon. "The Enemy Is Us: Democratic Capitalism in the Early Republic." *Journal of the Early Republic* 16.2 (1996): 293–308.
  The Creation of the American Republic, 1776–1787. Chapel Hill: University of North Carolina Press, 1998.
Wood, Neal. *Cicero's Social and Political Thought*. Berkeley: University of California Press, 1988.
Wootton, David. "Introduction: The Republican Tradition: From Commonwealth to Common Sense," in *Republicanism, Liberty, and Commercial Society, 1649–1776*, ed. David Wootton. Stanford, CA: Stanford University Press, 1994.
Worden, Blair. "The Commonwealth Kidney of Algernon Sidney." *The Journal of British Studies* 24.1 (1985): 1–40.

Index

Adair, Douglass, 32
Adams, John Q., 73, 86
Agrarianism, 27, 32–33, 38–40, 45–46, 49–50, 65, 69–75, 81, 89–92, 95
Anthony, Susan B., 134
Appleby, Joyce, 33n107, 65, 146
Aristotle, 24–26, 49
Athens, 18–27, 30–31
Authority, 28, 102–3
Autonomy (Legal), 51, 62–63, 104–5
Aveling, Edward, 160

Bache, Benjamin F., 73
Barry, Leonora, 160
Bebel, August, 134
Berlin, Isaiah, 11, 184
Blackstone, William, 79
Brown, David, 73
Brownson, Orestes, 92
Byllesby, Langdon, 31, 78, 83–88, 138–39, 151–52

Calhoun, John C., 18, 36, 38
Campbell, Justice John, 60
Cicero, 8, 23–24, 27–30, 32, 36, 38–39, 48–49
Civic Virtue: See Virtue
Clark, John Bates, 57
Colquhoun, Patrick, 84
Competition, 111, 116–19, 161–68
Cooley, Justice Thomas, 58–60
Cooperatives, Cooperation
  Consumers', 104, 120
  Knights of Labor, 3, 5–6, 87–88, 91, 119, 122, 125, 128, 133–35, 137, 160, 166–67

  and Labor Republicanism, 10, 17, 87, 99, 104, 118–20, 123–26, 128–31, 132–33, 137, 161, 166, 187–88
  as Political Movement, 86–88, 91, 121–23
  Producers', 86, 120, 128–30
  and Profit Sharing, 87, 130
  and Republican Liberty, 87, 91, 104, 118–21, 125–26, 128, 161, 167, 180–81, 188, 190
  and Solidarity, 148–49, 155, 161, 163, 165–67, 183
  and Strikes, 163, 165
  and The Labor Theory of Value, 131–32, 186
  and The State, 123–25, 131, 159, 179–81, 189
  and Women, 133–35
Coram, Robert, 73, 79
Cotlar, Seth, 72–73
Court Cases
  Allgeyer V. Louisiana, 62–63
  Ex Parte Jentzsch, 59
  Godcharles V. Wigeman, 56
  Holden V. Hardy, 61–62
  Lochner V. New York, 56, 63
  Re Jacobs, 60
  Re Morgan, 60–62
  Ritchie V. People, 57
  Slaughterhouse Cases, 52, 54–56
Cuno, Theodore, 158, 185n35
Currency Notes: See Labor Notes

207

Debt-Bondage, 21, 30, 81n78, 136
Democracy, 26, 145, 181–82, 188
Dew, Thomas, 36
Domination (See Also: Freedom, Republican Liberty, Slavery)
   "Moments of", 106–16
   Non, Versus Non-Interference, 10–11, 183–84
   Personal, 15–16, 103, 116, 137, 178–79
   Petit, Phillip, 11, 183
   in Republicanism, 10–12, 48, 102–3, 125–26, 136–37, 155–56, 183
   Skinner, Quentin, 10–11, 183
   Structural, 103, 106–9, 116, 137, 178–79
   in The Terms of Labor, 109–11
   Value of Non-, 131–32
   in The Workplace, 111–16, 175–76, 178
Duane, William, 74

Education (See Also: Virtue)
   and Knights of Labor, 138, 152, 156–57, 159–60, 165–66
   and Labor Press, 151, 156–60
   and Labor Republicanism, 140, 152, 160, 165, 171, 190
   and Reading Rooms, 134, 159–61, 171
   and Republicanism, 28–29, 39, 142, 152, 160–61, 171
   and Virtue, 138, 156–57, 159, 171–72
   and Workingmen's Parties, 165
Eight Hours Campaign (See Also: Leisure, Labor Republicanism)
   and Knights of Labor, 124n127, 128–30, 139, 147, 154
   and Labor Republicanism, 128–29, 147, 155–56, 179
   and Labor Theory of Value, 128, 147
   and Laissez-Faire Republicanism, 57, 60–62
   McNeill, George, 147, 154
   and Overwork, 154–55
   Powderly, Terence, 156
   Steward, Ira, 100, 128–29, 147, 154
   Sylvis, William H., 130, 147
   and Virtue, 139, 144–45, 147, 155–56
Equality
   Class Conflict, 67–68, 70–74, 80–81, 86–87, 137
   In Distribution of Means of Production, 70–72, 74, 84, 86–91, 94–95, 119, 126, 179
   and The Paradox of Slavery and Freedom, 14, 16, 19, 31–32, 35, 40, 182–83
   and Republicanism, 19, 31–32, 40–41, 119, 137, 175, 181, 184–85
   Political, 47, 54, 76, 97–98, 104–5, 150–51, 175, 181
   and Slavery, 4, 31–32, 35, 38, 47, 53, 74
Evans, George Henry, 44, 78, 92–95
Exploitation, 82–86, 109–10, 151

Ferguson, Adam, 145
Field, Justice Stephen J., 55
Filmer, Robert, 15
Fink, Leon, 50, 72
Fisk, Theophilus, 37
Fitzhugh, George, 36–38
Forbath, William, 51, 53, 66
Franklin, Benjamin, 3, 82
Free Labor
   Abolitionism, 38–40, 43–45
   and Cooperatives, 118–20, 125, 167
   Labor Republicanism, 17, 68–69, 82, 118, 133, 167, 183
   Laissez-Faire Republicanism, 17, 47, 51–56, 59–65, 183
   Paradox of Slavery and Freedom, 19, 41, 68, 133, 183
   and Wage-Labor, 17, 38–43, 46, 48–52, 64–66, 68, 101–3, 119, 183
Freedom (See Also: Domination, The Paradox of Slavery and Freedom, Republicanism)
   Ancient, 13, 20–31, 136
   Economic, 21–22, 56–61, 80–81, 167, 175, 180, 188
   and Equality, 19, 76, 97
   and Labor: See Free Labor
   Labor V. Laissez-Faire Republican Visions, 17, 48, 51–56, 82–86, 102, 106–16, 183
   Liberal and Republican, 10–12, 55–56, 62–66, 145
   Negative and Positive, 11–12, 183–84
   of Contract: See Laissez-Faire Republicanism
   Paradox of Slavery and Freedom, 16, 19, 31–32, 41, 49, 68, 133, 182–83
   Political, 21, 48, 57, 60, 133, 165–67, 175, 177
   and Property, 21, 80–81, 89, 94
   and Republicanism, 5, 10, 12, 14–15, 18–19, 23–24, 36–40, 43, 65–66, 133, 183
   and Slavery, 4, 13–14, 18–31, 33–35, 182
   Value of, 126–32, 155

Index

Garrison, William L., 41–45, 47, 52
Gender: See Women in Labor
George, Henry, 95, 160
Glickman, Lawrence, 147
Godkin, Edwin L., 58
Gompers, Samuel, 99, 147
Gray, John, 83–84, 87
Greece (Ancient): See Athens
Greeley, Horace, 94
Gunton, George, 147

Hamilton, Alexander, 73
Hammond, Henry, 37–38
Harrington, James, 70
Heighton, William (See Also: Workingmen's Parties, Labor Theory of Value), 67–68, 77–78, 80, 82–84, 86–88, 96, 138–39, 152
Herzog, Don, 142
Hobbes, Thomas, 11

Independence: See Domination, Freedom
Industry, Industrialization
  and Agrarian Ideal, 72, 92, 95, 117–18, 132
  and Class Conflict, 6, 8, 61, 68, 75, 84, 91, 95–98, 102, 163
  and Republican Liberty, 17, 45, 50–51, 55, 61, 65, 72, 75–78, 87–88, 97–98, 106, 116–17, 119–21, 123, 127–28, 132–33, 166, 183
  and Virtue, 127, 131–32, 140, 156, 166
Inheritance: See Law

Jay, William, 43
Jefferson, Thomas, 32–35, 38–39, 49, 65, 70–71, 75, 158
Jones, Marry Harris "Mother", 134
Journal of United Labor, 2–4, 14, 69, 100, 102–3, 105, 107–8, 119, 123–24, 138, 153, 158–60, 164, 166, 168–70

Kalyvas, Andreas, 65
Kant, Immanuel, 49
Katznelson, Ira, 65
Knights of Labor (See Also: Journal of United Labor, Cooperatives, Terence V. Powderly, George McNeill, Joseph Buchanan, Labor Republicanism)
  Convention of 1886, 2
  and Cooperatives, 3–6, 119, 121–25, 128, 160, 164, 188–89
  Eight Hours Campaign, 128–29, 164–65

  and Labor Republicanism, 6–7, 69, 99–101, 124, 157–58, 166, 185
  and the Law, 4, 51, 101
  McNeill, George, 6, 100, 104
  Membership, 2–3, 6, 8, 59, 99, 122–23
  Organization of, 1, 4, 6–8, 98, 160, 164, 172
  Origins of, 1, 15, 79, 98, 115
  Powderly, Terence V., 1–2, 100, 104, 121, 128, 163, 185
  and Race, 1–2, 4–5, 69, 98, 169–70
  Repression of, 2–5, 98–99, 101, 105
  and Republican Liberty, 4–6, 69, 102, 104, 114, 125, 173
  and Strikes, 2–3, 52, 59, 115, 122, 165
  and Virtue, 126–27, 138, 140, 145, 155, 163, 165–66, 173
  and Women, 2, 98, 133–35, 160
Kramnick, Isaac, 146

Labor Contract, 43, 58–59, 61, 82–83, 85, 103, 106, 109–13, 116, 177–78
Labor Notes, 88, 124
Labor Republicanism (See Also: Workingmen's Parties, Knights of Labor, Cooperatives, Republican Liberty)
  and Agrarianism, 45, 69–75, 93–95
  Cooperatives, 10, 17, 86–87, 99, 104, 118–26, 128–33, 137, 148, 161, 166–67, 179–82, 187–89
  Critique of Wage-Labor, 6, 17, 66, 68–69, 81–86, 99, 101–3, 106–16, 118–20, 130, 147, 177–79, 183
  Defensive V. offensive Republicanism, 136–37
  Eight Hours Campaign, 128–29, 147, 155–56, 179
  and Gender, 2, 98, 133–35, 160
  Heighton, William, 67–68, 77–78, 80, 82–84, 86–88, 96, 138–39, 152
  and Industrialization, 2–5, 98–99, 101, 105, 183
  Labor Theory of Value, 82–86, 186–88
  versus Laissez-Faire Republicanism, 17, 48, 51–56, 82–86, 102, 106–16, 183
  and the Law, 100, 174, 179
  and Leisure, 126–32, 144–45, 147, 154–55, 181–82
  McNeill, George, 97, 100–1, 104, 106–7, 113, 147, 154, 177
  and Personal Domination, 103, 116, 132, 137, 178–79

Labor Republicanism (cont.)
  and Political Corruption, 104–6
  and Producerism, 147–48
  Powderly, Terence V., 100, 104, 117–18, 121, 124, 128, 144, 147, 153, 156–57, 159, 161–63, 169, 185
  and Race, 98, 101, 169–71
  Repression of, 2–5, 98–101, 105, 174
  and Republican Liberty, 102–16, 118–19, 126–33, 148–49, 173, 175, 182–85
  and Slavery (See Also: Wage Slavery), 14–15, 101, 103, 121, 182–83
  Skidmore, Thomas, 67–68, 78–82, 84–85, 87–91, 93, 95, 151
  Steward, Ira, 100, 108, 128–29, 131, 146–47, 149, 152, 154, 156–57, 162
  and Structural Domination, 103, 106–9, 116, 132, 137, 178–79
  Sylvis, William H., 97–99, 101, 120, 127, 130, 137–38, 147, 152, 157, 159, 162–63
Labor Theory of Value (See Also: Labor Republicanism, Workingmen's Parties, Thomas Skidmore, Ira Steward, William Heighton, and Wage-Slavery)
  and Cooperatives, 131–32, 186–87
  and Labor Republicanism, 82–86, 186–88
  and Leisure 128–31
  Reduction of Hours, 128, 147
  and Workingmen's Parties, 82–86
Laissez-Faire Republicanism
  and Abolitionism, 47, 52, 58–59, 94
  Allgeyer V. Louisiana, 62–63
  and The Courts, 51–52, 54–64
  Godcharles V. Wigeman, 56
  Labor as Commodity, 17, 50, 52–54, 57–58, 60–61, 64–65
  Labor Market, 48, 53, 64–65
  and Labor Repression, 56–64
  and Labor Republicanism, 17, 48, 51–56, 82–86, 102, 106–16, 183
  Legal Autonomy, Freedom of Contract, 45, 51, 56–57, 59–64
  Lochner V. New York, 56, 63
  Slaughterhouse Cases, 52, 54–56
  Sumner, William Graham, 53, 121
  Thirteenth Amendment, 47, 54–55
  and Wage-Labor, 17, 47–66, 82, 183
Land
  Abolitionists v. National Reformers, 41–46
  and Agrarianism, 38–39, 43–44, 49–50, 70–72, 91–93
  Evans, George H., 44, 78, 92–95
  and National Reform Association, 44, 45, 50, 92–95, 106
  Pickering, Thomas, 93–94
  Redistribution of, 70–72, 74, 84, 86–91, 94–95, 119, 126, 179
  and Republican Liberty, 21, 27–28, 30, 33–34, 39, 43–44, 49, 73, 89–95
  West, William H., 44–45
Lassalle, Ferdinand, 158
Lause, Mark, 93
Law
  and Property Rights, 79, 93, 108–9, 178, 181
  and Labor Republicanism, 91, 94, 104–5, 108–9, 113, 149, 177–80
  and Repression of Labor, 56–64, 101, 105, 174
  Inheritance Law, 70–71, 74
  Labor Legislation, 51–53, 56–64, 101, 105, 111, 156, 158, 174, 177, 179
  Laissez-Faire Republicanism, 51–52, 54–64
  Martial Law, 4, 174
  Roman Law, 13, 22–23, 29, 57
Layton, Robert, 156
Leisure
  and Labor, 104, 129–32, 181–82
  and Labor Republicanism, 126–32, 144–45, 147, 154–55, 164–65, 181–83
  As Freedom from Labor, 104, 126, 133, 145, 181
  Eight Hours Campaign, 128–29, 147, 154–56
  Knights of Labor, 128–30, 154–55, 164–65
  McNeill, George, 147, 154
  Steward, Ira, 100, 128–29, 147, 154
  Virtue, 25–28, 127–28, 130–32, 139, 144–45, 147, 155–56
Liberalism, 10–12, 18, 48, 51, 63–66, 143–45, 147–48, 172, 183–84
Lincoln, Abraham, 38–39, 41, 46, 49, 117
Livy, 30, 136
Lloyd, Henry Demarest, 175
Lloyd, Thomas, 73, 79
Locke, John, 82
Lowell, Francis, 75
Luther, Seth, 68, 77

Machiavelli, Niccolo, 32, 136–37, 183
Madison, James, 32–34, 49, 76
Manning, William, 73, 149–52, 158
Marx, Eleanor, 36
Marx, Karl; Marxism, 10, 36, 185–88

Index

Mclelland, John, 114
McNeill, George
  and Equality, 104, 154
  and Knights of Labor, 100, 147, 154
  and Labor Journalism 19
  and Leisure, 147
  and the Eight Hours Campaign, 147, 154
  and Republican Government, 97, 101
  and Virtue, 147, 154
  and Wage Labor, 106–7, 113, 177
Mill, John S., 154, 158
Miller, Justice Samuel F., 54–55
Monroe, James, 86
Moore, Ely, 37
Morgan, Edmund, 34

National Reform Association (NRA), 44, 45, 50, 92–95, 106
Neo-Republicanism (See Also: Pettit, Skinner, Republicanism), 10–14, 23–24, 27, 40–41, 57, 64–65, 137, 141, 174, 182–83

Oldfield, Adrian, 141
Owen, Robert, 86–87, 123

Paine, Thomas, 71–72, 89
Paradox of Slavery and Freedom
  and Abolitionism, 38–46
  and Agrarianism, 38–40
  and Cooperatives, 87, 91, 118–20, 123–25, 132–37, 183
  In Early Modern Republicanism, 32–36
  and Equality, 14, 16, 19, 31–32, 35, 40, 182–83
  and Industrialization, 17, 72–73, 75–76, 87–88, 91, 116–17, 119–20, 132–37
  and Labor Republicanism, 17, 68–69, 96, 116, 126–27, 132–37, 173
  and Laissez-Faire Republicanism, 17, 50–51, 65, 133, 182–83
  and Land Reform 41–46
  Lincoln, Abraham, 38–41, 49
  as Modern Problem, 19, 31–32, 40, 132
  and Republicanism, 16–17, 19, 32–36, 40–41, 182–83
  In Virginia, 32–36
  and Wage-Labor, 19, 41–46
Peckham, Justice Rufus W., 62–64
Pettit, Phillip, 11, 13, 23, 27, 64, 183
Phillips, Wendell, 44–45
Pickering, John, 93–94
Pinkertons, 5–6, 99

Pocock, John G.A., 143, 145
Political Economy, 79, 81–86, 91, 128–31, 133, 144, 156–59, 166, 185
Political Theory of the Dependent Classes, 149–61
Powderly, Terence
  and Cooperatives, 117–18, 121, 124, 128, 153, 161–63
  and Knights of Labor, 1–2, 100, 104, 121, 128, 163, 185
  Labor Republicanism, 100, 104, 117–18, 121, 124, 128, 144, 147, 153, 156–57, 159, 161–63, 185
  and Republican Liberty, 50, 104, 121, 128, 153, 161–62
  and Virtue, 144, 147, 153, 156–57
Primogeniture: See Law

Rensselaer, General Stephen Van, 76
Repression (of Labor), 2–5, 56–64, 98–101, 105, 174
Republicanism (See Also: Laissez-Faire Republicanism, Labor Republicanism, Pettit, Skinner, Neo-Republicanism)
  Ancient and Modern, 7, 18–38, 136–37
  Civic Virtue, 10, 104, 140–49, 153–54, 164, 167, 170–71, 183
  and Cooperatives, 87, 103–4, 118–21, 125, 130–31, 148, 155, 183, 189
  and the Law, 51–52, 54–64, 71, 91, 94, 104–5, 108–9, 113, 149, 177–80
  Liberty, 8, 10–17, 19, 38–46, 48, 57, 60, 65–66, 72–75, 79, 87, 90, 95–96, 102–4, 111–13, 115–16, 130–33, 136–37, 140–43, 145, 152, 167, 170–71, 173, 183–85
  On Private Property, 9, 12–13, 33, 40, 49–50, 52, 74–77, 79–81, 87, 89, 91–93, 102, 106–7, 110, 124, 164, 188
  and Slavery, 6–7, 9–10, 19–38, 40–46, 53, 78–79, 81–82, 86, 94, 97–98, 101–3, 113, 132, 182–83
  and Wage Labor, 6–7, 10, 41–46, 48–50, 52–53, 57, 64–65, 72–75, 77, 81, 91–96, 98, 100–1, 104, 111, 136, 147, 151–52, 183
Ricardo, David, 82, 160
Roediger, David, 142, 170
Rome, Roman, 13, 18–24, 27–30, 35–36, 40, 57, 90–91, 136, 165
Rush, Benjamin, 142

Sallust, 27
Samuel, John, 119
Sandel, Michael, 64–65, 144–45
Self-Interest: See Virtue
Seward, William, 101
Sharpe, Henry, 109, 124
Shklar, Judith, 145
Sidney, Algernon, 11, 15–16, 32, 103, 115
Simpson, Stephen, 78, 80, 87–88
Skidmore, Thomas, (See Also: Workingmen's Parties, Workingman's Advocate), 67–68, 78–82, 84–85, 87–91, 93, 95, 151
Skinner, Quentin, 10–13, 27, 64, 141, 174, 183
Slavery (See Also: Freedom, Domination, Wage Slavery)
  American South, 16, 18, 32–36, 41, 45–46, 75
  Ancient Practices, 18–31
  Athens, 19–26, 30–31
  and Freedom, 4, 13–14, 18–31, 33–35, 38–39, 44, 69, 182
  Labor Republicanism, 14–15, 69, 101–3, 116, 121, 167, 182–83
  Laissez-Faire Republicanism, 47–48, 52–55, 58–59
  and the Market, 9–10, 53, 77, 82, 113
  Paradox of Slavery and Freedom, 8, 16–17, 19, 40–41, 45–46, 69, 182–83
  Pro-Slavery, Republican Arguments, 36–38, 170
  and Republican Liberty, 11–13, 18–19, 31–32, 38–40, 43, 69, 77–80, 101–2, 169, 182–83
  Rome, 19–24, 26–31
  Slave Society, 20, 39–40
  Wage-Slavery, 10, 17, 42–46, 50, 53, 68–69, 77, 81, 94, 103, 105–16, 119–21, 130, 156–57, 168, 185
Smith, Adam, 82, 145–46, 160
Solidarity
  Civic Virtue, 17, 140, 149, 161, 164–65, 183
  Cooperatives, 148–49, 155, 161, 163, 165–67, 183
  and Knights of Labor, 138–39, 157, 163–65, 170–71
  and Labor Republicanism, 17, 137, 148, 157, 162–64, 170–71, 183
  and Republican Liberty, 149–53, 163–64, 170
  Selfishness v. Self-Interest, 139–40, 161–62
Spencer, Herbert, 160

Stephens, Uriah, 98, 164, 169
Steward, Ira, 7, 10, 17, 100, 108, 128–29, 131, 146–47, 149, 152, 154, 156–57, 162
Stimson, Frederic J., 59
Sumner, William G., 53, 121
Supreme Court (U.S.), 51, 54–55, 62
Swinton, John, 105, 158, 167
Sylvis, William H., 97–99, 101, 120, 127, 130, 137–38, 147, 152, 157, 159, 162–63

Technology 22, 51, 75, 114–15, 127–28, 133, 181–82
Thibodaux, Masacre of, 1, 4–7, 10, 56, 122
Thompson, William, 83–84, 87
Tiedeman, Christopher, 58–60
Tucker, St. George, 31, 35

Vigilantism, 4–6
Virtue (See Also: Labor Republicanism, Republicanism)
  in Contemporary Political Philosophy, 24, 140–48, 168–72
  and Cooperatives, 17, 137, 153, 163, 166–70, 183
  and Desire, 143–44, 153–54, 169
  and Education, 138, 156–57, 159, 171–72
  and Freedom, 17, 137, 139–42, 170–71
  Knights of Labor, 126–27, 138, 140, 145, 155, 163, 165–66, 173
  and Labor Press, 151–52, 158–61, 171
  Labor Republicanism, 17, 137, 139–40, 145, 147–49, 153–54, 166, 170–71, 173
  and Leisure 25–28, 127–28, 130–32, 139, 144–45, 147, 155–56
  and Political Theory of The Dependent Classes, 148–49, 151–53, 161, 170–72
  and Politics, 24–25, 138–41, 145–46, 153, 156, 166
  Powderly, Terence V., 144, 147, 153, 156–57
  and Reading Rooms, 159–61, 171
  and Republican Liberty, 14, 24–25, 33, 137–39, 141, 155–56, 167, 170–71
  and Self-Emancipation, 137–39, 152, 170, 172
  and Self-Organization, 17, 137, 140, 148, 161–68, 171
  Selfishness V. Self-Interest, 139–40, 161–62
  and Solidarity, 17, 140, 149, 161, 164–65, 183
Stephens, Uriah, 164, 169
Steward, Ira, 17, 146–47, 157
Sylvis, William H., 138, 147, 159, 162–63

Index

Wage Slavery, 10, 17, 42–46, 50, 53, 68–69, 94, 103, 105–16, 119–21, 130, 156–57, 168, 185
Wage-Labor (See Also: Wage Slavery)
  and Abolitionism, 6, 42–47, 52, 69, 80, 101
  and Domination, 77–78, 109–11, 115, 124, 133, 179
  and Industry, 6, 45, 50–51, 75, 87–88, 95–96, 107–8, 124, 132
  and the Labor Market, Commodification of Labor, 48, 53, 57–58, 77, 80, 82, 84–85, 106–7, 119
  Labor Republican Critique, 6, 17, 66, 68–69, 81–86, 99, 101–3, 106–16, 118–20, 130, 147, 177–79, 183
  Laissez-Faire Republican Defense, 17, 47–66, 82, 183
  and National Reformers, 45, 50, 92–95, 106
  and Paradox of Slavery and Freedom, 19, 41–46
  and Political Economy, 81–86, 91
  and Republican Liberty, 5–6, 17, 25, 48, 64–65, 104, 124, 132
  and Workingmen's Parties, 68–69, 75–96
  as Free Labor, 17, 38–43, 46–52, 56–57, 64–66, 68, 101–3, 119, 183
  as Wage-Slavery, 10, 17, 66, 68–69, 77, 81, 94, 103, 105–16, 119–21, 130, 156–57, 168, 185

Walker, Francis A., 57–58
Warren, Josiah, 88
Weir, Robert, 164
West, William, 44–45
Women in Labor, 2, 57, 61–62, 75, 90, 98, 106, 122, 133–35, 160, 172
Working Man's Advocate, 78, 81, 92, 94, 152
Workingmen's Parties
  Byllesby, Langdon, 31, 78, 83–88, 138–39, 151–52
  and Cooperatives, 86–90, 163
  Evans, George Henry, 44, 78, 92–95
  Heighton, William, 67–68, 77–78, 80, 82–84, 86–88, 96, 138–39, 152
  History of, 42–43, 68, 77, 92, 158
  and Labor Theory of Value, 82–86
  Mechanics' Free Press, 67, 78, 84, 88, 91, 152
  National Reform Association, 45, 50, 92–95, 106
  of New York, 68, 78, 81, 90, 92, 169
  of Philadelphia, 67–68, 78, 138
  Political Economy, 79, 81–86, 91
  and Slavery, 42, 77, 79–81, 93
  Skidmore, Thomas, 67–68, 78–82, 84–85, 87–91, 93, 95, 151
  and Wage-Labor, 68–69, 75–96
  Working Man's Advocate, 78, 81, 92, 94, 152